Hellenic Studies 68

LITERARY HISTORY IN THE PARIAN MARBLE

Recent Titles in the Hellenic Studies Series

http://chs.harvard.edu/chs/publications

LITERARY HISTORY IN THE PARIAN MARBLE

Andrea Rotstein

Center for Hellenic Studies
Trustees for Harvard University
Washington, D.C.
Distributed by Harvard University Press
Cambridge, Massachusetts, and London, England
2016

Literary History in the Parian Marble
  Andrea Rotstein
Copyright © 2016 Center for Hellenic Studies, Trustees for Harvard University
All Rights Reserved.
Published by Center for Hellenic Studies, Trustees for Harvard University,
  Washington, D.C.
Distributed by Harvard University Press, Cambridge, Massachusetts, and London,
  England
Production: Nancy Wolfe Kotary
Cover design: Joni Godlove
Printed by Edwards Brothers Malloy, Ann Arbor, MI, and Lillington, NC

EDITORIAL TEAM

Senior Advisers: W. Robert Connor, Gloria Ferrari Pinney, Albert Henrichs, James
  O'Donnell, Bernd Seidensticker
Editorial Board: Gregory Nagy (Editor-in-Chief), Casey Dué (Executive Editor), Mary
  Ebbott (Executive Editor), Scott Johnson, Olga Levaniouk, Leonard Muellner
Production Manager for Publications: Jill Curry Robbins
Web Producer: Noel Spencer
Multimedia Producer: Mark Tomasko

On the cover: The view from Paroikia. Photo by the author.

ISBN: 9780674417236
Library of Congress Control Number: 2014953139

To Tamar

Contents

Contents

List of Plates
(Pages 139–146)

Plate 1. The Parian Marble, section A. Ashmolean Museum, University of Oxford, inv. ANChandler.2.23.
Photo ©Ashmolean Museum.

Plate 2. The Parian Marble, section A.
Drawing after Felix Jacoby, *Das Marmor Parium* (Berlin 1904), Beilage II.

Plate 3. The Parian Marble, section B. Archaeological Museum of Paros, inv. no. A26.
Photo © Hellenic Republic, Ministry of Culture and Sports, General Directorate of Antiquities and Cultural Heritage / Ephorate of Antiquities of the Cyclades.

Plate 4. The Parian Marble, section B. Archaeological Museum, Paros.
Drawing after Felix Jacoby, *Das Marmor Parium* (Berlin 1904), Beilage III.

Plate 5. Chronicon Romanum, recto (3a) and verso (3b). Capitoline Museum, Rome, inv. MC 342/S.
Photo courtesy of the Capitoline Museum.

Plate 6. Getty Table, or "Tabula Iliaca" inscription, obverse (4a) and reverse (4b). The J. Paul Getty Museum, Villa Collection, Malibu, California, inv. 81.AA.113. Gift of Vasek Polak.
Photos courtesy of the Getty Museum's Open Content Program (obverse) and the Getty Museum (reverse).

Plate 7. Mnesiepes Inscription, blocks E1 (7a) and E2 (7b). Archaeological Museum of Paros, inv. no. 175.
Photo © Hellenic Republic, Ministry of Culture and Sports, General Directorate of Antiquities and Cultural Heritage / Ephorate of Antiquities of the Cyclades.

Plate 8. Mnesiepes Inscription, E1 III, lines 27–36. Original inscription in the Archaeological Museum of Paros.

Squeeze photo courtesy of the Inscriptiones Graecae archive.

Plate 9: Comparison of squeezes from the Parian Marble, Section B (top) and the Mnesiepes Inscription (bottom).

Squeeze photos courtesy of the Inscriptiones Graecae archive.

Acknowledgements

I never dreamt of writing a book on the Parian Marble, but intellectual adventures are not always foreseen. It was on the very soil of Paros, at a conference on Archilochus in 2005, that the inscription beckoned and the fields of poetry and chronology converged in my mind. My interests in ancient literary history found an appropriate channel.

For encouraging me to brave this fascinating document I owe a debt of gratitude to Dwora Gilula, Margalit Finkelberg, Gregory Nagy, Jonathan Price and Ralph Rosen. Warm thanks go to the friends and scholars whose comments and discussions helped me on my way: Krystina Bartol, Ewen Bowie, Robert Cioffi, Andrew Ford, John Franklin, Sylvie Honigman, Dániel Kiss, Astrid Möller, Douglas Olson and Rachel Zelnick-Abramovitz. Special thanks are due to Astrid Möller, who unadvertedly set in motion my interest in chronology through her work on Eratosthenes, and to Richard Burgess, Paola Ceccarelli, Giambattista D'Alessio, John Franklin and Veit Rosenberger, who generously shared with me some of their published and unpublished work.

Several of my former students helped me in this project. Barak Blum, Dafna Cohen (Baratz) and Jonathan Schabbi proofread the manuscript of this book at different stages; Naomi Michalowicz and Ronnie Hirsch made numberless errands to the university library. Thanks are due to the CHS staff for their keen and professional assistance; to Sarah Lannom, Bruce King and most particularly to Jill Curry Robbins for her absolutely endless patience.

I gained valuable insights from the audiences at the Center for Hellenic Studies and the Ohio State University. Reactions to my presentations at Northwestern University, Tel Aviv University, Yale University, and the Epichoreia workshop in Ancient Greek Music (NYU) made possible some last minute fine tuning.

Invaluable institutional assistance came from the Israel Science Foundation (grant no. 169/11) that supported all stages of my research, and Tel Aviv University, that granted a sabbatical leave in 2011-2012 and funded research trips to Athens, Paros, Oxford and Berlin. A fellowship by the Center for Hellenic Studies provided access to wonderful resources, including the CHS and other Harvard libraries, as well as opportunities for discussing my work with friends and colleagues. The DAAD made possible a research stay at the University of Freiburg's Department of Ancient History.

As ever, libraries, museums and archives have proven more than repositories of knowledge. I am grateful to the American School of Classical Studies for enabling me to work at the Blegen library; to the Ashmolean Museum at Oxford and the Paros Archaeological Museum for the opportunity to study the Parian Marble and other Greek inscriptions; to Charles Crowther of the Centre for the Study of Ancient Documents in Oxford for access to squeezes. I am much obliged to Klaus Hallof, research leader of the Inscriptiones Graecae, for facilitating access to squeezes, photographs and unpublished materials at the Research Centre for Primary Sources of the Ancient World of the Berlin-Brandenburg Academy of Sciences and Humanities. Conversations with him and his colleagues, Jaime Curbera and Daniela Summa, were truly inspiring.

I would like to end with a personal note. When I started to juggle with issues of chronology my daughter Michal was learning to master the mysteries of time: the difference between yesterday and tomorrow, the weekly rhythms of work, play and rest, the recurrent cycle of the Jewish holidays, the irreversible nature of time. As I conclude revising this book, her six years of age have given her a sense of her own past. I treasure the privilege of holding Michal's hand, as we visit the times before she was born and envision possible futures.

Finally, I dedicate this book to my partner Tamar. As with most of the good things in our life together, her love has made this book possible.

Jerusalem, 2014

Preface

For most philologists working on ancient Greek poetry, the Parian Marble is not usually a final destination, but a series of stopovers. Indeed, a chronological list is hardly the kind of thing that one reads from beginning to end. Hence, the common tendency to approach the inscription as a repository of information and to mine it for specific dates of people and events. Only the few specialists in the field of ancient chronography would see the inscription as a text in its own right. This book will do precisely that: look at the Parian Marble as a continuous text, with eyes trained for philological and literary criticism.

My interest in the Parian Marble was initially prompted by its mention of a great number of poets and literary events (though not always those that one might have expected). Was that a regular feature of ancient Greek chronography? What attitudes towards the literary past does the selection of poets reveal? How was the information acquired, and to what extent can we trust it? My chapter on literary history (Chapter 6 below), which gives this book its title, takes up these questions. The emphasis on dating literary matters is, in my view, connected to the purpose and original location of the inscription. In my first chapter, after looking into the history of the discovery of the inscription and its study, I endorse and expand the hypothesis that it was displayed in a Parian site related to literary activities, such as the Archilocheion. Admittedly, the Parian Marble belongs to the family of ancient Greek chronography, but the counting down of years and the striking interest in poets set it in a *sui generis* category. Thus, in Chapter 3, I examine the literary genre to which the Parian Marble belongs. Chapter 4 analyzes the textual qualities of the inscription. The way the Parian Marble conceptualizes time is treated in Chapter 5.

The Parian Marble is the earliest extant instance of ancient Greek chronography, yet neither a critical edition nor a line-to-line commentary has been published since Jacoby's work.[1] The text I offer in Chapter 2 is intended to make a

---

[1] Critical editions of the Greek text can be found in IG XII.5 444 (1903), Jacoby 1904a, and FGrH 239. Most collections of inscriptions and historical sources only print excerpts: Tod 1946:308–315 (no. 205), Pfohl 1966:120–125 (no. 110), Harding 1985:1–3 (no. 1. A), Austin 2006:19–22 (no. 1).

contribution towards that end. With the optimism of a past era, Jacoby included many supplements, some of them long and speculative. This calls for reconsideration, especially in the first forty-five lines of the inscription, which survive only in a transcription of 1628.[2] There is a point of principle regarding restoration. Conjectures build on what is attested elsewhere. The Parian Marble can, however, be proven wrong at times. Occasionally it contains unorthodox dates and figures otherwise unknown, none of which we could have guessed; conjecture can hardly provide the unexpected. Extensive restoration poses also a practical problem. Supplements tend to become canonical, especially when cited in translation, and to acquire authority similar to what was actually written on the stone. I decided therefore to avoid substantial restoration, in the hope of giving more by giving less, and thus encourage further work on the text of the Parian Marble. For those who are not very familiar with ancient Greek, I offer a literal English translation with some epigraphical marks, reminders of the conjectural character of the text.

This book deals with a text surviving on stone, but is written for non-epigraphists. Similarly, it addresses non-specialists in ancient chronography, even though focusing on a chronicle. I have tried to spell out some of the conventions and basic knowledge that professional epigraphists and chronographers take for granted, in the hope of making this fascinating text accessible to both students and scholars working on classical Greek history, literature, and archaeology.

Unacknowledged translations are my own.

Bertrand 1992:17–22 offers a partial French translation. A reader-friendly translation can be found in Burgess and Kulikowski 2013:301-309. Jacoby's text without critical apparatus is freely available in Ulrich Harsch's *Bibliotheca Augustana* (http://www.hs-augsburg.de/~harsch/graeca/Chronologia/S_ante03/MarmorParium/mar_intr.html). An English translation by Gillian Newing is available in the Ashmolean Museum's website http://www.ashmolean.museum/ash/faqs/q004/.

[2] The inconsistent treatment of lacunae in the *editio princeps* truly complicates the constitution of the text (cf. Munro 1901a:150, Jacoby 1904b:63–76, and see introduction to chap. 2 below).

List of Abbreviations

BNJ   I. Worthington, ed., *Brill's New Jacoby: The Fragments of the Greek Historians* I–III (Jacoby Online), http://www.brill.com/publications/online-resources/jacoby-online.

BNP   H. Cancik, M. Landfester, H. Schneider, *Brill's New Pauly: Encyclopaedia of the Ancient World*, (New Pauly Online), http://referenceworks.brillonline.com/browse/brill-s-new-pauly.

CIG   *Corpus Inscriptionum Graecarum* (Berlin, 1825–1877).

CIL   *Corpus Inscriptionum Latinarum* (Berlin, 1863–).

DK   H. Diels and W. Kranz, *Die Fragmente der Vorsokratiker*, 6th ed. (Berlin, 1951).

DTC2   A. W. Pickard-Cambridge, *Dithyramb, Tragedy and Comedy*, 2nd ed. revised by T. B. L. Webster (Oxford, 1962).

FGrH   F. Jacoby, *Die Fragmente der griechischen Historiker* (Leiden, 1954–1969).

FHG   K. Müller, *Fragmenta Historicorum Graecorum* (Frankfurt, 1841–1938).

GL   D. Page, *Greek Literary Papyri* (Cambridge, MA, 1942).

IDelos   F. Durrbach, P. Roussel, M. Launey, J. Coupry, and A. Plassart, *Inscriptions de Délos*, I–VII (Paris, 1927–72).

IEph   H. Wankel, R. Merkelbach et al., *Die Inschriften von Ephesos* I–VII. *Inschriften griechischer Städte aus Kleinasien 11-17*, (Bonn 1979-81).

IMagnesia   O. Kern, *Die Inschriften von Magnesia am Maeander* (Berlin, 1900).

ISmyrna   G. Petzl, *Die Inschriften von Smyrna I-II. Inschriften griechischer Städte aus Kleinasien 23-24* (Bonn, 1982–90).

IG   *Inscriptiones Graecae* (Berlin, 1873–).

IGUR   L. Moretti, *Inscriptiones Graecae Urbis Romae* (Rome, 1968-1979).

IvO   W. Ditenberger, K. Purgold, *Inschriften von Olympia* (Berlin, 1896).

LIMC   *Lexicon Iconographicum Mythologiae Classicae*, 18 vols (Zurich, 1981–1999).

LP   E. Lobel and D. Page, *Poetae Melici Graeci* (Cambridge, 1962).

LSJ   H. G. Liddell, R. Scott, and H. S. Jones, *A Greek-English Lexicon*, 9th ed., with a Supplement (Oxford, 1925–1940).

NP   H. Cancik, H. Schneider, M. Landfester, eds., *Der Neue Pauly*, http://referenceworks.brillonline.com/browse/der-neue-pauly

P.Lips.   L. Mitteis, *Griechische Urkunden der Papyrussammlung zu Leipzig* I (Leipzig, 1906).

P.Oxy.   Bernard P. Grenfell and Arthur S. Hunt, eds., *The Oxyrhynchus Papyri* (London, 1898–). Ongoing series; individual volumes may have different editors.

PEG   A. Bernabé, *Poetarum Epicorum Graecorum Testimonia et Fragmenta* I (Stuttgart, 1996) and II (Munich, 2004–2005).

PMG   D. L. Page, *Poetae Melici Graeci* (Oxford, 1962).

SEG   *Supplementum Epigraphicum Graecum* (Leiden, 1923–).

SIG   W. Dittenberger, *Sylloge Inscriptionum Graecarum* (Leipzig, 1915-1921).

TrGF   B. Snell, R.Kannicht, and S. Radt, *Tragicorum Graecorum Fragmenta* (Göttingen, 1971–).

Chapter 1
The Parian Marble

1. Introduction

The Parian Marble is a monumental inscription written in Attic Greek on a stele that was originally over two meters tall,[1] dating from some time after 264/3 BCE.[2] It has reached us in two sections, ninety-three and thirty-three lines long. There is a gap of nineteen years between the sections, and the final thirty-five years are entirely missing.[3]

We have no information about the author. An Athenian origin would, perhaps, be the natural assumption, given the overall Athenian orientation of the text and the dating by Athenian archons.[4] Jacoby, however, noting the deviations from Attic usage, suggested that the author was a Parian or someone living in Paros, even though the stele contains no references to Parian history.[5]

---

[1] The extant section A is 0.34 m high on the right side and 0.57 m high on the left side, 0.81–0.82 m wide and 0.12–0.15 m deep. Before the loss of the upper part, section A, comprising 93 lines, was 0.92 m high on the right and 1.13 m on the left (or perhaps higher, if it was not complete, as Jacoby suggested). Section B, 33 lines long, is 0.39 m at its highest. Considering that section B renders 38 years in 33 lines, that letters are about 8 mm high, and that there may have been a closing paragraph at the end, by a conservative computation at least 0.55 m are necessary for the missing 54 years. The complete stele was, therefore, a bit more than 2 m high (1.13 + 0.39 + 0.55 = 2.07 m). Section B is 0.83 m wide and 0.16 m deep (Krispi and Wilhelm 1897:183–184, IG XII.5 444, Jacoby 1904a:v). The Chronicle of Lindos (99 BCE), which is 2.37 m high, 0.85 m wide, and 0.32 m deep (Higbie 2003:6), can help us to visualize the Parian Marble when it was still complete. In terms of layout, a good parallel is the 250 BCE Delian inventory IG XI.2 287 B, a tall stele (2.18 m) with long lines (between 105 and 135 letters) and small lettering (7 mm, images available in Prêtre and Brunet 2002, plates VIII–XI).

[2] Jacoby's comment that the lettering of the inscription would suggest a date fifty years later than the terminus established by content (Jacoby 1904a:v and 1904b:90–91n1) was rejected by Wilhelm 1909:288n11 (see Rotstein 2014).

[3] Lines are long, but the number of letters (110–130) in them is irregular (Jacoby 1904b:74, with a thorough analysis in his 1904 edition), as is the size of letters, with small ΘΟΩ (Dopp 1883:2–3, Jacoby 1904a:v) located in the middle of the line, and contrast in the width of broad letters (with Σ and M ca. 8 mm wide, A and H and N between 5 and 6 mm wide). The width of letters and the space between them is not regular.

[4] On the use of an Athenian chronographic framework in local history, see Clarke 2008:213–214.

[5] Jacoby 1904b:76–80, 102–104, FGrH 239 (commentary):666. Jacoby refers to the author as "the Parian," and many have followed him.

We know of two men who were involved with historical and literary research in Paros, Demeas and Mnesiepes, and both have been proposed as possible authors.[6] However, language and content are not enough for settling the question of origins, since an Athenian could follow local usage, and a Parian could adopt the point of view of Athens as a cultural center.[7] Perhaps it is best to leave the author of the Parian Marble anonymous.[8] We may still characterize him as an educated man with an interest in both history and literature who, if not a native, may have been living in Paros for some time before composing the chronicle. Jacoby further claimed that the author was not a professional historian or chronologist but rather a *dilettante* who put forward the results of his own reading.[9] Indeed, the inscription shows deficiencies from a chronographic point of view, such as departures from chronological orthodoxy and inconsistencies in the use of inclusive and exclusive computation.[10] We may well agree with Munro that the chronicle is "popular and superficial,"[11] while still considering it an example of the chronological knowledge typical of an educated man of the time. The author could have been one of the travelling historians attested at the time, who seem to have sometimes dealt with local history, if not a teacher, a poet, or a rhapsode.[12]

The surviving text does not illuminate the purpose for setting up the inscription. The opening is perhaps the most cited part of the chronicle, including the supplements that were given by Jacoby strictly *exempli gratia*. Let us look into the text without substantial restoration:

[- - -]ΟΥ[- - -]ν παν[τοί]ων [- - -]νων ἀνέγραψα τοὺς ἀν[- - -] | 2
[- - -] ἀρξάμ[εν]ος ἀπὸ Κέκροπος τοῦ πρώτου βασιλεύσαντος Ἀθηνῶν εἴως ἄρχοντος ἐμ Πάρωι [μὲν] [- - -] | 3 [- - -]υάνακτος, Ἀθήνησιν δὲ Διογνήτου. (vac. ca. 5)

---

6   Hypothesis of Demeas's authorship: Hiller von Gärtringen IG XII.5 (p. 115); also Lanzillotta 1987:32–34 (rejected by Jacoby 1904b:77 and FGrH 239 [commentary]:666, Chaniotis 1988:88–89); hypothesis of Mnesiepes's authorship: Peek 1955:46 (rejected by Chaniotis 1988:89).
7   Berranger 2000:115 emphasizes the provincial character of the author. The qualification of poetic victories as achieved "in Athens" without further details suggests composition for a non-Athenian audience, see chap. 6, sec. 2.IV below.
8   Chaniotis 1988:88.
9   Jacoby 1904b:84, 90–91, 99–102.
10   Different principles of time reckoning are applied before and after 399 BCE, see Jacoby 1904b:82–84 and FGrH II B pp. 668–671, Dinsmoor 1939:46, Cadoux 1948:83–86. Jacoby (1904b:89–91) believed that although chronographic deficiencies stood against the hypothesis of a professional chronographer or historian, the author was not simply an epitomizer, as had been suggested by Dopp 1883:7–8. Inconsistencies may result from the author's drawing on multiple sources (Robert Cioffi, personal communication). Jacoby also noted the inattentive work of the cutter, whose mistakes are not always corrected (Jacoby 1904b). Text is written in erasures at A37, A38, A46, A47, A48, A49, A54, A59, B9.
11   Munro 1905:269; cf. Jacoby's "populäre Universalchronik," FGrH 239 (commentary):666.
12   See Chaniotis 1988:366, Chaniotis 2009, Zelnik-Abramovitz 2014, with further references.

... [from / of / on account of] all sorts ... I recorded the ..., starting from Cecrops, the first king of Athens, until ... uanax was archon in Paros, and Diognetus in Athens.

The text was the work of an individual, as the first person of the verb ἀνέγραψα, "I recorded," indicates. That is, it was a private document, even if intended for public display (the verb means both "to register," as well as "to set up in public").[13] The scope of the inscription is clear from lines 2 and 3. The first line may have included the author's name, or a general statement of sources and purposes. It is, however, extremely damaged, and not much can be gained from Selden's transcription, with only twenty-five letters for the first line—that is, about a third of the line (assuming with Jacoby that it contained characters bigger than in most of the text).[14] Before ἀνέγραψα a complement with genitive, possibly ἐκ / ἐξ ... παν[τοί]ων [- - -]νων, may have indicated sources, provenance, or general subject (περί). The nature of what is being inscribed is missing (τοὺς ἀν[), and possibly one line or more are missing at the beginning.[15] As for the lost end of the inscription, after reaching year 1, a closing section may have specified the motives for setting it up and the place where it was set, perhaps including a dedication, as Jacoby suggested from comparison with the philosophical inscription by Diogenes of Oinoanda (second century CE).[16]

2. The Discovery of the Parian Marble

The Parian Marble survives in two sections. The tale of their discovery and publication epitomizes the diverse ways archaeology and epigraphy were practiced in the early seventeenth and late nineteenth centuries.[17]

The story of the upper part of the inscription, known as A (Plates 1–2), begins at the crossroads of trade, diplomacy, and the Western European passion

---

13 Cf. περὶ δὲ ὧν ἠβουλήθημεν ἀναγράψαι ..., Mnesiepes inscription, E1 (A) col. II l. 20. In contrast, the Lindian Chronicle gives extensive details about the motivation and procedure for the production and display of a public document (FGrH 532 A, 99 BCE).

14 Jacoby 1904a:26; cf. Higbie 2003:155 for a similar feature on the Lindian Chronicle.

15 Jacoby 1904a:27.

16 Jacoby 1904b:101–102. There are, however, significant differences between the Parian Marble and Diogenes's inscription, which was carved on a wall in short columns (letters between 1.8 cm and 3 cm tall) and included punctuation marks (paragraphoi and spaces). Thus, unlike the Parian Marble, the inscription of Diogenes of Oinoanda resembled a papyrus-roll (see Smith 1996 and 2003 for the text and further references).

17 For brief English accounts of the discovery and early editions, see Tod 1951:172–174, Connor 1990, Athanassakis 2001, Vickers 2006:6–13, 24–27, 38–40 (and the prefaces to Boeckh's, Hiller von Gärtringen's, and Jacoby's editions). Liddel 2014:2-4, which came to my knowledge after completion of this book, examines the reception of the Parian Marble from its discovery to the mid-nineteenth century. I thank Christy Constantakopoulou for the reference.

for collecting Greek antiquities. The stone arrived at the Earl of Arundel's palace in London in 1627, along with other pieces of sculpted or inscribed marble (*marmora*).[18] John Selden (1584–1654) published them in a quarto volume in 1628, the *Marmora Arundelliana*.[19] The introduction to the first edition says little about where and how the Parian Marble was found, except that it was among the objects collected by William Petty, whom the Earl had sent to the East to collect antiquities. From the reference to the Parian archon in the opening part of the inscription, Selden rightly conjectured that it originated from Paros. Smyrna was first linked to the Parian Marble in 1641, when Pierre Gassendi (1599–1655) published a biography of his patron, the politician and polymath Nicolas-Claude de Peiresc (1580–1637).[20] Gassendi credits Peiresc as the first who found and bought the marbles through "a certain Samson, who took care of his affairs in Smyrna."[21] According to Gassendi, when the marbles were about to be shipped, "I do not know by what stratagem of the sellers, Samson was imprisoned."[22] Gassendi, however, emphasizes Peiresc's gentlemanly reaction when he found out that the marbles were in good hands. Gassendi suggests that the sellers were to blame, but in his 1676 edition Prideaux made minor changes to Gassendi's story by blaming the Turks (*turcarum fraude*) and noting that Petty bought the marbles for a higher price. Later editors, Boeckh (CIG 2374), Hiller von Gärtringen (IG XII.5 444), and Jacoby (1904a:vi) repeat a conflation of Gassendi's story with Prideaux's additions almost word by word.[23]

The "certain Samson" who seems to have been instrumental in collecting the Peiresc or Arundel marbles was Samson Napollon (1583–1633), a Marseille merchant who became a diplomat.[24] On a mission to Constantinople, he visited Smyrna at least twice, in 1624 and early 1625, and was officially appointed consul in that city.[25] Samson sent antiquities to Peiresc at some point,[26] but in the surviving correspondence with him there is no mention of the marbles or

---

[18] The more famous one is the treaty between Smyrna and Magnesia (CIG 3137 = ISmyrna 573).

[19] Selden 1628. Selden studied the inscriptions with the help of Patrick Young (royal librarian to King Charles I) and Richard James. Selden's edition was published again in the same format in 1629.

[20] Gassendi 1641:239–240 (notes to year 1629).

[21] *per Samsonem quendam ipsius negotia Smyrna procurantem*, Gassendi 1641:239.

[22] *nescio qua venditorum arte, Samsonem conjectum in carcerem fuisse*, Gassendi 1641:239.

[23] Michaelis (1882:17) paraphrases Gassendi's stories focusing on Selden. Gassendi is cited by Prideaux as a source, but Boeckh and later editors use the information without mentioning him. In his recent biography of John Selden, Toomer (2009:361) suspects that Petty actually bribed the local officials in Smyrna.

[24] Samson is best known for the Truce of Treaty with Algiers in 1628. He was governor of the Bastion de France from 1630 until his death in 1633 (Miller 2005a:108–111 and 2005b:119–120).

[25] Miller 2005b:109–110.

[26] Miller 2005a:120n3.

the imprisonment.[27] As for Petty, although it is not impossible that he obtained the Parian Marble in Paros itself while travelling through Greece,[28] he could as well have interacted with Samson after he arrived in Smyrna in the last months of 1624.[29] Still, we have only Gassendi's testimony for the purchase of the Parian Marble at Smyrna. The city is not an improbable location, since at the time it was emerging as an important harbor for those travelling across the Mediterranean. If indeed the inscription was purchased in Smyrna, it may have been brought there from Paros either by or for any of those who were travelling at the time, collecting antiquities for individual patrons. The story of the upper section of the Parian Marble epitomizes to some extent the history of early European appropriation of antiquities.

Once in London, section A of the Parian Marble (Plate 1), along with the other "marbles," was located in the garden of Arundel's palace. When Prideaux published his 1676 edition, what was left of the Marbles had already been donated to Oxford University.[30] Prideaux mentions the neglect that the marbles suffered in the gardens of Arundel during the Civil War: some were damaged, some were stolen, and some were used for repairing the building.[31] By then, the upper part of section A, containing the first forty-five lines, was lost,[32] and the extant part was extremely defaced.[33] The inscription is nowadays displayed in the Ashmolean Museum. More than a hundred years ago, Munro still hoped that the lost part of the inscription might be recovered,[34] and perhaps so should we.

The second section of the stone, known as B (Plates 3–4), had a more straight-forward history. Indeed, B never left Paros. It was found on a private property southeast of Paroikia in 1897 and was published the same year by Krispi, with a commentary by Wilhelm. The discovery confirmed the hypothesis that Paros was the place where section A had originated. The Archaeological Museum of Paros houses the bottom section of the Parian Marble to this day.

---

[27] "Supporting documentation seems not to have survived" (Miller 2005b:109).

[28] Thomas Roe, ambassador in Constantinople, wrote to the Earl of Arundel that Petty "hath visited Pergamo, Samos, Ephesus, and some other places, where hee hath made your Lordship greate provisions, though hee lately wrote to mee he had found nothing worth" (20–30 October 1625).

[29] Michaelis 1882:11.

[30] The donation was made by Henry Howard in 1667 (Vickers 2006:38–40).

[31] Prideaux 1676:ix.

[32] Prideaux 1676:ix adds between brackets that the upper part was used to restore the palace's fireplace (preface), but it is unclear how Prideaux acquired this information.

[33] Already Dopp 1883 and Flach 1884 regretted the state of the Ashmolean section. They used a squeeze made by H. F. Pehlman (cf. IG XII.5 [p. 100]), now lost (Klaus Hallof, personal communication).

[34] "Prideaux says in his preface that this fragment was used to repair a fireplace in Arundel House, presumably a marble chimney-piece. If so, it may yet be recovered, for such a piece of furniture would be likely to be removed entire, and the slab may have been made into a panel or shelf and still retain the inscription on its inner face" (Munro 1901a:149n1).

3. Scholarship on the Parian Marble

Early editions of the upper section of the Parian Marble (A) appeared in books devoted to physical collections of statues and reliefs, as well as of Greek and Latin inscriptions: the *Marmora Arundelliana* by John Selden (1628, 1629), and the *Marmora Oxoniensia* by Humphrey Prideaux (1676), Michael Maittaire (1732) and Richard Chandler (1763).[35] After Selden, scholars mostly exercised conjecture rather than autopsy.[36] Their editions were based on Selden's transcription and (except for Chandler) they offered an incremental body of interpretation that summed up most scholarship on the Parian Marble current at the time.[37] In the eighteenth century, a few monographs discussed whether the Parian Marble might be a forgery.[38] The issue of authenticity, a forgotten chapter in the history of scholarship on the Parian Marble, was definitely settled with the discovery of section B. In the nineteenth century, section A of the Parian Marble was published in the then new and comprehensive corpora of inscriptions and fragments: by Boeckh in the *Corpus Inscriptionum Graecarum* (CIG 2374, 1843)[39] and by Müller in the *Fragmenta Historicorum Graecorum* (1853).[40] The studies of Dopp (1883) and Flach (1884, including an edition) followed.

With the discovery of B in 1897, new energies were directed towards the Parian Marble, which could now be seen as a nearly whole text. John A. Munro and Friedrich Hiller von Gärtringen carried out autopsy of the Ashmolean and the Parian sections.[41] While Munro published his own notes in two articles

---

[35] Prideaux 1676, Maittaire 1732, Chandler 1763 (Roberts 1791 reprinted the Greek inscriptions published by Chandler). I am grateful to the Houghton Library (Harvard University) for the opportunity to consult these early editions. The materials are also available online. They are, in principle, accessible to everybody, since copyrights expired long ago. But here we encounter a paradox of our current era. As digital technology advances and humanistic studies recede, accessibility is but an illusion. One still has to be able to read Latin to make use of them!

[36] From Prideaux's reading πρῶτος at A43, Connor (1990:28) infers that he must have seen the stone.

[37] Prideaux includes notes and commentary by Selden and Thomas Lydiatus, as well as his own. Maittaire's edition includes his own notes and commentary and those already included by Prideaux in his edition, adding those by Jacques Le Paulmier (written in 1668), John Marsham, Richard Bentley, and an Italian translation by Scipione Maffei.

[38] E.g. Robertson 1788, Hewlett 1789.

[39] Boeckh's edition is held in high esteem. However, he himself did not inspect the stone, but used unpublished notes by Reinhold Forster, who may have seen it. Boeckh gives no details of the Berlin manuscript containing Forster's notes, except that it was found in the Real Library of Berlin. Recovery of that manuscript would be an important contribution to the constitution of the Parian Marble's text. Jacoby, at any rate, took Forster as an important witness to the lost fragment.

[40] FHG 1:533–590, with introduction and notes, Latin translation and chronological tables.

[41] In the introduction to his IG edition, Hiller von Gärtringen acknowledges the help and erudition of Munro. He reports inspecting the Parian section in 1899 and spending five days examining the Ashmolean section together with Munro in October 1901.

(1901),[42] Hiller von Gärtringen provided the first critical edition of the complete Parian Marble in 1903, in the twelfth volume of the *Inscriptiones Graecae* (IG XII.5 444).[43] Both scholars reported the difficulties in getting any good readings out of A. Jacoby himself saw only pictures of the inscription when he published his *Habilitation* thesis in 1904,[44] at the age of twenty-eight, but he profited from the work of Hiller von Gärtringen, Munro, and others.[45] Although Jacoby's edition of 1904 was superseded by his own FGrH 239 (hereafter referred to as Jacoby's edition), the authoritative critical edition until today, the former remains useful for its fuller list of parallel passages, its discussion of sources, and its more complete report of the textual tradition. Similarly, his companion article published in *Rheinisches Museum* in 1904 is still fundamental for such issues as the constitution of the text, the author and his sources, language, chronographic method, possible reasons for setting up the inscription, and possible locations.

English translations of the complete inscription are not readily available. At the time I began this project, only the English translation made by Gillian Newing for the Ashmolean Museum's website was available,[46] whereas Robertson and Hewlett include only section A.[47] The situation changed with the recent publication of Burgess's translation,[48] which addresses a non-specialist public, and will change further with the one expected to appear in Brill's New Jacoby, for a more specialized audience.

No study of the Parian Marble has challenged Jacoby's monumental contribution. After Laqueur's comprehensive treatment in *RE* (1930), scholars have

---

[42] Munro 1901a and 1901b. Of the edition Munro was preparing nothing is known. Many of his readings, not to be found in his 1901 articles (including information in erasures), have reached us through Hiller von Gärtringen's notes. The IG archive does not hold any correspondence between the two.

[43] The Addenda et Corrigenda from 1909 acknowledge Jacoby's 1904 edition, as well as Munro's and Dopp's reviews (Munro 1905, Dopp 1905). In *Der Neue Pauly* and *Brill's New Pauly*, s.v. "Marmor Parium," references to Hiller von Gärtringen's edition should be corrected to IG XII (instead of XIII), and IG XII Suppl. 1909 (instead of 1939).

[44] The drawings of A2 and B provided by Hiller von Gärtringen and Jacoby 1904a:appendix 2 and 3 are probably based on the ones currently held at the IG archive in Berlin (Klaus Hallof, personal communication).

[45] Jacoby was then in Berlin and seems to have counted on Hiller von Gärtringen's advice, as well as that of Munro, with whom he corresponded (Jacoby 1904a:ix). Wilamowitz, to whom Jacoby dedicated his *Das Marmor Parium*, was his academic advisor; his readings must derive from personal communication. The IG archive holds a letter that Holleaux wrote to Jacoby on 3 November 1903, from which Jacoby derived a reading in line 57 (ὑποχείριον ἠσφαλίστο, A42). A sense of collaboration among scholars of different nationalities and ages emerges from the introductions to Hiller von Gärtringen's and Jacoby's editions. In turn, Munro 1905 and Dopp 1905 offer the perspective of senior scholars on the accomplishments of the young Jacoby.

[46] Michael Vickers, personal communication.

[47] Robertson 1788, Hewlett 1789.

[48] Burgess and Kulikowski 2013:301-309.

tended to focus on individual issues. Thus Chaniotis saw the inscription as an isolated example of epigraphical universal history and re-assessed the issue of authorship, rejecting Demeas and Mnesiepes.[49] He also argued against the location of the Parian Marble in the Archilocheion (see below). Rosenberger examined the issue of identities in the Parian Marble.[50] Clarke studied the inscription in the context of the ancient Greek chronographic tradition, pointing out the central role played by intellectuals and endorsing the location at the Archilocheion.[51] Ornaghi compared the Parian Marble to the Mnesiepes inscription, setting both in the context of the Parian cult of Archilochus.[52]

4. The Chronographic System of the Parian Marble

The Parian Marble records a variety of events and figures: the rise to power of rulers and states, battles fought, cities founded, temples built, games established, first victories at poetic contests, births and deaths of political and cultural figures. Information is given in entries with repeated formulae: "From when X happened, Y years, when Z was archon [or king] at Athens," for example:[53]

ἀφ' οὗ Ὅμηρος ὁ ποιητὴς ἐφάνη, ἔτη ΓΗΔΔΔΔΙΙΙ, βασιλεύοντος Ἀθηνῶ[ν Δ]ιογνήτου. [A29]

From when Homer the poet appeared, 643 years, when Diognetos was king of Athens.

The opening of the inscription announces that the text has a definite time-span: from the kingship of Cecrops until the archonship of Diognetus in Athens and the archonship of an individual in Paros whose name ended in -υαναξ.[54] The archonship of Diognetus sets a time limit equivalent to the year 264/3 BCE.[55] The text counts down years between events in the past and that ending point, beginning

---

[49] Chaniotis 1988:87–89.

[50] Rosenberger 2008.

[51] Clarke 2008:330–331, 325–335.

[52] Ornaghi 2009:273–279.

[53] For variation within the entries' default structure, see chap. 4, sec. 1 below.

[54] Selden 1628:72 suggested Astyanax; Boeckh considered other alternatives, such as Euryanax and Polyanax. A prosopographic work by Berranger (2000:34, 168) takes Astyanax for granted. A Parian archon list was used by Demeas on his work on Archilochus; cf. the Sosthenes inscription, IG XII.5 445, line 9.

[55] Diognetus is not attested elsewhere. The date 264/3, which depends on the assumption that the author was counting years exclusively (Cadoux 1948:83–86), is widely accepted (sometimes 263/2 is preferred, as in Hiller von Gärtringen's edition and Hazzard 2000).

from 1318 (equivalent to 1581/0 BCE).[56] As items progress, the number of years decreases.[57] The use of Athenian kings and archons, instead of Olympiads, may be surprising in a chronicle of panhellenic scope. However, the absence of the Olympiadic framework in the Parian Marble should not be understood as a rejection of a dominant system. The Olympiad system hardly became a standard for ancient historiography before the second century BCE,[58] and even after it was established, local lists of magistrates continued to be written and employed by officials, as well as by local historians all over the Greek-speaking world. The Athenian archon list, probably compiled and published by 420 BCE, may have been the only chronological system available to the author of the Parian Marble and his sources.[59] We shall return to this topic in Chapter 5, section 1 below.

While the Parian Marble uses as its diachronic axis a well-established system, namely, the Athenian archon list, its counting down to a year 1 is rather unusual. Herodotus uses his own present as a point of reference when speaking about the past,[60] but his expression "up to my own time" (ἐς ἐμέ) was not part of a systematic chronography.[61] And yet, from Jacoby on, many scholars have been satisfied by citing Herodotus for the Parian Marble's count-down of years to a present date, whereas only two such instances are known among Greek chronographic materials: the Roman Chronicle (*Chronicon Romanum*) and the Getty Table (*Getty Tabula*). Although the latter was unknown to Jacoby, only these use the expression μέχρι τοῦδε (*Chronicon Romanum* col. A, line 31; Getty Tabula col. IIB, lines 6, 10, 18),

---

56 It has been argued that the year 1581/0 BCE may be the starting point of an alternative system of numbering Olympic games (Lämmer 1967, Christesen 2005:344–345n63). An inscribed discus dedicated at Olympia (IvO 240, 241) refers to the 255th Olympiad (= 241 CE) on one side, and to the 456th Olympiad (*sic*) on the other, implying two different starting points for the Olympic games, the usual one, 776 BCE, and another at 1581/0 BCE. An honorary inscription from Ephesus (CIG 2999 = IEph 1121, 245 CE) seems to use the same year as a starting point, if the corrected number is right (υνζ' instead of υνε'). Ebert 1987, however, sets the mythical beginning of the Olympic games *ca.* 1,600 BCE. I am grateful to Klaus Hallof for these references.

57 The only reference to the present time appears in A5, where the place of the Amphictyons' sacrifice (at Delphi, though it is not made explicit) is said to be the same "where they still sacrifice nowadays" (οὖ[περ] καὶ νῦν ἔτι θύουσιν Ἀμφικτύονες). We cannot say, however, whether the present time is that of the author or his sources.

58 The list of winners at the stadion in Olympia was compiled by Hippias of Elis in the late fifth century BCE. The numbers of the Olympiads were added in the early third century by Timaeus of Tauromenium, while Eratosthenes based his chronological system on it in the late third century (Christesen 2007:8-13, see chap. 3, sec. 1 below). Incidentally, the Olympic games are not mentioned in the extant text, even though the inscription refers to the most important panhellenic festivals (unless the beginnings of the Olympic games are considered to coincide with or antedate the opening of the chronicle, see n. 56 above). Hiller von Gärtringen supplemented a reference to Olympia in A17, Boeckh in A18.

59 On the Athenian archon list, see Dinsmoor 1939, Merrit 1977, Mosshammer 1979:100–104, Osborne 1989, with further references. See also chap. 5, sec. 1 below.

60 Jacoby 1904b:85–88, Cobet 2002:397 with n. 25, van Wees 2002:322 with n. 2, Möller 2006:269.

61 Fowler 1996:73, 76–77, van Wees 2002:322n2.

which seems to suggest that the time of writing is taken as year 1 (I discuss these two chronicles in detail in Chapter 3, section 2 below).

Chronicles tend to be cumulative. In fact, ancient chronographic materials leave the impression that time is open, in the sense that lists could be, at least in principle, continued. A number of epigraphic eponymous lists and victor lists, where additions were made by different hands, illustrate this open quality.[62] In contrast, our inscription announces that it will end at a specific point in time. Thus, the Parian Marble has "closure," as literary and historiographical works do. Whatever sources the author of the Parian Marble used,[63] he was the one who probably made the effort to convert chronographic references into intervals from the point of closure. Such efforts make sense if that point is meaningful: if, that is, the series of years ends with it and something new begins.[64] Is it possible that our chronicle marks the beginning of a chronographic era? Hazzard combined numismatic evidence with the Parian Marble in order to put forward precisely that argument.[65] Indeed, more than a hundred coins showing Ptolemy I's head had for some time been understood as possibly marking an unknown era beginning between 265 and 255 BCE.[66] Hazzard suggests the Parian Marble points to the beginning of that era, which he denominates the "Soter Era," an era that Ptolemy Philadelphos would have introduced in 263/62 BCE in order to commemorate his father.[67] This roughly coincides with the appearance of the expression "son of Ptolemy Soter" in legal documents that Ptolemy II issued from 259 BCE until the end of his reign.[68] Hazzard's hypothesis was received with some skepticism among scholars,[69] and it cannot be confirmed without the end of the inscription. Yet support may be found, in addition to the

---

[62] For various hands in archon lists, see Bradeen 1963:198–200; for the Athenian Fasti and Didascaliae, see Millis and Olson 2012:5–6, 77, 134–135. On the general lack of closure in annals and chronicles, see White 1987.

[63] On the sources of the Parian Marble, see Dopp 1983:5–42, Jacoby 1904a *passim* and 1904b:xi–xviii.

[64] "What makes the year 264/3 so important?" asks Rosenberger. His answer—the Chremonidean War—is consistent with the interesting proposition that "the Marmor Parium was an attempt to establish the alliance between Athens and Alexandria by underlining the cultural importance of Athens in the Greek world, thus giving a historical-cultural explanation for a war against Macedonia" (Rosenberger 2008:230).

[65] Hazzard 2000:25–46, 161–176.

[66] Mørkholm 1975–76:52, though he assigns the coins to an Aradian era. Lorber 2007 suggests that the era commemorated events unrelated to Ptolemy II.

[67] Hazzard 2000:25–46. Hazzard dates year 1 of the Parian Marble to 263/2 BCE. The Soter Era would have begun in year 262 BCE, when the Great Ptolemaic procession was celebrated, to which the island league was invited.

[68] Hazzard 2000:3–24.

[69] Huss 2001:320–323, Chaniotis 2007. Hazzard's conclusions seem to have been rejected especially because of his manipulation of dates for the Grand Procession to coincide with the proposed Soter Era (cf. Marquaille 2008:54 with further references). More sympathetic to Hazzard's hypothesis is Ornaghi 2009:273–279.

numismatic evidence, in the Ptolemaic bias of the chronicle, already noted by Jacoby.[70] Moreover, Paros seems to have been under Ptolemaic government at the time, as a member of the League of the Islands.[71]

Although the evidence is circumstantial, Hazzard's hypothesis is the most plausible explanation for the Parian Marble's chronographic system. The non-scholarly nature of the inscription precludes, in my view, direct Ptolemaic commission.[72] Still, the author may well have wanted to align himself with Ptolemaic ideology by combining political and cultural interests with a Ptolemaic chronographic framework, i.e. the newly established era. If the hypothesis of the Parian Marble using this era is rejected, we are left with the possibility that the author of the Parian Marble may have counted years down to an event of local interest that is now lost to us.[73]

5. The Location of the Parian Marble

Where was the stele containing the Parian Marble originally displayed? A certain answer to this question cannot be provided.[74] As I noted at the beginning of this chapter, there is no information on the finding of the inscription that might help us locate it in a specific archaeological site. I suggest that the unusual prominence of poets and musicians, which I discuss in detail in Chapter 6, indicates the type of location we should be looking for—one that is related to literary activities. We know of one such plausible location on the island of Paros, where other instances of monumental historiography have also been found. Indeed, in addition to the Parian Marble, Paros has yielded some of the earliest and more impressive instances of ancient Greek historical inscriptions. Two narratives on the life and work of Archilochus have come down to us: the Mnesiepes

---

[70]   Jacoby 1904b:79–80 (cf. B8, B19, B23), Hazzard 2000:162–163.

[71]   CIG 3655, Pausanias 1.25.3; cf. Krispi and Wilhelm 1897:207–208 (Wilhelm), Jacoby FGrH 239 (commentary):666, Bagnall 1976:150, Berranger 2000:116–118, Constantakopoulou 2012:57, 67. For Paros in the third century BCE, see Lanzillotta 1987:157–173.

[72]   A case for comparison is the Egyptian priest Manetho, who wrote a chronicle of the Egyptian dynasties that may have been partly inspired by Ptolemaic interests (cf. a dedication to Ptolemy Philadelphus reported by Syncellus pp. 40-41 Mosshammer, cf. Waddell 1956:208–211, which many consider the work of a pseudo-Manetho). Manetho's fragments are available in Waddell 1956 and Verbrugghe and Wickersham 1996. For a comparison between Manetho and ancient Greek historiography, see Dillery 1999. I thank Jennifer Gates-Foster for suggesting the comparison.

[73]   Perhaps, as Rosenberger (2008:230; see n. 64 above) suggests, to the Chremonidean war.

[74]   Chaniotis 1988:102–112 points at the lack of evidence for the path followed in this section. His conclusions (p. 112) are very similar to those reached by Jacoby 1904b:101–102: namely, that the inscription was a private donation for display in a public place, either the agora or the foyer of a gymnasium, or in the sacred area of a temple. Chaniotis, however, rejected the possibility of a gymnasium.

inscription and the Sosthenes inscription. Whereas the Sosthenes inscription (early first century BCE), has been known from 1900, the Mnesiepes inscription (third century BCE, Plates 7–8),[75] was only found half a century later. From the time it was discovered (1949) and published (1955), scholars have linked the Mnesiepes inscription to the Parian Marble. To begin with, the Parian Marble provides a suitable *comparandum*. Similarity of lettering with the Parian Marble supports the dating of the Mnesiepes inscription to the mid-third century BCE (Plate 9).[76] At the same time, the Mnesiepes inscription is suggestive of a plausible location for the Parian Marble. Indeed, both the Mnesiepes and the Sosthenes inscriptions were written on orthostats and were therefore part of walls, of a temenos or of a building. The nature of this site is illuminated by the Mnesiepes inscription itself. The text makes clear that it comes from an Archilocheion, a precinct built as a place to honor Archilochus along with Apollo, the Muses, and other gods:

χρήσαντος δὲ τοῦ Ἀπόλλωνος ταῦτα τόν τε τόπον
καλοῦμεν Ἀρχιλόχειον καὶ τοὺς βωμοὺς ἱδρύμεθα
καὶ θύομεν καὶ τοῖς θεοῖς καὶ Ἀρχιλόχωι καὶ
τιμῶμεν αὐτόν, καθ' ἃ ὁ θεὸς ἐθέσπισεν ἡμῖν.

Since Apollo declared these things, we call the place the Archilocheion and we set up altars and we sacrifice both to the gods and to Archilochus and we honor him in accordance with the god's oracular response to us. [lines 16–19][77]

---

[75] IG XII.5 445, with Suppl. pp. 212–214 (Sosthenes), Kontoleon 1952 [1955], Peek 1955, SEG 15.517 (1958), Clay 2004 (Mnesiepes). References to the substantial bibliography dealing with these inscriptions can be found in Clay 2004, Hawkins 2009, Ornaghi 2009:38–65, Kivilo 2010:88–89. 95–102, 107–109, Rotstein 2010:294–298, and Lefkowitz 2012:167.

[76] Kontoleon's dating (1952 [1955]:36, 1956:399 and 1964a:44, 46, 52–54) has never been challenged (cf. Peek 1955:5, Robert and Robert 1955:248, Parke 1958:90, SEG 15.517 (1958), Treu 1959:205, Clay 2004:12). The two inscriptions, however, were cut by two different letter-cutters. Lettering of the Parian Marble displays early Hellenistic characteristics: rather small round letters (O and Ω), a geometric aspect in letters with straight strokes (Σ, Δ, Η, Ε), and occasional curving of the straight verticals of Ε and Μ. The Mnesiepes inscription displays a bigger Ο and Θ, a bigger and more open Ω, the three usually aligned to the top of the line; more curving of straight verticals, minor signs of apicature, and the cross-bar of alpha slightly broken. All in all, the Mnesiepes inscription has a more regular lettering and less contrast between narrow and broad letters (Α and Λ six to seven mm wide, Σ five mm wide, Μ five to six mm wide, cf. three mm on the Parian Marble). Letters in the Mnesiepes inscription are one to two mm shorter than on the Parian Marble. See Rotstein 2014 for a fuller comparison of formal features in both inscriptions.

[77] Translated by Gerber 1999:19. Hiller von Gärtringen postulated an Archilocheion on the basis of the Sosthenes inscription, before the discovery of the Mnesiepes inscription (IG XII.5 445). That both inscriptions refer to the same Archilocheion is the most reasonable assumption, though this need not coincide with an earlier burial place (see Clay 2004:35–38, with further references).

The precise location of the Archilocheion is difficult to establish because of the dispersion and the secondary use of the remains.[78] However, we can attempt to understand the nature of the Archilocheion by comparison with other shrines named after poets. There was a building named Homereion in second-century BCE Delos.[79] In the same period, a gymnasion named Homereion is attested in Notion, near Colophon,[80] and later on in Chios too.[81] Smyrna had two gymnasia linked to the cult of poets: a Homereion[82] and a Mimnermeion.[83] In late third-century Thespiae, Hesiod was honored along with the Muses,[84] and a boundary stone mentions a religious association of Hesiodians, in relation to the cult of the Muses.[85] These testimonies indicate that shrines honoring poets in Hellenistic Greece, as other hero shrines, were linked to gymnasia and mouseia.[86] They strongly support the notion that the Archilocheion was an institution related to literary activities, namely a gymnasion or a mouseion, a hypothesis put forward by Kontoleon, which has elicited much scholarly agreement.[87] If the Archilocheion was such an institution, it could have been a place for classes,

---

[78] Perhaps the most attractive hypothesis is that of Ohnesorg (1982 and 2008), who reconstructed the architectural form of a fourth century BCE Doric temple, identified it as the Archilocheion, and suggested that it was originally located in the Elitas valley near the Tris Ekklesies. Clay 2004:36–38 proposed a location along the banks of the Elitas (see p. 123 for other possible locations).

[79] IDelos 2.443, 178 BCE, cf. Farnoux 2002.

[80] Cf. a decree in honor of Athenaeus (Macridy 1905:161–163), which Gauthier (2006:486–488) dates to 180–160 BCE.

[81] CIG 2221, first century CE, cf. Peek 1976. See also Aelian *Historical Miscellanies* 13.22, for the temple to Homer built by Ptolemy Philopator in Alexandria.

[82] ISmyrna 214, Strabo 14.1.37.

[83] ISmyrna 215 (= CIG 3376), first century CE.

[84] IG VII 4240.

[85] IG VII 1785 (= SEG LIV 511), Tanagra, late third century BCE. The site may have been called Hesiodeion. See IG VII 4240, found near Thespiae for a stele dedicated to the Muses, where the personified Helicon gives an oracle regarding the blessings awaiting those who follow Hesiod's teaching.

[86] A long inscription from Thera provides the best example of a Mouseion including a shrine for hero cult, a provision of Epicteta for her husband and sons (IG XII.3 330, ca. 210–195 BCE). Similarly, a third-century inscription from Istria witnesses both cult and mouseion (IIstria 1, no. 1.15–26); cf. Fraser 1972:312–313, Clay 2004:72–74, with n83 for further references. On the cult of poets, see Clay 2004:63–98 and Kimmel 2008:547–675, with further references. Kimmel 2008:63–248 offers a useful collection of testimonies for Homer, Hesiod, Archilochus, Pindar, Aeschylus, Sophocles, and Euripides.

[87] Kontoleon 1952 [1955]:48–53, 1956, 1964a:51–52, and 1964b:200, Robert and Robert 1955:248 (favoring a mouseion rather than a gymnasion), Tarditi 1956:124, Treu 1959:205–207, Privitera 1966, Fraser 1972:313n57, Berranger 2000:114. Jacoby (1904b:102), who favored a gymnasium or the agora as possible locations for the Parian Marble, was not persuaded by the Mnesiepes inscription that the Parian Marble was set up in the Archilocheion (Jacoby 1955). See Chaniotis 1988:102–112 for arguments against the hypothesis that the Archilocheion was a gymnasion or mouseion.

lectures, meetings, recitals, and perhaps even poetic contests, by local as well as by itinerant performers.[88] The shrine may have been maintained by a professional association, similar to the Hesiodians in Thespiae. Indeed, Mnesiepes's use of plural verbs for the establishment of Archilochus's cult suggests that he is a member of a group. Such a *synodos* or *thiasos*, as has been suggested, could be a guild of rhapsodes,[89] similar to the Homeridai, a guild that possibly claimed descent from Archilochus. As in other shrines, the Archilocheion may have guarded Archilochus's works,[90] and it may have also housed a collection of books, as mouseia and gymnasia did.[91]

In such a place where the Muses and Archilochus were honored, where literary activities and meetings of an association of poets or rhapsodes may have taken place, where a collection of books was possibly kept and the results of literary research displayed, the Parian Marble would have been entirely in place.

Kontoleon's hypothesis that the Parian Marble was displayed at the Archilocheion has been given serious scholarly consideration.[92] Chaniotis objected to it on several grounds, in particular, that the Parian Marble seems not to know Archilochus, while the Mnesiepes and the Sosthenes inscriptions celebrate him.[93] However, in the type of setting that we have reconstructed, the Parian Marble may have had a different purpose altogether: not to celebrate

---

[88] Of the sort amply described in Hunter and Rutherford 2009. The cult of the Muses and, more specifically, mouseia were often associated with literary activities, such as recitals or poetic competitions; cf. Fraser 1972:313, Cameron 1995:24–70.

[89] Peek 1955:13–14, Tarditi 1956:124, 139, Nagy 1979:304, Clay 2004:10, Lefkowitz 2012:32.

[90] Pohlmann 1994:14–15.

[91] E.g. Demeas's work on Paros and Archilochus, mentioned at the beginning of the Sosthenes inscription. It is possible that the Archilocheion kept not only the poems of Archilochus, but also a book collection. The most famous instance of a mouseion housing a library is, of course, that of Alexandria. Temples are known to have housed books (e.g. Pausanias 9.31.3–5, on Hesiod's work), and this may have been the case of the Homereia (cf. Strabo 14.1.37) and the Mimnermeion. On book collections kept in Hellenistic gymnasia and libraries attached to gymnasia (e.g. at the Ptolemaeum in Athens, in Rhodes, Pergamon, Teos, Cos, and probably in Tauromenium), see Burzachechi 1963 and 1984, Nicolai 1987, Yegül 1992:7, 14–15, Scholz 2004:125–127, Ameling 2004:153–154 with n162.

[92] Kontoleon 1964a:52–53, Kontoleon 1964b:199–200 (first in 1952[1955]:52), Peek 1955:46, Vanderpool 1955:186, Graham 1978:83, Rosenberger 2008:228, Clarke 2008:330, Ornaghi 2009:273–274, Hawkins 2011.

[93] Chaniotis 1988:102–112. Chaniotis rejected the notion that the Archilocheion was a gymnasion and that it was founded by an association of rhapsodes. Instead, he postulated that it was a hero-shrine established by a private fund. Consequently he objected to the thesis that the Parian Marble was displayed at the Archilocheion, for which, admittedly, there is no direct evidence. Following Jacoby 1904b:103, who was reluctant to link the Parian Marble to the Archilocheion (FGrH 502), even after the discovery of the Mnesiepes inscription (Jacoby 1955), Chaniotis favors the hypothesis of display at a public place such as the agora (though Jacoby considered a gymnasion a possible location).

Archilochus, but to advertise the role of poets in history. Its purpose may have also been practical: a reference work for readers to consult.[94] Indeed, the complete layout of history in one stele may not have been significantly more difficult to consult than a papyrus roll. Still, whether or not the inscription was read from beginning to end, it had symbolic value nonetheless, as a visual representation of the reckoning of times past.

Given the state of our evidence, any answers to questions regarding the location of the Parian Marble remain speculative.[95] However, if it is granted that the Parian Marble was composed for display at the Archilocheion, and if this shrine was a site of literary learning, the large number of poets in the inscription certainly starts making sense.

---

[94]   Niese 1888:95 suggested the work was set up for use at a school (*contra* Chaniotis 1988:111).

[95]   The issue partly depends on the perception of similarities and differences with other types of inscriptions, such as the Tabulae Iliacae (see chap. 3, sec. 2 below) and the Athenian record of dramatic performance (see chap. 6, sec. 1, 2.IV below).

Chapter 2
Text and Translation

1. Introduction

For more than a century, Jacoby's has been the authoritative text of the Parian Marble, first through his 1904 *Habilitation* thesis, later through the collection of historical fragments (FGrH 239), hereafter referred to as Jacoby's edition. His work was timely, indeed. By 1904, section B of the inscription, just discovered (1897), had already been edited by Krispi and commented upon by Wilhelm, and two outstanding scholars, Munro and Hiller von Gärtringen, had performed autopsies of both the Ashmolean and the Parian fragments.[1] Although Jacoby did not see the inscriptions but worked with photographs, he was in a position to examine the entire tradition with the tools and perspectives of philology and epigraphy. He established the value of the main witnesses for the constitution of the text by detailed philological analysis.[2] Furthermore, Jacoby, in addition to his own experience of working on ancient Greek chronography,[3] counted on Wilamowitz's supervision and on the insights of Hiller von Gärtringen, Munro, and other scholars through correspondence and personal communication.[4] Yet his edition, as with most scholarly work, cannot be definitive—although not because new readings have emerged from autopsy. The damage to the Ashmolean section is so extensive that nothing new can be gained from it (although innovative digitization techniques may bring some unexpected surprises), whereas the Parian section is in relatively good shape, except for major lacunae at the center of the last twelve lines. The problem with Jacoby's edition is that it gives too much, especially for the lost part of the inscription.

---

[1] See chap. 1, sec. 3 above.

[2] For the lost fragment, Jacoby depends mainly on Selden, with a number of readings by Reinhold Forster and Chandler, although some of them, particularly Chandler's, may have resulted from conjecture.

[3] Möller 2006.

[4] Jacoby 1904a:ix (Jacoby believed that little could be read on the stone beyond what Hiller von Gärtringen and Munro reported from autopsy).

Indeed, the situation of the first forty-five lines (twenty-nine entries) of the Parian Marble is often desperate. For its constitution we depend entirely on Selden.[5] His majuscule and minuscule transcriptions, published at the beginning of the seventeenth century, do not conform to current standards of epigraphical notation and are not equivalent to diplomatic and edited transcriptions of texts. A crucial difference lies in the use of dots for signaling the presence of lacunae, rather than the probable number of missing letters based on traces seen on the surface.[6] The unreliable nature of Selden's dots has been made clear by the control of the Ashmolean section.[7] Sometimes the number of dots exceeds the number of letters missing.[8] Occasionally Selden has dots for lacunae that cannot be seen on the stone.[9] In most cases, it seems that the number of Selden's dots is significantly smaller than the size of the lacunae (e.g. A41), or lacunae are omitted where traces can be seen, especially at the end of lines (e.g. A45).[10] Indeed, Jacoby's detailed study of line-length indicates that even if the average line of A was between 90 and 110 letters long[11] (in B, between 110 and 130), in many cases a quarter of the line is missing, if not more. Often Selden simply made mistakes, as Jacoby's detailed comparison of his transcription against Munro's autopsy of the Ashmolean fragment suggests.[12] To the problems in the *editio princeps* one should add a difficulty inherent in the inscription itself—namely,

---

[5] Selden 1628 provided two transcriptions: one in majuscule, one in minuscule (the latter with parallel Latin translation). Modern editors (Boeckh, Hiller von Gärtringen, Jacoby) consider only the majuscule transcription relevant for the constitution of the text, as well as the *Errata* at the end of his 1628 edition (Jacoby 1904b:75–76). Selden's minuscule edition, aimed at aiding the reader, offers no division into lines or entries (epochae), unlike the majuscule text that was divided by lines. The minuscule edition rarely includes supplements or conjectures, which can be found in his notes.

[6] In many cases, numbers of dots in the majuscule transcription differ from the minuscule one. For example, at the end of A23 (lines 38–39) the dating formula requires supplementing six or eight letters: βασιλεύοντος Ἀθη‖[νῶν (or Ἀθή‖[νησιν) Μεν]εσθέως. Selden has ΒΑΣΛΕΥΟΝΤΟΣ ΑΘΗ | ... ΕΣΘΕΩΣ and βασιλεύοντος Αθ ...., with three and seven dots respectively.

[7] Line 54 (A38–A39) is a good example of Selden's arbitrary allocation of lacunae (Lacunae falso indicatae, cum de supplementis vix dubitari possit. Vides hic quoque quid Seldeni punctis tribuendum sit, Hiller von Gärtringen's note to line 54); cf. Jacoby "S' unbrauchbare lückenangaben" (1904a:105).

[8] At the beginning of line 8, for example, Selden has two dots where a single broad letter must be missing: .. TH and .. τη for ἔτη. Similarly, Selden's transcription of the end of line 48, HP.. EN .. P .. ΩΝΕΤ .. ΗΗΗΗΔΔ, later reported by Munro's autopsy as ΗΡΞΕΝΟΑΡΧΩΝ, represents ἦρξεν ὁ ἄρχων, ἔτη ΗΗΗΗΔΔ. That is, in the first, third, and fourth places, the pair of dots stand for single broad letters, Ξ, Χ, Η, and in the second place for two letters, ΟΑ. At the beginning of line 69, Selden has 5 dots, where Munro (1901b:358) confirms that only one letter is missing.

[9] As in A48 (line 62), after Πέρσας (Munro 1901b:357).

[10] Jacoby 1904b:72.

[11] Jacoby (1904a:26) suggests that letters in the first three lines of the inscription may have been slightly bigger, so as to facilitate reading.

[12] Jacoby 1904b:63–76.

the irregularity in the lines' length, due to a marked contrast in the width of letters.[13]

Jacoby was acutely aware of the hazardous nature of restoration when the number of missing characters is unclear, and thus gives supplements as examples,[14] but he operates differently in each section. In his edition of the Parian fragment (B), he was extremely cautious and rejected some of the supplements proposed by Wilhelm.[15] In the lost and the Ashmolean fragments (A), however, although his judgment is in most cases sound, he often indulged in over-restoration, perhaps under the burden of a long philological tradition.[16] There is also a difference between the 1904 and the FGrH editions. In the early edition, the conjectural character of supplements was graphically marked by the use of a smaller font,[17] but his FGrH edition, following the general style of the collection, displays both transmitted and restored text in the same font size.

A declaration that supplements are given *exempli gratia* is not enough. Jacoby's text has become canonical, including everything printed between square brackets.[18] As my predecessors were well aware, without knowing the exact length of lacunae, restoration is little more than guesswork. Nor can we predict where the author followed or departed from known traditions. I therefore avoid the more substantial supplements, indicating in footnotes where I depart from Jacoby's FGrH edition. Similarly, maintaining the *editio princeps*'s dots for most of A, as Jacoby did, would wrongly encourage restoration (as if the

---

[13] Jacoby 1904b:73–74, Rotstein 2014:7.

[14] Jacoby 1904a:xi and 1904b:72–75, FGrH 239 (commentary):665. For lacunae that could not be confirmed, Hiller von Gärtringen also notes the maximum number of dots found in Selden. The problem was already discussed by Dopp 1883:2 regarding Boeckh's edition.

[15] B20 (Demetrius of Phalerum) is the only long supplement that Jacoby allowed in the Parian fragment.

[16] Munro's review (1905) of Jacoby's 1904 edition relates precisely to this flaw.

[17] Jacoby's 1904 apparatus offers a more comprehensive review of the history of restoration than his FGrH one. Some omissions are tendentious, for example, in A17 and A18 restorations pointing at the Olympic games are rightly omitted from the text (Hiller von Gärtringen includes it in A17), but not so from the apparatus. I note some of those omissions in the notes on the Greek text.

[18] So, for example, restored sections of the Parian Marble are cited as evidence for the origins of the Nemean Games in Opheltes's funerary games (BNP s.v. 'Opheltes', by A. Ambühl, cf. notes to A22), or tragedy and the City Dionysia having being held under Pisistratus (e.g. DTC² 69 based on A43, cf. Connor 1990:26–32). Munro's comments (1901a:149–150) regarding Boeckh's edition, which he deeply admired, can be applied to Jacoby's: "It is the foundation on which all later editors have built, and enjoys such unquestioned acceptance that even in scholarly works Boeckh's restorations are commonly quoted as if they had the authority of the Marble itself. Boeckh has indeed done more for the restoration and interpretation of the text than anyone since Selden, and more than anyone will ever be able to do again. But his edition has not the finality which has sometimes been attributed to it. Perhaps no edition can ever be final, for the reconstruction of the text is a very difficult matter."

dots did represent the precise number of missing characters).[19] I have therefore avoided dots in the lost part of the inscription, marking instead the presence of lacunae of unknown size. When possible, I add Jacoby's or my own approximate figures for the sizes of those lacunae. The result is less of the Parian Marble than we used to have. Yet by giving a more precise account of our witnesses and by omitting speculation, we may nonetheless get closer to the original text.

I have used the Leiden system, which sometimes differs from Jacoby's sigla:

[αβγ]	restoration of missing letters
⟨αβγ⟩	addition and substitution
{αβγ}	suppression of letters seen on the stone (instead of Jacoby's ⟦αβγ⟧)
[- - -]	lacuna of unknown extent, instead of Jacoby's asterisk (I use it also for places, especially in A, where Jacoby gives dots, even though the extent of missing characters is unknown)
[- - - ca. 20 - - -]	lacuna with estimate number of missing letters
⟨⟨abc⟩⟩	erasures (which Jacoby mentions only in his apparatus)
α β γ	in the lost section of A, dots mark departures from Selden's *editio princeps*;[20] from A35 on they indicate uncertain letters
ΑΒΓ	letters of uncertain interpretation

I omit underlining to mark letters seen by earlier authors, which can no longer be seen (the case of the first 45 lines). Question marks signal the more tentative character of restoration, as in Jacoby's edition, though not necessarily in the same places. To aid reading and consultation, the text is structured upon entries with vertical lines and accompanying line numbers (e.g. |²) indicating line breaks on the stone.[21]

My English translation attempts to render the formulaic style of the inscription. It includes square brackets marking restoration, three dots signaling lacunae, and minor additions between round brackets. To aid the readers, I give Jacoby's conversion of years to the Common Era.

---

[19] Munro 1905 and Dopp 1905 criticized the young Jacoby precisely for that.
[20] As in Jacoby's edition, e.g. μετ' Ἀδράσ[του instead of Selden's ΝΕΥΑΔΡΑΣ (A22, line 37); Jacoby 1904 uses square brackets to mark the μ and the τ.
[21] As in Jacoby's edition. Jacoby 1904a is organized upon lines.

2. Greek Text

A1. The Lost Fragment

[- - -]ΟΥ[- - -]ν παν[τοί]ων [- - -]νων ἀνέγραψα τοὺς ἀν[- - -] |² [- - -]²²
ἀρξάμ[εν]ος ἀπὸ Κέκροπος τοῦ πρώτου βασιλεύσαντος Ἀθηνῶν εἵως
ἄρχοντος ἐμ Πάρωι [- - -] |³ [- - -]υάνακτος,²³ Ἀθήνησιν δὲ Διογνήτου.
(vac. ca. 5)²⁴

1. ἀφ᾽ οὗ Κέκροψ Ἀθηνῶν ἐβασίλευσε, καὶ ἡ χώρα Κεκροπία ἐκλήθη
τὸ πρότερον καλου|⁴μένη Ἀκτικὴ ἀπὸ Ἀκταίου τοῦ αὐτόχθονος, ἔτη
ΧΗΗΗΔΓΙΙΙ.

2. ἀφ᾽ οὗ Δευκαλίων παρὰ τὸν Παρνασσὸν ἐν Λυκωρείαι ἐβασίλευσε,
[βα]σιλε[ύ|⁵ο]ντος Ἀθηνῶν Κέκροπος, ἔτη ΧΗΗΗΔ.

3. ἀφ᾽ οὗ δίκη Ἀθήνησι [ἐγέ]νετο Ἄρει καὶ Ποσειδῶνι ὑπὲρ Ἁλιρροθίου
τοῦ Ποσειδῶνος, καὶ ὁ τόπος ἐκλήθη |⁶ Ἄρειος Πάγος, ἔτη ΧΗΗΓ̄ΔΓΙΙΙ,
βασιλεύοντος Ἀθηνῶν Κρ[ανα]οῦ.

4. ἀφ᾽ οὗ κατακλυσμὸς ἐπὶ Δευκαλίωνος ἐγένετο, καὶ Δευκαλίων τοὺς |⁷
ὄμβρους ἔφυγεν ἐγ Λυκωρείας εἰς Ἀθήνας πρὸ[ς - - -]ΟΝ, καὶ τοῦ Διὸ[ς
- - -]ΥΟ[- - -]ΜΤΟΥ τὸ ἱ[ε]ρὸν ἱδ[ρύσατ]ο (?)²⁵ [καὶ] τὰ σωτήρια ἔθυσεν,
|⁸ ἔτη ΧΗΗΓ̄ΔΓ, βασιλεύοντος Ἀθηνῶν Κραναοῦ.

5. ἀ[φ᾽ οὗ Ἀμφι]κτύων²⁶ Δευκαλίωνος ἐβασίλευσεν ἐν Θερμοπύλαις
καὶ συνήγε[ι|⁹ρε²⁷ τ]οὺς περὶ τὸ [ἱε]ρὸν οἰκοῦντας καὶ ὠνόμασεν
Ἀμφικτύονας καὶ π[- - -]ν²⁸ οὕ[περ] καὶ νῦν ἔτι θύουσιν Ἀμφικτύονες |¹⁰
ἔτη ΧΗΗΓ̄ΔΓΙΙΙ, βασιλεύοντος Ἀθηνῶν Ἀμφικτύονος.

---

22 Jacoby has * ΟΥ * [ἐξ ἀναγραφῶ]ν (?) παν[τοί]ων [καὶ ἱστοριῶν κοι]νῶν (?) ἀνέγραψα τοὺς
ἄν[ωθεν] χρό|νους] ἀρξάμενος.
23 Jacoby's apparatus has Selden's Ἀστ]υάνακτος (Selden 1628:72), omitting Boeckh's Εὐρ]υάνακτος
and Πολ]υάνακτος.
24 On the likelihood that the space left by Selden was seen on the stone, see chap. 5, sec. 2 below.
25 Jacoby has πρὸ[ς Κραναό]ν, καὶ τοῦ Διὸ[ς το]ῦ Ὀ[λυ]μ[πί]ου τὸ ἱ[ε]ρὸν ἱδ[ρύσατ]ο [καὶ] τὰ
σωτήρια ἔθυσεν (Prideaux and Chandler combined). Selden's transcription reads: ΠΡΟ . . .
ΟΝΚΑΙΤΟΥΔΙΟ . . ΥΟ . . Δ . . . ΜΤΟΥΤΟΙΡ . . ΟΝΙΑ . . . . . . Ο . . ΤΑΣΩΤΗΡΙΑΕΘΥΣΕΝ. Chandler's το]ῦ
Ὀ[λυ]μ[πί]ου requires too many corrections and overlooks gaps; more probable is Prideaux's τὸ
ἱ[ε]ρὸν ἱδ[ρύσατ]ο.
26 Here, in A66 (Socrates), A69 (Philoxenus), and B15 (Sosiphanes), the inscription omits the article
ὁ, but only here and in A66 Jacoby supplements it.
27 Jacoby has συνῆγε (Selden). Wilamowitz's συνήγειρε, preferred by Hiller von Gärtringen, may be
better for Selden's three dots at the beginning of line 9.
28 Jacoby marks Hiller von Gärtringen's π[ροέθυσε]ν with a question mark. Jacoby 1904a has Le
Paulmier's Π[υλαία]ν.

6. ἀφ᾽ οὗ Ἕλλην ὁ Δευκ[αλίωνος Φθι]ώτιδος ἐβασίλευσε, καὶ Ἕλληνες |**11** ὠνομάσθησαν τὸ πρότερον Γραικοὶ καλούμενοι, καὶ τὸν ἀγῶνα {Παναθ⟨η⟩ναι} [- - -]ΩΙ[29] [ἔτη] ΧΗΗ𐅄𐅃ΙΙ, βασιλεύοντος |**12** Ἀθηνῶν Ἀμφικτύονος.

7. ἀφ᾽ οὗ Κάδμος ὁ Ἀγήνορος εἰς Θήβας ἀφίκετο [- - - ca. 30 - - -] [καὶ] ἔκτισεν τὴν Καδμεί|**13**αν, ἔτη ΧΗΗ𐅄𐅃, βασιλεύοντος Ἀθηνῶν Ἀμφικτύονος.

8. ἀφ᾽ οὗ [- - - ca. 40 - - -]νικης (?) ἐβασίλευσαν, |**14** ἔτη ΧΗΗ𐅄ΙΙ, βασιλεύοντος Ἀθηνῶν Ἀμφικτύονος.

9. ἀφ᾽ οὗ ναῦ[ς - - - ca. 40 - - - κωπ]ῶν[30] ἐξ Αἰγύπτου |**15** εἰς τὴν Ἑλλάδα ἔπλευσε καὶ ὠνομάσθη πεντηκόντορος, καὶ αἱ Δαναοῦ θυγατέρες [- - - ca. 20 - - -]ΩΝΗ καὶ ΒΑ[- - -] |**16** [- - -]ΛΑΡΕΥΩ καὶ Ἑλίκη καὶ Ἀρχεδίκη ἀποκληρωθεῖσαι ὑπὸ τῶν λοιπῶν [- - - ca. 45 - - -]αντ[ο][31] |**17** καὶ ἔθυσαν ἐπὶ τῆς ἀκτῆς ἐμ ΠΑΡΑ.ΑΔΙ[32] (?) ἐν Λίνδωι τῆς Ῥοδίας, ἔτη ΧΗΗΔΔΔ𐅃ΙΙ, βασιλεύο[ντος Ἀθηνῶν - - -].[33]

10. [ἀφ᾽ οὗ Ἐριχ]|**18**θόνιος Παναθηναίοις τοῖς πρώτοις γενομένοις ἅρμα ἔζευξε καὶ τὸν ἀγῶνα ἐδείκνυε καὶ Ἀθηναίους [- - - ΟΝ - - -],[34] κ]αὶ [ἄγαλμα |**19** θ]εῶν μητρὸς ἐφάνη ἐγ Κυβέλοις, καὶ Ὕαγνις ὁ Φρὺξ αὐλοὺς πρῶτος ηὗρεν ἐγ Κ[- - -][35] τοὺς Φρύγας [καὶ ἁρμονίαν τὴν κ]α|**20**λουμένην Φρυγιστὶ πρῶτος ηὔλησε καὶ ἄλλους νόμους Μητρὸς Διονύσου Πανὸς καὶ τὸν ΕΠ[- - - ca. 30 - - -] |**21** [- - -], ἔτη ΧΗΗΔΔΔΙΙ, βασιλεύοντος Ἀθηνῶν Ἐριχθονίου τοῦ τὸ ἅρμα ζεύξαντος.

29 Jacoby has {τὸν ἀγῶνα Παναθ . . ναι . . . . ωι}. Since the first Panathenaic games are mentioned in entry 10, a reference to the Panathenaea must be a mistake, either Selden's or probably the cutter's, but τὸν ἀγῶνα may not be part of the mistake (cf. Boeckh's Πανελλήνια ἔθεσαν). Selden's two dots in Παναθ . . ναι may represent a broad letter such as H. After Παναθ⟨η⟩ναι a large lacuna must be assumed (the line has only seventy-eight letters).

30 Jacoby has ναῦ[ς κατασκευασθεῖσα ὑπὸ Δαναοῦ πρώτη πεντ]ή[κοντα κωπ]ῶν, partly based on Chandler (Selden locates an H in the middle of the lacuna). The reference to the ship's name with consecutive καί supports the supplement κωπ]ῶν.

31 Jacoby has [τῆς Ἀθηνᾶς τῆς Λινδίας τὸ ἱερὸν * * ἱδρύσ]αντ[ο].

32 Selden marks two dots, but as his suggested corrections (1628:74) indicate (ΠΑΡΑΡΑΔΙ or ΠΑΡΑΓΑΔΙ), they probably represent a single broad letter.

33 Jacoby has Le Paulmier's Ἐριχθονίου, but Hiller von Gärtringen's Ἀμφικτύονος (apparatus) cannot be ruled out.

34 Jacoby has [ὠν]όμ[ασε (with Boeckh and Hiller von Gärtringen).

35 Jacoby has Κ * * ΝΑΙΩΝ (Selden's own correction to Κ . . ΑΝΝΑΙ). If the supplement [καὶ ἁρμονίαν τὴν κ] is correct, at least ten letters are missing after the K.

11. ἀφ' οὗ Μίνως [- - -] πρ[- - - ἐ]βα[σίλευσε - - -]³⁶ |²² Ἀ[πολ]λωνίαν
(?)³⁷ ὤικισε καὶ σίδηρος ηὑρέθη ἐν τῆι Ἴδηι, εὑρόντων τῶν Ἰδαίων
Δακτύλων Κέλμιος κ[αὶ Δαμναμενέως - - - ca. 30 - - -,³⁸ βα|²³σι]λεύοντος
Ἀθηνῶν Πανδίονος.

12. ἀφ' οὗ Δημήτηρ ἀφικομένη εἰς Ἀθήνας καρπὸν ἐφύ[τευ]σεν,³⁹ καὶ
πρ[οηροσία (?)⁴⁰ ἐ]πρά[χθη πρ]ώτη, δ[- - - ca. 25 - - - |²⁴ Τ]ριπτολέμου
τοῦ Κελεοῦ καὶ Νεαίρας, ἔτη ΧΗΔΔΔΔΓᴵ⟨Ι⟩,⁴¹ βασιλεύοντος Ἀθήνησιν
Ἐριχθέως.

13. ἀφ' οὗ Τριπτό[λεμος - - - ca. 20 - - -] |²⁵ [- - -]⁴² ἔσπειρεν ἐν τῆι
Ῥαρίαι καλουμένηι Ἐλευσῖνι, ἔτη Χ[Η]ΔΔΔΔΓᴵ, βασιλεύοντος Ἀθηνῶν
['Ἐριχθέως].

14. [ἀφ' οὗ Ὀρφεὺς - - -]⁴³ |²⁶ υἱὸ[ς - - -]ν[- - - ἑ]αυτοῦ⁴⁴ πόησιν⁴⁵ ἐξέθηκε,
Κόρης τε ἁρπαγὴν καὶ Δήμητρος ζήτησιν καὶ τὸν αὐτου[- - - |²⁷ - - -]θος⁴⁶
τῶν ὑποδεξαμένων τὸν καρπόν, ἔτη ΧΗΔΔΔΓᴵ, βασιλεύοντος Ἀθηνῶν
Ἐριχθέως.

15. [ἀφ' οὗ Εὔμολπος (?)⁴⁷ - - -] |²⁸ [- - -]ΝΟΥ τὰ μυστήρια ἀνέφηνεν
ἐν Ἐλευσῖνι καὶ τὰς τοῦ [πατρὸς Μ]ουσαίου ποιήσ[ει]ς ἐξέθηκ[εν - - -⁴⁸
βασιλεύοντος Ἀθηνῶν |²⁹ Ἐριχθέ]ως τοῦ Πανδίονος.

---

36 Jacoby has [ὁ] πρ[ότερος (?) ἐ]βα[σίλευσε Κρήτης καὶ] (Boeckh). At least thirty letters are missing
at three different points of the line.

37 Jacoby's correction of Selden's reading in the Errata: Δ . . . ΑΩΝΙΑΝ; Hiller von Gärtringen conjectured Κνωσὸν καὶ Κυδω]νίαν.

38 Jacoby has ἔτη ΧΗ * *, but the precise location of the year number in the lacuna is unclear.

39 Jacoby has ἐφ[εῦρ]εν. Hiller von Gärtringen's ἐφύ[τευσ]εν is consistent with the inscription's
preference for the aorist, but the imperfect cannot be ruled out (cf. Selden's ἐφύ[τε]υεν for his
repported ἐφύ . . υεν / ΕΦΥ . . . ΥΕΝ, see chap. 4, n. 21 below).

40 With Hiller von Gärtringen I omit Boeckh's and Jacoby's δ[είξαντος and add a question mark
after Munro's πρ[οηροσία.

41 Assuming that the chronicle never gives the same number to two different entries, Munro
supplements the numeral ⟨Ι⟩ (ΧΗΔΔΔΔΓᴵ⟨Ι⟩= 1146) to distinguish it from the following
ΧΗΔΔΔΔΓᴵ = 1145 (but Lydiat and Boeckh read ΙΙ instead of Γᴵ in A13, i.e. ΧΗΔΔΔΔΙΙ = 1142).

42 Jacoby has Τριπτό[λεμος ἐθέρισε τὸν καρ|πόν, ὄν. A longer piece of text is missing, probably
including the word καρπόν.

43 Prideaux's supplementation of Orpheus is highly probable, see chap. 6, n. 44 below.

44 Jacoby's ΥΙΟ . . [τ]ὴ[ν ἑ]αυτοῦ (for Selden's ΥΙΟ . . . Ν . . . ΑΥΤΟΥ) does little justice to the lacuna
in line 26, where at least thirty-five letters are missing.

45 Jacoby and Hiller von Gärtringen regularize the word into πο⟨ί⟩ησιν.

46 Jacoby has αὐτου[ρηγηθέντα ὑπ' αὐτῆς σπόρον | καὶ τὸ πλῆ]θος (combining Diels's and
Wilamowitz's conjectures). In line 27, at least thirty-five letters are missing at the beginning and
the end.

47 I added a question mark.

48 Jacoby has ἔτη ΧΗ * in the lacuna. Almost forty letters are missing in line 28, at the beginning,
before Μ]ουσαίου, and at the end.

16. ἀφ’ οὗ καθαρμὸς πρῶτον ἐγένετο [- - -]ου πρώτωι (?) ΑΟΝ[- - -]ΕΑΝΤ
[- - -]⁴⁹ |³⁰ [ἔτη - - -]ΔΙΙ,⁵⁰ βασιλεύοντος Ἀθηνῶν Πανδίονος τοῦ Κέκροπος.

17. ἀφ’ οὗ ἐν Ἐλευσῖνι ὁ γυμνικὸς [ἀγὼν - - -] ΑΦΟΥ⁵¹ [- - -] |³¹ [- - - ΑΙ
- - -] τὰ Λύκαια ἐν Ἀρκαδίαι ἐγένετο καὶ Λ [- - - ΚΚΕ - - -] Λυκάονος
ἐδόθησαν [- - -]⁵² τοῖς Ἑλλ[η]σι[ν - - - Η - - - Ν - - -]⁵³ βασιλεύον|³²τος
Ἀθηνῶν Πανδίονος τοῦ Κέκροπος.

18. ἀφ’ οὗ κα[- - - Γ - - -]ησιαι Ἡρακλῆς [- - - Ν - - - Ω - - - ΔΟΣΤ - - -]⁵⁴ |³³
βασιλεύοντος Ἀθήνησιν Αἰγέως.

19. ἀφ’ οὗ Ἀθήνησι [σπάνι]ς τῶν καρπῶν ἐγένετο καὶ μαντευομένο⟨ι⟩ς
[- - -] Ἀθην[αίοις Ἀπό]λλων ἔχρη[σε (?)⟩⁵⁵ |³⁴ δίκα]ς ὑποσχε⟨ῖ⟩ν [- - -]
ἂ[ς] ἂμ Μίνως ἀξιώσει, ἔτη ΧΔΔΔΙ, βασιλεύοντος Ἀθηνῶν Αἰγέως.

20. ἀφ’ οὗ Θησ[εὺς - - - βασιλεύσας] |³⁵ Ἀθηνῶν τὰς δώδεκα πόλεις εἰς
τὸ αὐτὸ συνώικισεν καὶ πολιτείαν καὶ τὴν δημοκρατίαν παρέδω[κε
- - -]⁵⁶ |³⁶ [- - -]ΟΣ Ἀθηνῶν τὸν τῶν Ἰσθμίων ἀγῶνα ἔθηκε Σίνιν ἀπο-
κτείνας, ἔτη ႃᄆΗΗΗΗᄆΔΔΔΔႃᄆ.

21. ἀπὸ τῆς Ἀμ[αζ]όν[ων ? - - -] ΤΗ[- - -, ἔτη |³⁷ ᄆΗΗΗΗᄆ]ΔΔΔΔΙΙ,⁵⁷
βασιλεύοντος Ἀθηνῶν Θησέως.

---

⁴⁹ With at least forty-five letters missing, Jacoby, following Hiller von Gärtringen, avoids restoration; the word πρώτωι may be distinguished.

⁵⁰ A numeral ending with twelve. Jacoby has Lydiat's supplement: [ἔτη ΧΓᄆ]ΔΙΙ; Hiller von
Gärtringen's Χ[- -]ΔΙΙ is less speculative.

⁵¹ At least thirty letters are missing in line 30. Hiller von Gärtringen's supplement ἀφ’ οὗ [τὰ
Ὀλύμπια ἐν Ἤλιδ]ι [κ]αὶ τὰ Λύκαια is omitted from Jacoby's apparatus. On the question whether
ΑΦΟΥ could mark the beginning of a new entry, see Jacoby 1904a:77–79.

⁵² Selden reports two dots in the majuscule transcription, none in the minuscule. Jacoby omits
them, while Hiller von Gärtringen has [ἐν (?)].

⁵³ Jacoby has τοῖς Ἑλλ[η]σι[ν ἔτ]η .. Ν .. βασιλεύον|³²τος. At least thirty letters are missing in nine
different spots of line 31.

⁵⁴ Among the long and daring supplements that Jacoby omits from his FGrH apparatus, is one by
Boeckh, alluding to Olympia: ἀφ’ οὗ κα[τερ]γ[ασάμενος τὰ ἐν] Ἤ[λ]ι[δ]ι Ἡρακλῆς [τὸ τέμε]ν[ος
καθιέρ]ω[σε τοῦ] Δ[ι]ός (at least forty-five letters are missing in line 32).

⁵⁵ Jacoby follows Hiller von Gärtringen in combining Le Paulmier's and Boeckh's restorations
(Hiller von Gärtringen gives more detail: ἔχρη[σε τοῦ Ἀνδρόγεω φό|νου δίκα]ς), which requires
omitting two lacunae (which Selden reports by two dots each) and ignoring a lacuna between
the end of line 33 and the beginning of 34. I mark the lacunae but leave the restoration, adding
a question mark. There is scope for rethinking Ἀπό]λλων ἔχρη[σε | δίκα]ς ὑποσχε⟨ῖ⟩ν [- - -] ἂ[ς]
ἂμ Μίνως for Selden's .. ΑΛΩΝΕΝΗ ..| . . . . ΣΥΠΟΣΧΕΝ . . Α . . ΑΜΜΙΝΩΣ. The syntax of the
restored entry is more complex than usual in the inscription.

⁵⁶ Hiller von Gärtringen, following Boeckh, has ἀπ[έδ]ω[κε (Selden's transcription: ΑΠΡΕΩ . . . . .).

⁵⁷ Selden's majuscule transcription has ΑΠΟΤΗΣΑΜΜΟΝ . . . ΤΗ . . . . | . . . . ΔΔΔΔ. Jacoby
has ἀπὸ τῆς Ἀμαζόν[ων εἰς τὴ[ν Ἀττικὴν στρατείας, ἔτη ᄆΗΗΗΗᄆ]ΔΔΔΔΙΙ, the text "brilliantly

22. ἀφ' οὗ Ἀργεῖοι μετ' Ἀδράσ[του ἐπὶ Θή]βας [ἐστράτ]ευσαν καὶ τὸν ἀγῶνα ἐν [Νεμέ]α[ι ἔ]θ[εσ]αν [- - - |**38** - - -],⁵⁸ ἔτη ⌐ΗΗΗΗ⌐ΔΔΔΓΙΙ, βασιλεύοντος Ἀθηνῶν Θησέως.

23. ἀφ' οὗ οἱ ['Έλλη]νες εἰς Τροίαν ἐ[στ]ράτευσ[αν], ἔτη ⌐ΗΗΗΗ⌐ΙΙΙΙ, βασιλεύοντος Ἀθη[νῶν |**39** Μεν]εσθέως τρεισκαιδεκάτου ἔτους.

24. ἀφ' οὗ Τροία ἥλω, ἔτη ⌐ΗΗΗΗΔΔΔΔΓ, βασιλεύοντος Ἀθηνῶν [Μενεσθέ]ως δευτέρου ⟨καὶ εἰκοστοῦ⟩⁵⁹ ἔτους μηνὸς Θ[αρ|**40**γηλιῶ]νος ἑβδόμηι φθίνοντος.

25. ἀφ' οὗ Ὀρέστη[ι - - -]ΙΟΙΑΙΤΩΝΑΥΤΟ[- - - καὶ τῆι Α]ἰγίσθου θυγατρὶ ['Ηριγ]όν[ηι - - - Αἰ]γίσθου καὶ ΑΥ[- - - δίκη |**41** ἐγένε]το ἐν Ἀρείωι Πάγωι, ἢν Ὀρέστης ἐνίκησεν [- - -]ων[- - -], ἔτη [⌐]ΗΗΗΗΔΔ[ΔΙΙ]ΙΙ (?), βασιλεύοντος Ἀθηνῶν Δημοφῶντος.⁶⁰

26. ἀφ' οὗ [Σαλαμῖνα |**42** τὴν ἐγ] Κύπρωι Τεῦκρος ὤικισεν, ἔτη ⌐ΗΗΗΗΔΔΓΙΙΙ, βασιλεύοντος Ἀθηνῶν Δημοφῶντος.

27. ἀφ' οὗ Νη[λ]εὺς ὤικισ[ε Μίλη]τ̣[ον - - -]ΑΛΑΗΧΑΡ . . . ΣΙ |**43** - - -]αν,⁶¹ 'Έφεσον Ἐρυθρὰς Κλαζομενὰς Π[ρι]ήνην Λέβεδον Τ̣έω Κολοφῶνα Μυοῦντα [Φώκ]α[ιαν] Σάμον [Χίον καὶ] τὰ [Παν]ιώνι[α] ἐγένετο,

---

restored by Boeckh," as Jacoby (1904a:87) puts it; Jacoby adds that Selden's corruption of AZ into M is apparent. I add a question mark to the restored word Ἀμαζόνων. The attested numbers for the previous and following entries support the restored number of years (992). At least twenty-five letters are missing from line 36, part at the beginning of entry 21.

⁵⁸ Jacoby has [Νεμέ]α[ι ἔ]θ[εσ]αν (with Le Paulmier and Chandler), highly probable in the context, but with line 37 missing at least thirty-five letters, the spaces represented by Selden's dots (ΚΑΙΤΟΝΑΓΩΝΑ . Ν . . Α . . . ΗΘ . . ΑΝ . . . |) may be bigger. Jacoby also accepts Boeckh's supplement [ἐπ' Ἀρχε|μόρωι], whose speculative nature is marked by Hiller von Gärtringen with a question mark. Jacoby and Hiller von Gärtringen are probably right in suspecting that Selden omitted a lacuna at the end of line 38.

⁵⁹ Since the thirteenth year of Menestheus's reign is mentioned in entry 23, and there is a nine-year interval between entries 23 and 24 (i.e. years 954 and 945), it is highly probable that the Parian Marble dated the fall of Troy to the twenty-second year of Menestheus's reign. The omission of εἰκοστοῦ may have been the cutter's or Selden's, pace Munro 1901a:154.

⁶⁰ Jacoby restores the entry as follows: ἀφ' οὗ Ὀρέστη[ι τ]ῶι Ἀ[γαμέμνονος (?) καὶ τῆι Α]ἰγίσθου θυγατρὶ ['Ηριγ]όν[ηι ὑπὲρ Αἰ]γίσθου καὶ Κλυ[ταιμήστρας δίκη |**41** ἐγένε]το ἐν Ἀρείωι πάγωι, ἢν Ὀρέστης ἐνίκησεν [ἴσων γενομένων τ]ῶν [ψήφων], ἔτη [⌐]ΗΗΗΗΔΔΔ[ΔΙ]ΙΙ (?), βασιλεύοντος Ἀθηνῶν Δημοφῶντος. At least 25 letters are missing from line 40 (granting a space of five letters between entries 24 and 25), and at least twenty-five letters are missing from line 41. In addition to Jacoby's numeral (= 944), [⌐]ΗΗΗΗΔΔ[ΔΙ]ΙΙ (= 943) and [⌐]ΗΗΗΗΔΔ[ΓΙΙ]ΙΙ (= 939) have been suggested.

⁶¹ Jacoby gives Boeckh's restoration: Νη[λ]εὺς ὤικισ[ε Μίλη]τ̣[ον καὶ τὴν] ἄλλην ἄπ[α]σ[αν | 'Ιωνί]αν, 'Έφεσον. Selden's transcription reads: ΑΦΟΥΝΗ . . ΕΥΣΩΙΚΙΣ . . . . . . Γ . . . . ΑΛΑΗΧΑΡ . . . ΣΙ . . | . . . . . . ΑΝΕΦΕΣΟΝ. Miletos was probably the subject of ὤικισ[ε, perhaps by zeugma, but not

ἔτ[η |⁴⁴ ⌐ᴴΗΗΗ]ΔΙΙΙ, βασιλεύοντος Ἀθηνῶν Μέ⟨δοντο⟩ς {νεσθ⟨έ⟩ως τρεισκαιδεκάτου [ἔτο]υς}.⁶²

28. ἀφ’ οὗ [Ἡσ]ίοδος ὁ ποιητὴς [ἐφάν]η, ἔτη ⌐ᴴΗ⌐ᴰΔΔ[- - -],⁶³ βασιλεύοντος Ἀθηνῶν [- - -] |⁴⁵ [- - -].

29. ἀφ’ οὗ Ὅμηρος ὁ ποιητὴς ἐφάνη, ἔτη ⌐ᴴΔΔΔΔΙΙΙ, βασιλεύοντο Ἀθηνῶ[ν Δ]ιογνήτου.

A2. The Ashmolean Fragment

30. ἀφ’ οὗ Φ[εί]δων ὁ Ἀργεῖος⁶⁴ ἐδήμευσ[ε τὰ] μέτ[ρα καὶ |⁴⁶ στ]αθμὰ⁶⁵ κατεσκεύασε καὶ νόμισμα ἀργυροῦν ἐν Αἰγίνηι ἐποίησεν, ἑνδέκατος ὢν ἀφ’ Ἡρακλέους, ἔτη ⌐ᴴΔΔΔΙ, βασιλεύοντος Ἀθηνῶν |⁴⁷ [Φερεκλ]είους.

31. ἀφ’ οὗ Ἀρχίας Εὐαγήτου δέκατος ὢν ἀπὸ Τημένου ἐκ Κορίνθου ἤγαγε τὴν ἀποικίαν [καὶ ἔκτισε] Συρακού[σσας, ἔτη - - - |⁴⁸ β]α[σι]λεύ[ο]γτος Ἀθηνῶν Αἰσχύλου ἔτους εἰκοστοῦ καὶ ἑνός.

32. ἀφ’ οὗ κατ’ ἐνιαυτὸν ἦρξεν ὁ ἄρχων, ἔτη ΗΗΗΗΔΔ.

---

necessarily represented by the Γ (corrected into T). Restoration of Priene, Lebedos, and Teos is plausible given the context, but cf. Selden’s reported ΗΝΚΑΤΑΓΡΟΝΟΝΥΠΟ.

⁶² Jacoby has Μέ{νεσθέως τρεισκαιδεκάτου} ⟨δοντος⟩ [ἔτο]υς (Selden: ΜΕΝΕΣΘΩΣΤΡΕΙΣ-ΚΑΙΔΕΚΑΤΟΥ . . . ΥΖ. Munro (1901a:154) suggests reading ἐννεακαιδεκάτου instead of τρεισκαιδεκάτου, thus the nineteenth year of Menestheus’s reign. I include the restored name of Medon but seclude the reference to thirteen years as a repetition from entry 23 (editors have proposed correcting the number 13 into 10, 11, 13, and 19).

⁶³ I follow both Jacoby FGrH and Hiller von Gärtringen in avoiding restoration of the year number in entry 28. The Parian Marble makes Hesiod earlier than Homer, but the precise time span is unattested. Selden has two dots after the numerals, not necessarily representing two missing letters. Possible restorations imply an interval of one generation: ⌐ᴴΗ⌐ᴰΔΔ[Δ] (= 680, Selden), ⌐ᴴΗ⌐ᴰΔΔ[ΙΙ] (= 672, Lydiat), ⌐ᴴΗ⌐ᴰΔΔ[ΙΙΙ] (= 673, Boeckh, followed by Jacoby 1904a), ⌐ᴴΗ⌐ᴰΔΔ[ΓΙ] (= 676, Jacoby in the apparatus of his FGrH edition).

⁶⁴ Jacoby adds *cruces* before Pheidon’s and Archias’s names, indicating a possible confusion of entries 30 and 31, which he proposes to read as follows (see the apparatus to his 1904 edition):

30. ἀφ’ οὗ Ἀρχίας Εὐαγήτου ἐκ Κορίνθου ἤγαγε τὴν ἀποικίαν καὶ ἔκτισε Συρακούσσας, ἑνδέκατος ὢν ἀφ’ Ἡρακλέους, ἔτη ⌐ᴴΔΔΔΙ, βασιλεύοντος Ἀθηνῶν Φερεκλείους.

31. ἀφ’ οὗ Φείδων ὁ Ἀργεῖος δέκατος ὢν ἀπὸ Τημένου ἐδήμευσε τὰ μέτρα καὶ σταθμὰ κατεσκεύασε καὶ νόμισμα ἀργυροῦν ἐν Αἰγίνηι ἐποίησεν ἔτη * * βασιλεύοντος Ἀθηνῶν Αἰσχύλου.

Jacoby switched the order of the entries, placing Pheidon as tenth from Temenos (instead of eleventh from Heracles) and Archias eleventh from Heracles (instead of tenth from Temenos). He attributes the mistake to the stone-cutter or the author. I omit Jacoby’s *cruces*. Indeed, disagreement with Ephorus (FGrH 70 F 115 20–24) is not necessarily an indication of textual corruption.

⁶⁵ From here up to the end of section A, the constitution of the text follows not only Selden’s transcription, but also the legible sections of the Ashmolean fragment, with the aid of the autopsy reported by Munro 1901a and b, and Hiller von Gärtringen.

33. ἀφ’ οὗ [- - -]ο[- - -]υ[- - - ⁶⁶|**49** - - -] ἔτη ΗΗΗΗΔΓΙΙΙ, ἄρχοντος Ἀθήνησι Λυσιά[δου].

34. ἀφ’ οὗ Τέρπανδρος ὁ Δερδένεος ὁ Λέσβιος τοὺς νόμους τοὺ[ς κιθ]α[ρ]ωιδ[ικ]οὺς καὶ αὐλητ[ικ - - -⁶⁷|**50** - - -]λησε⁶⁸ καὶ τὴν ἔμπροσθε μουσικὴν μετέστησεν, ἔτη ΗΗΗΓᴨΔΔΔΙ, ἄρχοντος Ἀθήνησιν Δρωπίδου.

35. ἀφ’ οὗ Ἀ[λυάττη]ς Λυδ[ῶν⁶⁹ ἐβα]σίλευσ[εν, ἔτη |**51** Η]Η[Η]ΔΔΔΔΙ,⁷⁰ ἄρχοντος Ἀθήνησιν Ἀριστοκλε[ί]ους.

36. ἀφ’ οὗ Σαπφὼ ἐγ Μυτιλήνης εἰς Σικελίαν ἔπλευσε φυγοῦσα [- - -|**52** - - - ἄρχο]ντος⁷¹ Ἀθήνησιν μὲν Κριτίου τοῦ προτέρου, ἐν Συρακούσσαις⁷² δὲ τῶν γαμόρων κατεχόντων τὴν ἀρχήν.

---

⁶⁶ The stone is broken at this point. Jacoby has ἀφ’ οὗ . . . . ο . . υ * | . . . . , keeping the number of dots in Selden’s majuscule transcription, seven, two, and nine (the minuscule transcription has two, two, and seven). The supplement Archilochus, proposed by Baumgarten ([Ἀρχίλοχ]ο[ς ἐκ Πάρο]υ [εἰς Θάσον τὴν ἀποικ|ίαν ἤγαγεν]), suits the number of dots reported by Selden, though it is difficult to believe that the dots represent here an exact number of letters (see section 1 in this chapter). Although Selden does not mark dots after the Y, there probably was a lacuna at the end of the line (at least fourteen letters seem to be missing at the end of line 48). The supplement Archilochus should remain outside the text, as in Jacoby’s edition (though he includes it in 1904a, cf. Hiller von Gärtringen 1934:56: ἀφ’ οὗ [Τελεσικλῆς ὁ Πάριος Θάσον ᾤκισεν]; see chap. 6, sec. 2.I).

⁶⁷ Jacoby has τοὺς νόμους τοὺ[ς κιθ]α[ρ]ωιδ[ικ]οὺς {θαιαυλητ . . } [ἐκαι|⁵⁰νοτόμ]ησε (for Selden’s ΤΟΥΣΝΟΜΟΥΣΤΟ . . . . Α . . . ΩΝ . . . Δ . . ΟΥΣΘΑΙΑΥΛΗΤ . . ; since the top right part of the Ashmolean fragment is broken, we depend on Selden’s transcription for the text after τοὺς νό-). Hiller von Gärtringen’s τοὺ[ς κιθ]α[ρωι]δ[ικ]ούς is very plausible in the context. There is no need to excise θαιαυλητ, which may stand for καὶ αὐλητ-, perhaps καὶ αὐλητ[ικούς], if not αὐλητ[αῖς] (Le Paulmier) or αὐλητ[άς] (Chandler). These and other supplements are found only in Jacoby’s 1904 edition.

⁶⁸ Jacoby has [ἐκαι|νοτόμ]ησε. Many aorist verbs would do for Selden’s . . . ΛΗΣΕ if the lambda is corrected, but Le Paulmier’s συνηύ]λησε (or simply ηὔλησε ?) deserves attention, in the context of musical history.

⁶⁹ Thus Hiller von Gärtringen. Jacoy has Λυδῷ[ν, but from Selden’s reported ΣΛΥΔΟ Munro could see only ΣΛ (from correspondence with Hiller von Gärtringen, see his note to line 50).

⁷⁰ From this point on, dots underneath letters represent traces of characters partially seen (or reported to have been seen) on the stone.

⁷¹ Jacoby has φυγοῦσα . . . . . . ΟΛ . . . . . Θ . . . . . | ἄρχο]ντος (with wrong brackets: ἄρχο[ντος, and omitting an opening square bracket after φυγοῦσα). I follow Hiller von Gärtringen and Jacoby 1904a, omitting the doubtful majuscules and signaling a lacuna (Jacoby [1904a:100] considers Selden’s reported Θ to be a mistake, whereas from ΟΛ only the Ο could be partially seen). The year number, between 340 and 328, is missing. According to Hiller von Gärtringen, after φυγοῦσα 25/26 letters are missing, or 11/15 if ἔτη ΗΗΗΔΔ- is supplemented (Hiller von Gärtringen’s note to line 51). Schoene’s suggestion that Alcaeus was mentioned along with Sappho is not recorded in Jacoby’s apparatus ([καὶ Ἀλκαῖος] ὁ Λ[έσβιος ἐξέ]θ[ηκε τὰ στασιωτικά,), but cf. his 1904a edition.

⁷² “The double σ in Συρακούσσαις is plainly legible” (Munro 1901b:356).

37. [ἀφ' οὗ] Ἀμ[φικτ]ύο[νες ἔθ]υ[σαν κ]αταπο|⁵³[λεμή]σαντες⁷³ Κύρραν, καὶ ⟨⟨ὁ ἀγὼν ὁ γυμνικὸς ἐτέθη χρ⟩⟩⁷⁴ἡματίτης ἀπὸ τῶν λαφύρων, ἔτη ΗΗ[Η]ΔΔΓᴵΙΙ, ἄρχοντος Ἀθήνησιν Σίμω[ν]ος.

38. ἀφ' οὗ [ἐν Δελφοῖ]ς |⁵⁴ [ὁ στε]⟨⟨φανίτης ἀγὼν πάλιν ἐτέθη, ἔτη ΗΗΗΔΓᴵΙΙΙ, ἄρχοντο⟩⟩ς⁷⁵ Ἀθήνησιν⁷⁶ Δαμασίου τοῦ δευτέρου.

39. ἀφ' οὗ ἐν Ἀθ[ήν]αις κωμω[ιδῶν χο]ρ[ὸς ἐτ]έθη,⁷⁷ [στη]σάν|⁵⁵[των πρώ]των Ἰκαριέων, εὑρόντος Σουσαρίωνος, καὶ ἆθλον ἐτέθη πρῶτον ἰσχάδω[ν] ἄρσιχο[ς] καὶ οἴνου⁷⁸ με[τ]ρητής [- - - 23/24 - - - |⁵⁶ - - -].⁷⁹

40. ἀφ' οὗ Πεισίστρατος Ἀθηνῶν ἐτυράννευσεν, ἔτη ΗΗᴵᴵΔΔΔΔΓᴵΙΙ, ἄρχοντος [Ἀθήνη]σι Κ[ω]μ[έ]ου.

41. ἀφ' οὗ Κροῖσος [ἐξ] Ἀσίας [εἰς] Δελφοὺς ἀ[- - - ⁸⁰|⁵⁷ ἔτη Η]Η[Γᴵ]ΔΔΔΔΙΙ, ἄρχοντος Ἀθήνησιν Εὐθυδήμου.

---

73 Restoration depends on Munro's readings (as reported by Hiller von Gärtringen, note to line 52).
74 The text partially transmitted by Selden was written in an erasure (Munro, as reported by Hiller von Gärtringen, note to line 53).
75 The text transmitted by Selden was written in an erasure (Munro, as reported by Hiller von Gärtringen, note to line 54).
76 Jacoby has Ἀθήνησι, but a final N was reported by Munro 1901b:356.
77 Of Selden's ΑΦΟΥΕΝΑΘ . . . ΑΙΣΚΩΜΩ . . . . Ρ . . . ΕΘΗ . . . . . ΣΑΝΙ at the end of line 54, Munro could only read ΣΑΝ (1901b:356; Hiller von Gärtringen suggests that the final vertical stroke was a mistake). κωμω[ιδῶν χο]ρ[ός is Boeckh's conjecture, ἐτ]έθη is Le Paulmier's. Perhaps Le Paulmier's κωμω[ιδία π]ρ[ῶτον ἐτ]έθη, though not a performance term, deserves attention. Selden's ΚΩΜΩ stands in contrast with the spelling κωμοιδοποιός at B7 and B14. Boeckh's [ηύρ]έθη is missing from Jacoby's apparatus.
78 ἆθλον . . . οἴνου is Mill's reading, reported by Buckham 1830:176, οἴνου με[τ]ρητής is Munro's (1901b:356).
79 Jacoby has [ἔτη ΗΗ * *, ἄρχοντ]ος [Ἀθήνησιν |⁵⁶ . . . . It is highly likely that the dating formula was found in the lacuna of 23/24 letters, but the position of the ΟΣ reported by Selden is unclear (Munro 1901b:356).
80 Δελφούς instead of Selden's ΔΕΛΦΟΣ is partially secured by Munro's reading. Selden marks only two dots after ΔΕΛΦΟΣΑ for a lacuna of at least 15 characters. Jacoby supplements ἀ[πέστειλε θεωρούς (?) (ἀπέστειλε is Le Paulmier's supplement, θεωρούς is Flach's). Munro further suggested ἀ[πέπεμψε τὰ ἀναθήματα] (Munro 1901b:357). Although the entry most probably refers to the events told by Herodotus 1.85, it is preferable not to restore the precise phrasing.

42. ἀφ' οὗ Κῦρος ὁ Περσῶν βασιλεὺς Σάρδεις ἔλαβεν καὶ Κροῖσον ΥΠΟ - - - ΗΣΣΦΑΛ - - - [81] [- - - 40 / 44 - - -][82]|**58** [ἦν δὲ][83] καὶ Ἱππῶναξ κατὰ τοῦτον ὁ ἰαμβοποιός.

43. ἀφ' οὗ Θέσπις ὁ ποιητὴς [ὑπεκρίνα]το πρῶτος[84] ὃς ἐδίδαξε ΝΑΛ - - - ΣΤΙΝ[85] [καὶ ἆθλον ἐ]τέθη ὁ [τ]ράγος, ἔτη ΗΗΓᴾ[- - -],[86] ἄρχοντος Ἀθ[ήνη|**59**σι - - -]ναίου τοῦ προτέρου.

44. ἀφ' οὗ Δαρεῖος Περσῶν ἐβασίλευσε μάγου τελευτήσαντος, ἔτη [ΗΗ]ᴾᴹΓᴵⵏ , ἄρχοντος Ἀθήνησ[ι - - -].

45. ἀφ' οὗ Ἁρμόδιος καὶ [Ἀριστογε]ίτων ἀπέκτε[ιναν |**60** Ἵππα]ρχον Πεισιστράτου δ[ιά]δ̣[οχ]ον (?), καὶ Ἀθηναῖοι [ἐξανέστ]ησαν τοὺς Πεισιστρατίδας ἐκ τ̣[οῦ Π]ελασγικοῦ τείχους, ἔτη ΗΗΔΔΔΓΙΙΙ, ἄρχοντος Ἀθήνησιν Ἁ[ρ]π[ακ|**61**《τίδου].

46. ἀφ' οὗ χοροὶ πρῶτον ἠγωνίσαντο ἀνδρῶν, ὃν (?) διδάξας Υ》 πό[δι]κος[87] ὁ Χαλκιδεὺ[ς] ἐνίκ[α], ἔτη ΗΗΔΔΔΔΓᴵ (?), ἄρχοντος Ἀθήνησιν Λυσαγόρου.

47. ἀφ' οὗ Με[λαν]ιππίδ[ης] Μ[ήλιος][88] |**62** ἐνίκησ]《εν Ἀθήνησιν》,[89] ἔτη ΗΗΔΔΔΙ, ἄρχοντος Ἀθήνησι Πυθοκρίτου.

48. ἀφ' οὗ ἡ ἐμ Μαραθῶνι μάχη ἐγένετο Ἀθηναίοις πρὸς τοὺς Πέρσας Ἀρ[ταφ]έ[ρνην τε τὸ]ν Δαρείου ἀδελφι|**63**[δοῦν κα]ὶ [Δᾶ]《τ[ι]ν

---

[81] Jacoby has ὑπο . . . . . . ησσφαλ . . . . , with Selden's number of dots.

[82] Jacoby has [ἔτη ΗΗΓᴾᴹΔΔΓᴵΙΙ (?), ἄρχοντος Ἀθήνησι * * |**58**. The dating formula was most probably at the end of the line, but the result may be too long. The lacuna's size is given by Hiller von Gärtringen.

[83] The coordinant δέ seems to be the rule in postscripts (A36, A55, A60, A71, B7, B11, B12, B14; only A72 has καί, asyndeton in A48; cf. chap. 4, sec. 1).

[84] Munro reported seeing]το πρῶτος or even]ατο πρῶτος; [ὑπεκρίνα]το is Keil's restoration.

[85] Jacoby has ὃς ἐδίδαξε δρᾶμ[α ἐν ἄ]στει (similarly, Hiller von Gärtringen). Given the importance of this restoration for the history of tragedy and the City Dionysia, I follow Connor's more conservative text (1990:26–32). The lacuna indicated by Selden with three dots (ΟΣΕΔΙΔΑΞΕΝΑΛ . . . ΣΤΙΝ) was supplemented by him and by other early editors as Ἄλ[κη]στιν. The restoration ἐδίδαξεν Ἄλκηστιν was rejected by Boeckh, and is missing from Jacoby's apparatus. By the end of the seventeenth century no traces of ΑΛ . . . ΣΤΙΝ could be seen (Bentley *ap.* Connor 1990:29). The N may or may not belong to the verb ἐδίδαξε.

[86] Jacoby has Boeckh's ΗΗΓᴾ[ΔΔ .] (between two and four characters are missing).

[87] The text transmitted by Selden was written in an erasure (Munro, as reported by Hiller von Gärtringen, note to line 61).

[88] Με[λαν]ιππίδ[ης] ἐνίκησ]εν (Bergk) is supported by Munro, who reports also an M after Melanippides's name, which he supplements Μ[ήλιος (1901b:357).

[89] ΕΝΑΘΗΝΗΣΙΝΕ, transmitted by Selden, was written in an erasure, replacing [ΔΙ]ΘΥΡΑΜΒΟΠΟΙΟΣ (Munro, as reported by Hiller von Gärtringen, note to line 62).

στρατηγόν, ἣν ἐνίκων⟩⟩[90] Ἀθηναῖοι, ἔτη ΗΗΔΔΓΊΙΙ, ἄρχοντος Ἀθήνησιν
τ[ο]ῦ δευτέρου [Φ]α̣[ι]ν[ι]π[πίδ]ου· ἧι ἐν μάχηι συνηγωνίσατο Αἰσχύλος
ὁ ποιητής, |[64] ἐτῶν ὢν ΔΔΔΓΊ.

49. ⟨⟨ἀφ' οὗ Σιμωνίδης ὁ Σιμωνίδου πάππος τοῦ ποιητοῦ⟩⟩,[91] ποιητὴς
ὢν καὶ αὐτός, ἐνίκησεν Ἀθήνησι, καὶ Δαρεῖος τελευτᾶι, Ξέρξης δὲ ὁ υἱὸς
βασιλεύει, ἔτ[η |[65] ΗΗ]ΔΔΓΊΙ, ἄρχοντος Ἀθήνησι Ἀριστείδου.

50. ἀφ' οὗ Αἰσχύλος ὁ ποιητὴς τραγωιδίαι πρῶτον ἐνίκησε, καὶ
Εὐριπίδης ὁ ποιητὴς ἐγένετο, καὶ Στησίχορος ὁ ποιητὴς εἰς |[66] τὴν
Ἑλλάδα ἀ[φίκετ]ο,[92] ἔτη ΗΗΔΔΙΙ, ἄρχοντος Ἀθήνησι Φιλοκράτους.

51. ἀφ' οὗ Ξέρξης τὴν σχεδίαν ἔζευξεν ἐν Ἑλλησπόντωι καὶ τὸν Ἄθω
διώρυξε, καὶ ἡ ἐν Θερμο[πύ]|[67]λαις μάχη ἐγένετο, καὶ ναυμαχία τοῖς
Ἕλλησι περὶ Σαλαμῖνα πρὸς τοὺς Πέρσας, ἣν ἐνίκων οἱ Ἕλληνες, ἔτη
ΗΗΔΓΊΙΙ, ἄρχοντος Ἀθήνησι Καλλιάδου.

52. ἀφ' οὗ ἡ ἐν |[68] Πλαταιαῖς μάχη ἐγένετο Ἀθηναίοις πρὸς Μαρδόνιον
τὸν Ξέρξου στρατηγόν, ἣν ἐνίκων Ἀθηναῖοι, καὶ Μαρδόνιος ἐτελεύτησεν
ἐν τῆι μάχηι, καὶ τὸ πῦρ ἐρύη ἐ[ν] |[69] Σικελίαι περὶ τὴν Αἴτνην, ἔτη
ΗΗΔΓΊΙ, ἄρχοντος Ἀθήνησι Ξανθίππου.

53. ἀφ' οὗ Γ[έ]λων ὁ Δεινομένους Σ[υρακο]υ[σσῶν] ἐτυράννευσεν, ἔτη
ΗΗΔΓΊ, ἄρχοντος Ἀθήνησι Τιμοσθέν[ους]. |[70]

---

[90] Τ.ΝΣΤΡΑΤΗΓΟΝΗΝΕΝΙΚΩΝ in an erasure (Munro, as reported by Hiller von Gärtringen, note to line 63; Hiller von Gärtringen, however, omits the HN, which Munro [1901b:358] saw on the stone). Jacoby has [Δᾶ]τιν, but Munro suggests T.N, where Selden's majuscule transcription has ΤΟΝ.

[91] ΑΦΟΥΣΙΜΩΝΙΔΗΣΟΣΙΜΩΝΙΔΟΥΠΑΠΠΟΣΤΟΥΠΟΙΗΤΟΥ was written in an erasure (Munro, as reported by Hiller von Gärtringen, note to line 64). Jacoby added a crux before πάππος, indicating the implausibility of the reference, given that at A57 (= 468/7 BCE) the inscription states that Simonides died at ninety years of age. Accordingly, he would have been almost seventy years old by the time his grandfather won his victory in A49 (= 489/8 BCE). Perhaps the word πάππος is used in a general sense, indicating an uncle (Jacoby 1904a:113). At any rate, the Parian Marble presents Simonides the elder as a relative of the famous Simonides (mentioned again in A54 and A57).

[92] Selden's majuscule transcription reads ΤΗΝΕΛΛΑΔΑΑ . . . . (with four dots), but his Errata give ΤΗΝΕΛΛΑΔΑ . . . .; later editors disregard the correction. The supplement ἀ[φίκετ]ο goes back to Le Paulmier (1668, published in Maittaire 1732:217), whom Bergk and Flach credit, but not Jacoby and Hiller von Gärtringen. Le Paulmier further conjectured εἰς at the end of line 65, where no lacuna was reported by Selden. Hiller von Gärtringen has εἰ[ς] and Jacoby εἰς, suggesting that at least part of the preposition may have been seen, which in turn would support restoration of a verb of movement. One could infer *ab silentio* from Munro's note to A50 (1901b:358) that he did not object to the supplement on the basis of autopsy. The date is too late for Stesichorus, but see chap. 6, n. 76 below for further references to the traditions possibly underlying the entry.

54. ἀφ' οὗ Σιμωνίδης ὁ Λεωπρέπους ὁ Κεῖος ὁ τὸ μνημονικὸν εὑρὼν
ἐνίκησεν Ἀθήνησι διδάσκων, καὶ αἱ εἰκόνες ἐστάθησαν Ἁρμοδίου καὶ
Ἀριστογείτονος, ἔτη ΗΗΔΙ Ι Ι (?),[93] |⁷¹ ἄρχοντος Ἀθήνησιν [Ἀ]δειμάντου.

55. ἀφ' οὗ Ἱέρων Συρακουσσῶν ἐτυράννευσεν, ἔτη ΗΗΓ¹ΙΙΙ, ἄρχοντος
Ἀθήνησι Χά[ρ]ητος· ἦν δὲ καὶ Ἐπίχαρμος ὁ ποιητὴς κατὰ τοῦ|⁷²τον.

56. ἀφ' οὗ Σοφοκλῆς ὁ Σοφίλλου ὁ ἐκ Κολωνοῦ ἐνίκησε τραγωιδίαι,
ἐτῶν ὢν ΔΔΓ¹ΙΙΙ, ἔτη ΗΗΓ¹Ι, ἄρχοντος Ἀθήνησι Ἀψηφίωνος.

57. ἀφ' οὗ ἐν Αἰγὸς ποταμοῖς ὁ λίθος ἔπεσε, |⁷³ καὶ Σιμωνίδης ὁ
ποιητὴς ἐτελεύτησεν, βιοὺς ἔτη Γ¹ΔΔΔΔ, ἔτη ΗΗΓ¹, ἄρχοντος Ἀθήνησι
Θεαγενίδου.

58. ἀφ' οὗ Ἀλέξανδρος ἐτελεύτησεν, ὁ δὲ υἱὸς Περδίκ|⁷⁴κας Μακεδόνων
βασιλεύει, ἔτη ΗΓ¹ΔΔΔΔΓ¹ΙΙΙΙ,[94] ἄρχοντος Ἀθήνησιν Εὐθίππου.

59. ἀφ' οὗ Αἰσχύλος ὁ ποιητής, ⟨⟨βιώσας ἔτη Γ¹ΔΓ¹⟩⟩ΙΙΙΙ,[95] ἐτελεύτησεν
ἐγ [Γέ|⁷⁵λ]αι τῆς Σικελίας, ἔτη ΗΓ¹ΔΔΔΔΙΙΙ, ἄρχοντος Ἀθήνησι Καλλέου
τοῦ προτέρου.

60. ἀφ' οὗ Εὐριπίδης ἐτῶν ὢν ΔΔΔΔΙΙΙΙ (?)[96] τραγωιδίαι πρῶτον
ἐνίκησεν, ἔτη ΗΓ¹Δ[ΔΓ¹ΙΙΙΙ,[97] |⁷⁶ ἄρ]χοντος Ἀθήνησι Διφίλο[υ· ἦ]σαν δὲ
κατ' Εὐριπίδην Σωκράτης τε καὶ Ἀναξαγόρας.

---

[93] ΟΓΕΙΤΟΝΟΣΕΤΗΗΗ was written in an erasure (Munro, as reported by Hiller von Gärtringen, note
to line 70), but it is unclear what numerals Munro could actually see ("one would rather restore
214, but it is a tight fit," Munro 1901b:358). Jacoby's apparatus has ΟΓΕΙΤΟΝΟΣΗΗΔΙΙΙΙ, with
small question marks on top of the Δ and the second Ι, which may render what was in Munro's
unpublished work).

[94] Jacoby excises a numeral, giving ΗΓ¹ΔΔΔΔΓ¹ΙΙΙ{Ι} (not so Hiller von Gärtringen and Jacoby
1904a).

[95] The reading ΒΙΩΣΑΣΕΤΗΓ¹ΔΓ¹ (thus Selden's majuscule transcription) was written in an erasure
(Munro, as reported by Hiller von Gärtringen, note to line 74; the numeral ΗΓ¹ΔΓ¹ in Jacoby's
apparatus is wrong).

[96] Munro's reading ΔΔΔΔΙΙΙΙ, with small question mark on top of the first iota, is reported by Jacoby
(probably deriving from personal communication). If the date of the entry is right (see following
note), ΔΔΔΔΙΙΙ (Selden, Hiller von Gärtringen) would be the correct reading, since Euripides's
birth is dated in entry A50. Munro, however, may have seen the number forty-four, and noted
the inconsistency with A50 with a question mark.

[97] The restoration ΗΓ¹Δ[ΔΓ¹ΙΙΙΙ, unattributed in modern editions, goes back to Le Paulmier's
(Maittaire 1732) correction of Selden's ΗΓ¹Δ[ΔΔ (Selden 1628:111, in the *canon chronicus*; both
transcriptions give ΗΓ¹Δ). Le Paulmier's supplement was adopted by Chandler 1763:31, whereas
Boeckh, following a different computation, has ΗΓ¹Δ[ΔΓ¹ΙΙΙ.

61. ἀφ᾽ οὗ Ἀρχέλαος Μακεδόνων βασιλεύει Περδίκκου τελευτήσαντος, ἔτη Η[ᴾᴵΓᴵΙΙ, |⁷⁷ ἄρ]χοντος Ἀθήνησιν Ἀστυφίλου.

62. ἀφ᾽ οὗ Διονύσιος Συρακουσσῶν⁹⁸ ἐτυράννευσεν, ἔτη ΗΔΔΔΔΓᴵΙΙ,⁹⁹ ἄρχοντος Ἀθήνησιν Εὐκτήμονος.

63. ἀφ᾽ οὗ Εὐριπίδης βι[ώσας ἔτη - - -]¹⁰⁰ |⁷⁸ [ἐτ]ελεύτησεν, ἔτη ΗΔΔΔΔΓᴵ,¹⁰¹ ἄρχοντος Ἀθήνησι Ἀντιγένους.

64. ἀφ᾽ οὗ Σοφοκλῆς ὁ ποιητὴς βιώσας ἔτη ᴾᴵΔΔΔΔΙΙ ἐτελεύτησεν, καὶ Κῦρος ἀνέβη [ἔτη ΗΔΔΔΔΙΙΙ, |⁷⁹ ἄρχ]οντος Ἀθήνησι Καλλίου τοῦ † προτέρου.¹⁰²

65. ἀφ᾽ οὗ Τελέστης Σελινούντιος ἐνίκησεν Ἀθήνησιν, ἔτη ΗΔΔΔΓᴵΙΙΙΙ, ἄρχοντος Ἀθήνησιν Μίκωνος.

66. ἀφ᾽ οὗ [κατῆλθον οἱ Ἕλληνες οἱ |⁸⁰ μετ]ὰ Κύρου ἀναβάντες, καὶ Σωκράτης¹⁰³ φιλόσοφος ἐτελεύτησεν, βιοὺς ἔτη ᴾᴵΔΔ, ἔτη ΗΔΔΔΓᴵΙΙ, ἄρχοντος Ἀθήνησιν Λάχητος.

67. ἀφ᾽ οὗ Ἀρ[ι]στο[νους¹⁰⁴ - - - ca. 20 - - - ἐνίκη|⁸¹σεν] Ἀθήνησιν, ἔτη ΗΔΔΔΓᴵ, ἄρχοντος Ἀθήνησιν Ἀριστοκράτους.

---

⁹⁸ Munro's reading, as reported by Hiller von Gärtringen's commentary to line 72.

⁹⁹ Jacoby excises two numerals, giving ΗΔΔΔΔΓᴵ (not so Hiller von Gärtringen and Jacoby 1904a).

¹⁰⁰ Jacoby has βι[ώσας ἔτη ᴾᴵΔΔΓᴵ . . (?). The numeral has been restored as ᴾᴵΔΔΓᴵΙΙΙ (Boeckh), ᴾᴵΔΔΓᴵΙΙ (Hiller von Gärtringen), and ᴾᴵΔΔΓᴵΙΙΙΙ (Jacoby 1904a). Euripides's age at death, between seventy-seven and seventy-nine, cannot be retrieved, since the inscription is damaged at this point, but seventy-seven results from computation.

¹⁰¹ Jacoby adds a crux before the numeral, suggesting the reading ΗΔΔΔΔΙΙΙΙ, even though there are no doubts about the transmitted text, but about Euripides's date of death (see note above).

¹⁰² The qualification of Callias as "first" appears mistaken (Le Paulmier corrected it to δευτέρου), since "Calleas the first" was mentioned already (A59, and cf. Calleas at A70; it is unclear whether the orthographical difference between Callias and Calleas is significant). Munro, however, clearly read προτέρου (Munro 1901b:358), though it may have been a repetition from A59.

¹⁰³ Hiller von Gärtringen and Jacoby supplement the article (without noting it), namely Σωκράτης ὁ φιλόσοφος. According to Munro 1901b:358, however, there is no space for the article, and it was not in Selden's transcriptions either.

¹⁰⁴ Jacoby has Ἀρ[ι]στό[νους, following Wilamowitz (Hiller von Gärtringen's note to line 80). Munro read Ἀρ[ι]στ[ο or Ἀρ[ι]στ[α. The archon's name Ἀριστοκράτους is suspect of repetition. Hiller von Gärtringen, following Wilamowitz, has Ἀρ[ι]στο[νους ὁ κιθαρωιδὸς ἐνίκη|σεν], homeland (Jacoby) or patronymic may have been mentioned in the lacuna; cf. chap. 6, sec. 2.IV below, for a possible identification with a winner kitharode at Delphi (Plutarch *Life of Lysander* 18.5) and/or with Aristonous of Corinth (*contra* Jacoby).

68. ἀφ' οὖ Πολύιδος[105] Σηλυμβριανὸς διθυράμβωι ἐνίκησεν Ἀθήνησιν, ἔτη ΗΔ[- - - ἄρχοντος Ἀθήνησι - - -].

69. |[82] [ἀφ'] οὖ Φιλόξενος διθυραμβοποιὸς τελευτᾶι, βιοὺς ἔτη ΓᴾΓ, ἔτη ΗΔΓᴴΙ, ἄρχοντος Ἀθήνησιν Πυθέου.

70. ἀφ' οὖ Ἀναξανδρίδης ὁ κωμο[ιδοποιὸς - - - ca. 15 - - - ἄρχοντος][106] |[83] Ἀθήνησι Καλλέου.

71. ἀφ' οὖ Ἀστυδάμας Ἀθήνησιν ἐνίκησεν, ἔτη ΗΓᴾΙΙΙΙ, ἄρχοντος Ἀθήνησιν Ἀστείου. κατεκάη δὲ τότε κα[ὶ ὁ ἐν Δελφοῖς ναός].[107]

72. [ἀφ' οὖ ἡ ἐν Λεύκτροις μάχη |[84] ἐ]γένετο Θηβαίων καὶ Λακεδαιμονίων, ἥν ἐνίκων Θηβαῖοι, ἔτη ΗΓᴾΙΙ, ἄρχοντος Ἀθήνησιν Φρασικλείδου. καὶ Ἀλ[έξανδρος - - - ca. 20 - - - Μακεδόνων][108] |[85] βασιλεύει.

73. ἀφ' οὖ Στησίχορος ὁ Ἱμερ⟨α⟩ῖος ὁ δεύτερος ἐνίκησεν Ἀθήνησιν, καὶ οἰκίσθη Μεγάλη πόλις [ἐν Ἀρκαδίαι, ἔτη ΗΓᴾ[109], ἄρχοντος Ἀθήνησι - - -].

74. |[86] ἀφ' οὖ Διονύσιος Σικελιώτης ἐτελεύτησεν, ὁ δὲ υἱὸς Διονύσιος ἐτυράννευσεν, καὶ Ἀλεξάνδρ[ου - - - ca. 35 - - - Μακεδόνων βα][110]|[87]σιλεύει, ἔτη ΗΙΙΙΙ, ἄρχοντος Ἀθήνησιν Ναυσιγένους.

---

[105] Munro's reading, confirmed by Hiller von Gärtringen. Selden did not transmit the name of the poet, but Baumgarten suggested either Polyidus or Timotheus (Munro 1901b:358).

[106] Jacoby has κωμο[ιδοποιὸς ἐνίκησεν Ἀθήνησιν, ἔτη ΗΔΙΙΙ, ἄρχοντος] (for spelling, cf. κωμοιδοποιός at B7 and B14). A formulaic reference to victory, as well as the number of years, is most plausibly missing, but the resulting line is somewhat too long (135 letters). Boeckh's πρῶτον ἐδίδαξεν is omitted from Jacoby's apparatus (cf. his 1904a edition; Capps 1900:55n1).

[107] Munro (1901b:359) reports clearly seeing κατεκάη on the stone, the supplement κα[ὶ ὁ ἐν Δελφοῖς ναός] is his.

[108] Jacoby has Ἀ[μύντας τελευτᾶι, Ἀλέξανδρος δὲ ὁ υἱὸς Μακεδόνων], but Munro (1901b:359) saw traces of Ἀλ[, which suggests Ἀλ[έξανδρος. The phrasing of Hiller von Gärtringen's restoration (following Boeckh's) suits the general style of postscripts: Ἀλ[έξανδρος ὁ Ἀμυντοῦ κατὰ τοῦτον Μακεδόνων].

[109] The numeral could also be ΗΓᴾΙ (Hiller von Gärtringen).

[110] While Jacoby has Ἀλεξάνδρ[ου τελευτήσαντος Πτολεμαῖος ὁ Ἀλωρίτης Μακεδόνων βα], Hiller von Gärtringen, following Munro, prefers Perdiccas as the subject of the verb βασιλεύει, because "Ptolemy was not the legitimate sovereign" (Munro 1901b:359). However, the author's or his source's position on the matter cannot be guessed with confidence.

75. ἀφ' οὗ Φωκεῖς τὸ ἐν Δελφοῖς μα[ντεῖον κατέλαβον - - - ca. 25/30 - - - ἔτη - - -[111] ἄρχοντος Ἀθή]|[88]νησι Κηφισοδώρου.[112]

76. ἀφ' οὗ Τιμόθεος βιώσας ἔτη ⟨Π⟩ΔΔΔΔ ἐτελεύτησεν, ἔτ[η - - - ἄρχοντος Ἀθήνησι - - -].

77. [ἀφ' οὗ Φίλιππος ὁ Ἀμύντου Μα]|[89]κεδόνων βασιλεύει, καὶ Ἀρτοξέρξης ἐτελεύτησεν, Ὦχος δὲ ὁ υἱὸς β[ασιλεύει - - - ἔτη - - - ἄρχοντος Ἀθήνησι - - -].

78. [ἀφ' οὗ - - - Ἀθήνη|[90]σιν] ἐνίκησεν,[113] ἔτη ⟨Π⟩ΔΔΔΔIII, ἄρχοντος Ἀθήνησιν Ἀγαθοκλέους.

79. [ἀφ' οὗ - - - |[91] ἐγ]ένετο, ἔτη ⟨Π⟩ΔΔΔΔI, ἄρχοντος Ἀθήνησι Καλλιστ[ράτου - - -] |[92] . . . . . σοφος (?). . . . Τ . . . τούτου (?).[114]

80. ἀφ' οὗ Καλλι[115][- - -]|[93] [ἔτ]η ⟨Π⟩ - - - ἄρχοντος [Ἀθήνησι - - -].[116]

B: The Parian Fragment[117]

1. [- - -]ΔΟ[- - -] |[2] [- - - ca. 15 - - - Φίλιππος ἐτ]ε[λε]ύτη[σ]εν, Ἀλέ[ξανδρ]ος δὲ βασιλεύει, ἔτη ⟨Π⟩ΔΔII, ἄρχοντος Ἀθήνησι Πυθοδήλου.[118]

---

[111] Jacoby has ἔτη HII, the year of Kephisodorus (the name is "plainly legible," Munro 1901b:359). However, since our sources date the event to the archonship of Agathocles, it seems preferable to omit supplementation, with Hiller von Gärtringen.

[112] At the end of the Ashmolean section less than half the lines survive (fifty-four letters in line 88, fifty-two letters in line 89, forty-six letters in line 90, thirty-six letters in line 91, twenty letters in line 92, ten letters in line 93). The last two lines depend on Selden's transcription.

[113] This is most probably an agonistic victory (Munro 1901b:360, Jacoby 1904a:123), but the name of the poet is lost. None of Jacoby's editions record Capps's supplement of Alexis ([. . . . . καὶ Ἄλεξις ὁ κωμοιδοποιὸς τότε πρῶτον] ἐνίκησεν) (Capps 1900:60, cf. Wilhelm and Kaibel 1906:249).

[114] Jacoby has . . . . . ΣΟΦΟΣ (?) . . . . Τ . . . TOYTOY (?), both the reading and the number of dots derive from Selden's majuscule transcription. Hiller von Gärtringen prints | -ἐπὶ τού]του (for similar postscripts, cf. A42, A55 and chap. 4, sec. 1). Munro's reading (1910b:360) is of little help: . . . Σ . . . . . . ΕΥΤΟΥ ("the letter before Σ looks like A or H, and the letters next after Σ suggest ΑΓΩ or AM rather than Σ[ΟΦΟΣ]." Tod (1957:132n2) writes: "We should expect some reference to Plato, but I know no event in Plato's life dated in that year which would call for notice."

[115] Jacoby has ἀφ' οὗ ΚΑΛΛ * * * |, but Forster's reading supports Καλλι[, as in Hiller von Gärtringen's edition.

[116] The last line of section A disappeared by the time Munro and Hiller von Gärtringen examined it; the reading depends on Selden's transcription.

[117] Jacoby's text follows the first edition of Krispi and Wilhelm, with occasional contributions by Hiller von Gärtringen and Munro.

[118] The first line of this section is completely lost, except for the horizontal bottom strokes of some letters, from which Munro could make out ΔΟ. At the beginning of line 2, ca. fifteen letters are missing.

2. ἀφ' οὗ Ἀλέξανδρος εἰς Τριβαλλοὺς καὶ Ἰλλυριοὺς ἐστρά[τευσε][119] |[3] καὶ Θηβαίων ἐπαναστάντων καὶ τὴμ φρουρὰν πολιορκούντων ἐπανελθὼν κατὰ κράτος λαβὼν τὴν πόλιν κατέσκαψεν, ἔτη 𐅅ΔΔΙ, ἄρχοντος Ἀθήνησι Εὐαινέτου.

3. |[4] ἀπὸ τῆς Ἀλεξάνδρου διαβάσεως εἰς τὴν Ἀσίαν καὶ μάχης περὶ τὸν Γρανικόν, καὶ ἀπὸ τῆς ἐν Ἰσσῶι μάχης Ἀλεξάνδρωι πρὸς Δαρεῖον, ἔτη 𐅅ΔΔ, ἄρχοντος Ἀθήνησι |[5] Κτησικλείους.

4. ἀφ' οὗ Ἀλέξανδρος Φοινίκης καὶ Κύπρου καὶ Αἰγύπτου ἐκυρίευσε, ἔτη 𐅅ΔΠΙΙΙΙ, ἄρχοντος Ἀθήνησι Νικοκράτους.

5. ἀπὸ τῆς Ἀλεξάνδρου πρὸς Δαρεῖον μάχης |[6] τῆς περὶ Ἄρβηλα, ἣν ἐνίκησεν Ἀλέξανδρος· καὶ Βαβυλὼν ἥλω, καὶ ἀφῆκε τοὺς συμμάχους, καὶ Ἀλεξάνδρεια ἐκτίσθη, ἔτη 𐅅ΔΠΙΙΙ, ἄρχοντος Ἀθήνησιν Νικήτου.

6. ἀφ' οὗ |[7] Κάλλιππος ἀστρολογίαν ἐξέθηκεν, καὶ Ἀλέξανδρος Δαρεῖον ἔλαβεν, Βῆσον δὲ ἐκρέμασεν, ἔτη 𐅅ΔΠΙ, ἄρχοντος Ἀθήνησι Ἀριστοφῶντος.

7. ἀφ' οὗ Φιλήμων ὁ κωμοιδο|[8]ποιὸς ἐνίκησεν, ἔτη 𐅅ΔΙΙΙΙ, ἄρχοντος Ἀθήνησι Εὐθυκρίτου. ᾠκίσθη δὲ πρὸς τῶι Τανάι πόλις Ἑλληνίς.

8. ἀπὸ τῆς Ἀλεξάνδρου μεταλλαγῆς καὶ Πτολεμαίου Αἰγύπτου |[9] κυριεύσεως, ἔτη 𐅅Δ, ἄρχοντος Ἀθήνησι Ἡγησίου.

9. ἀπὸ τοῦ πολέμου τοῦ γενομένου περὶ ⟨⟨. .⟩⟩ Λαμίαν[120] Ἀθηναίοις πρὸς Ἀντίπατρον, καὶ ἀπὸ τῆς ναυμαχίας |[10] τῆς γενομένης Μακεδόσιν πρὸς Ἀθηναίους περὶ Ἀμοργόν, ἣν ἐνίκων Μακεδόνες, ἔτη 𐅅ΠΙΙΙΙ, ἄρχοντος Ἀθήνησιν Κηφισοδώρου.

10. ἀφ' οὗ Ἀντίπατρος Ἀ|[11]θήνας ἔλαβε, καὶ Ὀφέλας Κυρήνην ἀποσταλεὶς ὑπὸ Πτολεμαίου, ἔτη 𐅅ΠΙΙΙ, ἄρχοντος Ἀθήνησι Φιλοκλέους.

11. ἀφ' οὗ Ἀντίγονος εἰς τὴν Ἀσίαν διέβη, |[12] καὶ Ἀλέξανδρος εἰς Μέμφιν ἐτέθη, καὶ Περδίκκας εἰς Αἴγυπτον στρατεύσας ἐτελεύτησεν, καὶ Κράτερος, καὶ Ἀριστοτέλης ὁ σοφιστὴς ἐτελεύτη|[13]σεν, ἔτη 𐅅ΠΙΙ,

119 Jacoby has ἐστράτευσε. Although restoration seems correct, I prefer to render it as ἐστρά[τευσε] (with the first editors, Krispi and Wilhelm 1897, and Jacoby 1904a), since the stone is broken at the end of the line.

120 There is an erasure equivalent to two broad letters (17 mm, with traces) before the word ΛΑΜΙΑΝ, and the correction of -NA into -AN at the end of the word is still visible. The cutter seems to have corrected ΣΑΛΑΜΙΝΑ into ΛΑΜΙΑΝ (Munro 1901b:360).

βιοὺς ἔτη Ⱶᴵ, ἄρχοντος Ἀθήνησι Ἀρχίππου. ἐπορεύθη δὲ καὶ Πτολεμαῖος εἰς Κυρήνην.

12. ἀπὸ τῆς Ἀντιπάτρου τελευτῆς, Κασσάνδρου δὲ ἀποχωρήσεως |[14] ἐγ Μακεδονίας, καὶ ἀπὸ τῆς ἐγ Κυζίκωι πολιορκίας, ἣν ἐπολιόρκησεν Ἀριδαῖος, καὶ ἀφ' οὗ Πτολεμαῖος ἔλαβεν Συρίαν καὶ Φοινίκην, ἔτη ⱵᴵΓᴵ, ἄρχοντος Ἀθή|[15]νησι Ἀπολλοδώρου. τῶι δ' αὐτῶι ἔτει τούτωι καὶ Ἀγαθοκλῆν Συρακόσιοι εἵλοντο ἐπὶ τῶν ἐρυμάτων τῶν ἐν Σικελίαι αὐτοκράτορα στρατηγόν.

13. ἀπὸ τῆς Κλείτου |[16] ναυμαχίας καὶ Νικάνορος περὶ τὸ ἱερὸν τὸ Καλχηδονίων, καὶ ὅτε Δημήτριος νόμους ἔθηκεν Ἀθήνησιν, ἔτη ⱵᴵΙΙΙ, ἄρχοντος Ἀθήνησι Δημογένους.

14. ἀφ' οὗ |[17] Κάσσανδρος εἰς Μακεδονίαν κατῆλθεν, καὶ Θῆβαι οἰκίσθησαν, καὶ Ὀλυμπιὰς ἐτελεύτησεν, καὶ Κασσάνδρεια ἐκτίσθη, καὶ Ἀγαθοκλῆς Συρακουσ|[18]σῶν ἐτυράννευσεν, ἔτη ⱵᴵΙΙ, ἄρχοντος Ἀθήνησι Δημοκλείδ[ου]· ἐνίκα δὲ καὶ Μένανδρος ὁ κωμοιδοποιὸς Ἀθήνησιν τότε πρῶτον.

15. ἀφ' οὗ Σωσιφά|[19]νης[121] ποιητὴς τελευτᾶι, ἔτη ΔΔΔΔΓΙΙΙΙ, ἄρχοντος Ἀθήνησιν Θεοφράστου, βι[οὺ]ς ἔτη ΔΔΔΔΓ.

16. ἀφ' οὗ ὁ ἥλιος ἐξέλιπεν, καὶ Πτολεμαῖος Δημήτριον ἐνίκα ἐν |[20] Γάζει καὶ Σέλευκον ἀπέστειλεν εἰς Βαβυλῶνα, ἔτη ΔΔ[Δ]ΔΓΙΙΙ, ἄρχοντος Ἀθήνησιν Πο[λέμ]ωνος.

17. ἀφ' οὗ [Ν]ικοκρέων ἐτελεύτησεν καὶ Πτολεμαῖος κυρι|[21]εύει τῆς νήσου, ἔτη ΔΔΔΔΓΙΙ, ἄρχοντος Ἀθήνησιν Σι[μωνί]δου.[122]

18. ἀφ' οὗ Ἀλέ[ξ]α[νδρος ὁ Ἀλεξάνδρου] τελευτᾶι καὶ ἕτερος ἐκ τῆς Ἀρταβάζου θυγατρὸς Ἡρα|[22]κλῆς, καὶ Ἀγαθοκλῆς διέβη εἰς Καρχηδ[όνα - - - ca. 35 - - - ἔτη Δ]ΔΔΔΓΙ, ἄρχοντος Ἀθήνησι Ἱερομνήμονος.

19. ἀφ' οὗ Λ[υ|[23]σι]μάχεια πόλις ἐκτίσθη, καὶ Ὀφέλας εἰς [Κα]ρ-χ[ηδόνα - - - ca. 40 - - -][123] καὶ Πτολεμαῖος ὁ υἱὸς ἐγ Κῶι ἐγένετο,

---

[121] Jacoby has ⟨ὁ⟩ ποιητής, but there is no room for a regular omicron (before ποιητής there is a vertical scratch, perhaps a mistaken vertical stroke, that may conceal a small omicron). The article has been omitted in A5 too.

[122] From this point on, all lines have major lacunae in the middle.

[123] Jacoby has ΣΩΙ (?) after the lacuna, following a tentative reading of Wilhelm on a squeeze (who further proposed νό]σωι, Krispi and Wilhelm 1897:207), but Munro could not "make it out on the stone" (1901b:361). I omit the letters, with Krispi and Hiller von Gärtringen.

καὶ Κλ[εο|²⁴π]άτρα ἐν Σάρδεσιν ἀπέθαν[ε - - - ca. 35 - - - ἔτη ΔΔΔΔΓ',
ἄρχοντος Ἀ]θήνῃσ[ι Δ]ημητρίου.

20. ἀφ' οὗ Δημήτριος ὁ Ἀντιγόνου τὸ[μ|²⁵ Π]ειραιᾶ πολιορκήσας ἔλαβεν,
[- - - ca. 35 - - - ἔτη ΔΔΔΔΙΙΙΙ, ἄρχοντος]¹²⁴ Ἀθήνησι Καιρίμου.

21. ἀφ' οὗ Δημήτριος Μουνυχίαν κατέ|²⁶σκαψεν καὶ Κύπρον ἔλαβεν καὶ
Φιλλιπ¹²⁵[- - - ca. 22 - - - ΟΝ - - - ca. 18 - - - Σ.ΟΥ ἔτη Δ]ΔΔΔΙΙΙ, ἄρχοντος
Ἀθήνησιν Ἀναξικράτους.

22. |²⁷ ἀφ' οὗ Σωσιφάνης ὁ ποιητὴς ἐγέ[νετο (?)¹²⁶ - - - ca. 25 - - - ἔτη
ΔΔΔΔΙΙ, ἄρχοντος Ἀθήνη]σ[ι Κ]οροίβου.

23. ἀπὸ τῆς περὶ Ῥόδον πολιορκίας, καὶ ἀφ' ο[ὗ |²⁸ Πτ]ολεμαῖος τὴν
βασιλείαν παρ[έ]λ[α]β[εν, ἔτ]η [ΔΔΔΔΙ, ἄρχοντος Ἀθήνησι Εὐξενίππου].

24. [ἀπὸ τῶ]ν σε[ι[σ]μῶν τῶν [γ]ενομένων καθ' Ἰωνίαν, καὶ ὅτε
Δημήτριος Χαλκ[ί|²⁹δα ἔλα]βεν καθ' ὁμολογίαν καὶ πρεσ[- - - ca. 40 - - -
Δη]μητρίου, ἔτη ΔΔΔΔ, ἄρχοντος Ἀθήνησι Φερεκλείους.

25. ἀφ' οὗ |³⁰ [κομήτης ἀσ]τὴρ ἐφ[ά]ν[η],¹²⁷ καὶ Λυσίμαχ[ο]ς [εἰς τὴν
Ἀσίαν διέβη (?),¹²⁸ ἔτη ΔΔΔΓΙΙΙΙ, ἄρχοντος Ἀθήνησι] Λ[εωστ]ρ[άτου].

26. ἀ[φ'] οὗ [δ]ιάλυσις Κασσάνδρωι καὶ Δημητρίωι |³¹ [ἐγένετο]....ν...
....Κασσαν[δ]ρο [- - - ca. 45 - - - ἐτελεύτ]ησεν, [ἔτη] ΔΔΔΓΙΙΙ, ἄρχοντος
Ἀθήνησι Νικοκλείους.

---

¹²⁴ Jacoby has [καὶ Δημήτριος ὁ Φαληρεὺς ἐξέπεσεν Ἀθηνῶν, ἔτη ΔΔΔΔΙΙΙΙ, ἄρχοντος], combining
  Wilhelm's (καὶ Δημήτριος ὁ Φαληρεύς) and his own (ἐξέπεσεν Ἀθηνῶν) supplements. This is the
  sole substantial supplement that Jacoby includes in section B of the inscription.
¹²⁵ Jacoby has Φιλλ.π (?); I could make out the second iota. Munro (1901b:361) read ΦΙΛΛΠ, reading
  the second lambda as alpha and the mark before π as an accidental scratch ("one might be
  tempted to restore φ[υ]λ[αὶ π[ρος"); Krispi and Hiller von Gärtringen give Φίλα.
¹²⁶ Jacoby has ἐγέ[νετο (?) καί (with Krispi's [ἐγένετο καί] and Hiller von Gärtringen's ἐ]γ[ένετο).
  Munro suggested ἐτέ[λεύτησεν, or Sositheus instead of Sosiphanes, to avoid another Sosiphanes,
  otherwise unknown (Munro 1901b:361, *contra* Jacoby 1903 and Jacoby 1904a:127–128). Partial
  upper horizontal strokes are still visible in the squeezes at the IG archive, consistent with either
  ΕΓΕ or ΕΤΕ (a drawing at the IG archive, probably by Hiller von Gärtringen (Klaus Hallof, personal
  communication), suggests that he may have been able to recognize the vertical of Γ, perhaps
  the vertical of a following Ν). The text should not be corrected, even though a mistake by the
  cutter or the author, whether in the verb (ΕΓΕΝ-, ΕΤΕΛ-, ΕΝΙΚ-?) or the name of the poet, cannot
  be ruled out. Without further evidence, one must agree with Jacoby that the Parian Marble
  mentions two poets of similar name.
¹²⁷ Jacoby has ἐφάνη. I give ἐφ[ά]ν[η], with Hiller von Gärtringen (I can make out ΤΗΡΕΦ on one of
  the IG squeezes, there is space for eight to ten letters before).
¹²⁸ Krispi and Wilhelm's restoration, I add a question mark with Hiller von Gärtringen.

27. |³²[ἀφ' οὗ - - - ca. 75 - - - Δημη]τρίου εἰς Χαλκίδα ἀναβολῆς, Ἀθηναῖοι δὲ Κασ|³³[σάνδρ - - - ca. 80 - - -] ιοι Πτολεμαί . . . . ἔτη ΔΔΔΓᴵ, |³⁴ [ἄρχοντος Ἀθήνησι Εὐκτήμονος].

3. English Translation

A1: The Lost Fragment

The first part of the inscription, found in Smyrna in 1627 and published by Selden, is lost. The section containing the first forty-five entries depends on Selden's transcription.

> . . . of all sorts . . . I recorded the . . . , starting from Cecrops, the first king of Athens, until . . . uanax was archon in Paros, and Diognetus in Athens.

(A space of three to five letters possibly marks a new section)[129]

> 1. From the time Cecrops became king of Athens,[130] hence[131] the land formerly called Actica—from Actaeus, born from the earth—was called Cecropia, 1318 years (= 1581/0 BCE).[132]

> 2. From the time Deucalion became king on Mount Parnassus in Lycorea, when Cecrops was king of Athens, 1310 years (= 1573/2 BCE).

> 3. From the time a trial occured in Athens between Ares and Poseidon over Halirrhothius, Poseidon's son—hence the place was called Areopagos—1268 years (= 1531/0 BCE), when Cranaus was king of Athens.

> 4. From the time a flood (*kataklysmos*) occured in Deucalion's days, and Deucalion escaped the waters from Lycorea to Athens towards, . . . and es[tablished] the t[e]mple of Zeus (?) . . . [133] and made the sacrifices of deliverance, 1265 years (= 1528/7 BCE), when Cranaus was king of Athens.

---

[129] See chap. 5, sec. 2 below.

[130] A proleptic reference, since the Athenians get their name in A10 (FGrH 239 [commentary]:671).

[131] Inferential or consecutive καί, found also in A3, A5, A6, and A9. The feature appears only in these entries, which may suggest a provenance from sources used for the very early periods.

[132] Conversion to the Common Era (i.e. BCE) is that of Jacoby in his FGrH edition.

[133] Jacoby's restored text reads: "to [Crana]us, and es[tablish]ed the t[e]mple of Zeu[s] O[ly]m[pi]an, and made the sacrifices of deliverance."

5. From the time Amphictyon, son of Deucalion, became king in Thermopylae and gathered together those dwelling near the sanctuary—hence named them Amphictyons—and . . . where the Amphictyons still make sacrifices nowadays,[134] 1258 years (= 1521/0 BCE), when Amphictyon was king of Athens.

6. From the time Hellen, son of Deuc[alion], became king of [Phthi]otis—hence they were named Hellenes, being formerly called Greeks—and the contest . . . , 1257 years (= 1520/19 BCE), when Amphictyon was king of Athens.

7. From the time Cadmus, son of Agenor, went to Thebes . . . [and] founded the Cadmea, 1255 years (= 1518/7 BCE), when Amphictyon was king of Athens.

8. From the time . . . became kings, 1252 years (= 1515/4 years), when Amphictyon was king of Athens.

9. From the time a shi[p . . . o]ars[135] sailed from Egypt to Hellas—hence it was called *pentekontoros*—and Danaus's daughters . . . and . . . Helike and Archedike, chosen by lot by the rest . . . and made sacrifices on the shore in . . . in Lindos of Rhodes, 1247 years (= 1510/9 BCE), when . . . was kin[g of Athens].[136]

10. [From the time Erich]thonius yoked a chariot in the first Panathenaea that took place, and showed forth the contest and . . . the Athenians,[137] [a]nd [an image] of the Mother of the [g]ods appeared on the ridge of Cybele, and the Phrygian Hyagnis first invented the *auloi* in C[138]. . . the Phrygian ones . . . and he first played on the *auloi* [the mode (harmonia) c]alled Phrygian and the other *nomoi* of the Mother, of Dionysos, of Pan, and the . . . , 1242 years (1505/4 BCE), when Erichthonius, who yoked the chariot, was king of Athens.

11. From the time Minos . . . [bec]ame [k]ing . . . founded A[pol]lonia (?),[139] and iron was discovered on Ida, an invention of the Idaean

---

[134] The only reference to present time in the extant text, though it may have been drawn from a source.

[135] Jacoby's restored text reads: "a shi[p furnished by Danaus for the first time with fifty o]ars . . ."

[136] Jacoby supplements Erichthonius; Hiller von Gärtringen prefers (apparatus) Amphictyon.

[137] Jacoby's restored text reads: "and named the Athenians."

[138] A word beginning with C can be restored as Cybele (Jacoby) or Celaenae (Le Paulmier).

[139] Jacoby's restored text reads "From when Minos [the] fi[rst] (?) ru[led over Crete and] founded A[pol]lonia."

Dactyls, Celmis a[nd Damnameneus ... years], when Pandion was [ki]ng of Athens.

12. From the time Demeter, after arriving at Athens, planted grain,[140] and the [fi]rst [festival of ploughing (?)] was brought about . . . of [T]riptolemus, son of Celeus and Neaera,[141] 1146 ? years (= 1409/8 BCE), when Erichtheus was king in Athens.

13. From the time Tripto[lemus] . . . sowed (the grain?) in the Rarian land called Eleusis, 1[1]45 years (= 1408/7 BCE), when [Erichtheus] was king of Athens.

14. [From the time . . . Orpheus] . . . so[n] . . . made his poetry public, namely,[142] Kore's rape and Demeter's quest,[143] and the . . .[144] of those who received the grain, 1135 years (=1398/7 BCE), when Erichtheus was king of Athens.

15. [From the time Eumolpus (?)] . . . instituted the mysteries in Eleusis and made the po[e]ms of his [father M]ousaeus publ[ic], . . . [years, when Erichthe]us, son of Pandion, [was king of Athens].

16. From the time a purification first occured . . . 12 [years], when Pandion, son of Cecrops, was king of Athens.

17. From the time the gymnic [contest] at Eleusis . . . the Lycaea[145] occured in Arcadia and . . . of Lycaon were given . . . to the Hell[e]ne[s] . . . [years], when Pandion, son of Cecrops, was king of Athens.

18. From the time . . . Heracles . . . when Aegeus was king in Athens.

19. From the time there was a [deart]h of grain in Athens, and [Apo]llo advised (?) the Athe[nians] . . . consulting him to undert[a]ke the [compensa]tion . . . th[at] Minos would consider just, 1031 years (= 1294/3 BCE), when Aegeus was king of Athens.

---

[140] Jacoby has "invented grain."

[141] *Sic*, probably mistaken for Metaneira.

[142] Epexegetic or explanatory τε.

[143] The accusatives "rape" and "quest" are in apposition to "poetry." West (1983:24) suggests the poem could be the Homeric Hymn to Demeter. On the content of poetry attributed to Orpheus in antiquity, see Bernabé PEG II.1 frr. 379–402.

[144] Boeckh restored a reference to Orpheus's own descent to Hades.

[145] I.e. the Lycaean festival.

20. From the time Thes[eus] . . . [became king] of Athens and united the twelve cities and bestow[ed] the constitution and the democracy . . . of Athens . . . established the Isthmian contest after killing Sinis, 995 years (= 1259/8 BCE).[146]

21. From the . . . of the Am[az]on[s . . . 9]92 [years] (= 1256/5 BCE), when Theseus was king of Athens.

22. From the time the Argives with Adras[tus waged] war [against Th]ebes and [e]st[abl]ished the contest in [Neme]a . . . , 987 years (= 1251/0 BCE), when Theseus was king of Athens.

23. From the time the [Helle]nes w[a]ge[d] war against Troy, 954 years (= 1218/7 BCE), when [Men]estheus was king of Ath[ens], in his thirteenth year.

24. From the time Troy was conquered, 945 years (= 1209/8 BCE), when [Menesthe]us was king of Athens, in his ⟨twenty⟩[147] second year, in the month of Th[argeli]on, in the seventh day, (counting) from the end of the month.

(A space of 3 to 5 letters possibly marks a new section)[148]

25. From the time . . . [a trial occur]ed in the Areopagos (between) Orestes . . . and Ae]gisthus's daughter [Erig]on[e] . . . of [Aegisthus] and . . . , which Orestes won . . . , 944 ? years (= 1208/7 ? BCE), when Demophon was king of Athens.

26. From the time Teucer founded [Salamis in] Cyprus, 938 years (= 1202/0 BCE), when Demophon was king of Athens.

27. From the time Ne[l]eus founde[d Milet]u[s] . . . Ephesus, Erythrae, Clazomenae, P[ri]ene, Lebedus, Teos, Colophon, Myus, [Phoc]a[ea], Samos, [Chios, and] the [Pan]ioni[a] came into being,[149] 813 yea[rs] (= 1077/1075, 1087/1 BCE), when Me⟨don⟩ was king of Athens.[150]

---

[146] From here on Hiller von Gärtringen's conversion to BCE years differs from Jacoby's.

[147] On the plausibility of the supplement, see note on Greek text.

[148] See n. 24 above.

[149] The Panionian league. One could think of "the Panionian festival came into being," but the verb ἐγένετο is not the usual one for establishing games.

[150] The inscription reads "when Menestheus was king of Athens, in his thirteenth year." On the reasons for restoration, see note on the Greek text.

28. From the time [Hes]iod the poet [appear]ed, . . .[151] years (= 937/5 ? BCE), when . . . was king of Athens.

29. From the time Homer the poet appeared, 643 years (= 907/5 BCE), when [D]iognetus was king of Athen[s].

A2: The Ashmolean Fragment

The second part of A, the inscription found in Smyrna, currently in the Ashmolean Museum, Oxford.

30. From the time the Argive Ph[ei]don[152] mad[e] [the] meas[ures] public [and] determined [we]ights and produced silver coins in Aegina, being eleventh from Heracles, 631 years (= 895/3 BCE), when [Pherecl]es was king of Athens.

31. From the time Archias,[153] son of Euagetes, being tenth from Temenus, led the settlement from Corinth [and founded] Syracu[se, . . . years], when Aeschylus w[a]s [k]ing of Athens, in his twenty-first year.

32. From the time the archon held the magistracy yearly, 420 years (= 683/2 BCE).

33. From the time . . . ,[154] 418 years (= 682/1, 681/0 BCE), when Lysia[des] was archon in Athens.

34. From the time the Lesbian Terpander, son of Derdenes, . . . -ed the [kith]a[r]od[ic] *nomoi* and aulet[ic][155] . . . and changed the music of old, 381 years (= 645/3 BCE), when Dropides was archon in Athens.

---

[151] The number is incomplete. Several restorations are possible (672, 673, and 676, see note on the Greek text).

[152] Due to disagreement with ancient testimonies (see note on the Greek text), Jacoby marked Pheidon's and Archias's names with cruces. In his 1904a edition he suggested the following restoration:

30. From the time Archias, son of Euagetes, led the settlement from Corinth and founded Syracuse, being eleventh from Heracles, 631 years, when Pherecles was king of Athens.

31. From the time the Argive Pheidon, being tenth from Temenus, made the measures public and determined weights and produced silver coins in Aegina, . . . years, when Aeschylus was king of Athens, in his twenty-first year.

[153] See the note above.

[154] Some editors supplement Archilochus here; see note on the Greek text and chap. 6, sec. 2.I.

[155] Jacoby's restored text reads "made innovations in the kitharodic *nomoi,*" omitting a reference to the *aulos,* which cannot be ruled out (perhaps: "the kitharodic and auletic *nomoi*"? see note on Greek text and chap. 6, sec. 2.III below).

35. From the time A[lyatte]s [be]came kin[g] over the Lyd[ians], [3]41 years (= 605/3 BCE), when Aristocles was archon in Athens.

36. From the time Sappho sailed from Mytilene to Sicily, fleeing . . . , when the elder Critias was [arch]on in Athens, and in Syracuse the land-owners seized power.

37. [From the time] the Am[phict]yo[ns ma]de sacri[fices] [a]fter de[fe]ating Cyrrha in war, and the gymnic contest was established with money prizes[156] from the spoils, 327 years (= 591/0 BCE), when Simon was archon in Athens.

38. From the time [in Delph]i [the c]rown contest was reestablished, 318 years (= 582/1 BCE), when Damasius the second was archon in Athens.

39. From the time a [cho]r[os] of *komo[idoi]* was [esta]blished in Ath[en]s, the Icarians [setting it up fi]rst, an invention by Susarion, and the prize consisted at first[157] of a baske[t] of dried fi[gs] and a me[a]sure of wine . . .[158]

40. From the time Pisistratus became tyrant of Athens, 297 years (= 561/0 BCE), when C[o]m[e]as was archon [in Athe]ns.

41. From the time Croesus . . .[159] [from] Asia [to] Delphi, 292 [years] (= 556/5 BCE), when Euthydemus was archon in Athens.

42. From the time Cyrus, the king of Persia, seized Sardis and Croesus . . . And Hipponax too (lived) at that time, the iambic poet.

43. From the time Thespis the poet first [act]ed (?), who produced[160] . . . [and] the goat was established [as prize], . . . years,[161] when . . .-naeus the elder was archon [in] Ath[ens].

44. From the time Darius became king of Persia, after the magus died, [2]56 years (= 520/19, 519/8 BCE), when . . . was archon in Athen[s].

---

[156] "Chrematic," i.e. granting material rewards.
[157] Adverbial (at first), rather than attributive (first prize).
[158] The date is lacking. Jacoby gives an equivalent as 581/0–562/1.
[159] Supplements include "sent envoys" (ἀ[πέστειλη, Prideaux; θεωρούς, Flach) or "sent offerings" (ἀ[πέπεμψε τὰ ἀναθήματα, Munro).
[160] Jacoby's restored text reads: "who produced a play in town"; see note on the Greek text.
[161] The number of years is incomplete. Jacoby has 2[70] with a digit missing, a date he converts into 536/5–532/1.

45. From the time Harmodius and [Aristoge]iton kill[ed Hippa]rchus, s[uc]ces[sor] (?) of Pisistratus, and the Athenians [expell]ed the Pisistratids from t[he P]elasgian wall (= 511/0 BCE), 248 years, when Ha[r]p[actides] was archon in Athens.

46. From the time choruses of men first competed, which (?) Hypo[di]cus of Chalcis produced and won, 246 (?) years (= 510/8 BCE), when Lysagoras was archon in Athens.

47. From the time Me[lan]ippid[es] of M[elos wo]n in Athens, 231 years (= 494/3 BCE), when Pythocritus was archon in Athens.

48. From the time the battle in Marathon occured, the Athenians[162] (fighting) against the Persians and Ar[taph]e[rnes], Darius's neph[ew, an]d [Da]tis the commander, which the Athenians won, 227 years (= 490/89 BCE), when [Ph]a[i]n[i]p[pid]es t[h]e second was archon in Athens. In this battle fought Aeschylus the poet, being 35 years of age.

49. From the time Simonides, grandfather of the poet Simonides, himself a poet too, won in Athens, and Darius dies, and his son Xerxes becomes king, [2]26 years (= 489/8 BCE), when Aristides was archon in Athens.

50. From the time Aeschylus the poet first won in the tragic competition,[163] and Euripides the poet was born, and Stesichorus the poet a[rrive]d in Hellas, 222 years (= 485/4, 486/5 BCE), when Philocrates was archon in Athens.

51. From the time Xerxes erected the bridge in the Hellespont and crossed (Mount) Athos, and the battle in Thermo[py]lae occured, and the naval battle of the Hellenes against the Persians near Salamis, which the Hellenes won, 217 years (= 480/79 BCE), when Calliades was archon in Athens.

---

[162] Instrumental-comitative dative (not possessive dative, see also A52, B9, and B26). The pattern ἡ . . . μάχη ἐγένετο + dat. (Ἀθηναίοις) + πρός + acc. (πρὸς Πέρσας) seems to be equivalent to a construction of nominative (Ἀθηναῖοι) ἐμάχοντο πρός + acc. (τοὺς Πέρσας).

[163] This dative is locative (in the tragic competition) rather than instrumental (with a tragedy), cf. LSJ s.v. νικάω (πυγμῇ, *Iliad* 23.669, ἵππῳ, Herodotus 6.122, ἵππῳ ἢ συνωρίδι ἢ ζεύγει, Plato *Apology* 36d, λαμπάδι, 4.42, etc.). It also appears in A56, A60, and A68.

52. From the time the battle in Plataea occured, the Athenians (fighting) against Mardonius, Xerxes's commander, which the Athenians won, and Mardonius died in the battle, and the fire erupted [in] Sicily at the (Mount) Aetna, 216 years (= 479/80 BCE), when Xantippus was archon in Athens.

53. From the time G[e]lon, son of Deinomenes, became tyrant of S[yrac]u[se], 215 years (= 478/7 BCE), when Timosthen[es] was archon in Athens.

54. From the time the Ceian Simonides, son of Leoprepes, who invented the mnemonic art, won in Athens as producer, and the statues of Harmodius and Aristogeiton were set up, 213 (?) years (= 477/6 BCE), when [A]deimantus was archon in Athens.

55. From the time Hieron became tyrant of Syracuse, 208 years (= 472/1 BCE), when Cha[r]es was archon in Athens. And Epicharmus the poet too lived at this time.

56. From the time Sophocles, son of Sophillus, of Colonos, won in the tragic competition, being 28 years of age, 206 years (= 469/8 BCE), when Apsephion was archon in Athens.

57. From the time a meteorite fell in Aegospotami, and Simonides the poet died, being 90 years of age, 205 years (= 468/7 BCE), when Theagenides was archon in Athens.

58. From the time Alexander died, and his son Perdiccas became king of Macedonia, 199 years (= 461/0 BCE), when Euthippus was archon in Athens.

59. From the time Aeschylus the poet, being 69 years of age, died in [Gel]a on Sicily, 193 years (= 456/5 BCE), when Calleas the elder was archon in Athens.

60. From the time Euripides, being 44 (?) years of age, first won in the tragic competition, 1[79] years (= 442/1 BCE), when Diphil[us] was [ar]chon in Athens. Socrates and Anaxagoras too lived at Euripides's time.

61. From the time Archelaus becomes king of Macedonia after Perdiccas died, 1[57] years (= 420/19 BCE), when Astyphilus was [ar]chon in Athens.

62. From the time Dionysius became tyrant of Syracuse, 147 years (= 408/7 BCE), when Euctemon was archon in Athens.

63. From the time Euripides, being . . . years [of age, d]ied, 145 years (= 407/6 BCE), when Antigenes was archon in Athens.

64. From the time Sophocles the poet, being 92 years of age, died, and Cyrus went up (from the coast), [143 years] (= 406/5 BCE), when Callias the elder [was arch]on in Athens.

65. From the time Telestes of Selinus won in Athens, 139 years (= 402/1 BCE), when Micon was archon in Athens.

66. From the time [the Greeks who] went [wi]th Cyrus returned, and Socrates the philosopher died, being 70 years of age, 137 years (= 400/399 BCE), when Laches was archon in Athens.

67. From the time Ar[i]sto[nous . . . won] in Athens, 135 years (= 399/8 BCE), when Aristocrates was archon in Athens.

68. From the time Polyidus of Selymbria won in the dithyrambic competition in Athens, . . . years, . . . [when . . . was archon in Athens].

69. [From] the time the dithyrambic poet Philoxenus dies, being 55 years of age, 116 years (= 380/79, 379/8 BCE), when Pytheas was archon in Athens.

70. From the time Anaxandrides the com[edy-poet] . . . [when] Calleas [was archon] in Athens.

71. From the time Astydamas won in Athens, 109 years (= 373/2, 372/1 BCE), when Asteius was archon in Athens. And [the temple in Delphi] then burned down too.

72. [From the time the battle in Leuctra o]ccured, between Thebans and Lacedaemonians, which the Thebans won, 107 years (= 371/0, 370/69 BCE), when Phrasicleides was archon in Athens. Also, Al[exander . . .] became king [of Macedonia].

73. From the time Stesichorus of Himer[a], the second,[164] won in Athens, and Megalopolis was founded [in Arcadia, 105 years (= 370/68, 368/7 BCE), when . . . was archon in Athens].

74. From the time the Sicilian Dionysius died, and his son Dionysius became tyrant, and Alex[ander] . . . became [k]ing [of Macedonia], 104 years (= 368/7, 367/6 BCE), when Nausigenes was archon in Athens.

75. From the time Phocis [seized . . .] the o[racle] in Delphi, . . . [years] . . . when Cephisodorus [was archon in Ath]ens.

76. From the time Timotheus, being 90 years of age, died . . . yea[rs, when . . . was archon in Athens].

77. [From the time Philip, son of Amyntas] became king [of Ma]cedonia, and Artaxerxes died, and his son Ochos b[ecame king, . . . years, . . . when . . . was archon in Athens].

78. [From the time . . .] won [in Athens], 93 years (= 357/6, 356/5 BCE], when Agathocl[es] was archon in Athens.

79. [From the time . . . o]ccurred, 91 years (= 355/4, 354/3 BCE), when Callist[ratus] was archon in Athens . . . -*sophos* (?) . . . (at) that (time?).[165]

80. From the time Calli[. . . yea]rs, . . . when . . . was archon [in Athens].

B: The Parian Fragment

The second part of the inscription, found on Paros and published in 1897, is currently displayed at the Archaeological Museum of Paros. There is a gap of 19 years between this and the previous section.

1. . . . . [Philip d]ie[d, and Ale[xand]er became king, 72 years (= 336/5 BCE), when Pythodelus was archon in Athens.

2. From the time Alexander [waged] war against the Triballi and the Illyrians, and after the Thebans rose up and besieged the guard, he returned, conquered the city, and destroyed it, 71 years (= 335/4 BCE), when Euaenetus was archon in Athens.

---

[164] More than 100 years separate this otherwise unknown Stesichorus from the one mentioned in A50.

[165] On the possibility of a postscript naming a philosopher, see note on the Greek text.

3. From Alexander's crossing to Asia and the battle near the (river) Granicus, and from Alexander's battle against Darius in Issus, 70 years (= 334/3 BCE), when Ctesicles was archon in Athens.

4. From the time Alexander took possession of Phoenicia, Cyprus, and Egypt,[166] 69 years (= 333/2 BCE), when Nicocrates was archon in Athens.

5. From the battle of Alexander against Darius at Arbela, which Alexander won, and Babylon was conquered, and he discharged the allies, and Alexandria was founded, 68 years (= 332/1 BCE), when Nicetes was archon in Athens.

6. From the time Callippus made (his) astrology (i.e. astronomy) public,[167] and Alexander seized Darius, and hung Bessus, 66 years (= 330/29 BCE), when Aristophon was archon in Athens.

7. From the time Philemon the comic poet won, 64 years (= 328/7 BCE), when Euthycritus was archon in Athens. Also, the city of Hellenis was founded by the (river) Tanais.

8. From the time of Alexander's decease[168] and Ptolemy's dominion over Egypt, 60 years (= 324/3 BCE), when Hegesias was archon in Athens.

9. From the war[169] that occured near Lamia, the Athenians (fighting) against Antipater, and from the naval battle of the Macedonians against the Athenians that occured at Amorgos, which the Macedonians won, 59 years (= 323/2 BCE), when Cephisodorus was archon in Athens.

10. From the time Antipater seized Athens, and Ophelas was dispatched[170] by Ptolemy to Cyrene, 58 years (= 322/1 BCE), when Philocles was archon in Athens.

---

[166] The concept of "becoming lord, taking possession" (κυριεύειν) appears here with reference to Alexander and later in B8 (noun) and B17 with reference to Ptolemy.

[167] The verb "making public" appears in A14 and A15 with reference to Orpheus's and Mousaeus's poetry. The year coincides with the beginning of the first Callipean period (of 76 years, see chap. 5, n. 17).

[168] The word μεταλλαγή ("change," applied to death) appears only in relation to Alexander's death; otherwise the inscription has the verb τελευτάω ("bring to pass, finish," used absolutely, "die").

[169] Sole appearance of the word πόλεμος; otherwise the word μάχη is used.

[170] The Greek has the participle ἀποσταλείς.

11. From the time Antigonus crossed over to Asia, and Alexander was buried in Memphis, and after waging war against Egypt Perdiccas died, and Craterus, and Aristotle the sophist[171] died, 57 years (= 321/0 BCE), being 50 years of age, when Archippus was archon in Athens. Also, Ptolemy marched to Cyrene.[172]

12. From the death of Antipater, and Cassander's withdrawal from Macedonia, and from the siege of Cyzicus, which Aridaeus laid, and from the time[173] Ptolemy seized Syria and Phoenicia, 55 years (= 319/8 BCE), when Apollodorus was archon in Athens. Precisely in the same year the Syracusans appointed Agathocles as absolute commander of the Sicilian defence.

13. From the naval battle of Cleitus and Nicanor near the temple of the Calchedonians, and when Demetrius set laws in Athens, 53 years (= 317/6 BCE), when Demogenes was archon in Athens.

14. From the time Cassander returned to Macedonia, and Thebes was founded, and Olympias died, and Cassandreia was founded, and Agathocles became tyrant of Syracuse, 52 years (= 316/5 BCE), when Democleid[es] was archon in Athens. Also then Menander the comic poet won in Athens for the first time.

15. From the time Sosiphanes the poet dies, 49 years (= 313/2 BCE), when Theophrastus was archon in Athens, being 45 years of [age].

16. From the time the sun eclipsed, and Ptolemy prevailed over[174] Demetrius in Gaza and dispatched Seleucus to Babylon, [4]8 years (= 312/1 BCE), when Po[lem]on was archon in Athens.

17. From the time Nicocreon died and Ptolemy takes possession of the island (of Cyprus), 47 years (= 311/0 BCE), when Si[moni]des was archon in Athens.

---

[171] Tod (1957:135) suggests that the range of Aristotle's studies may partly explain why σοφιστής and not φιλόσοφος is used.

[172] A very dislocated entry. In addition to a postscript, Aristotle's age at death is separated from the reference to his death. There are no signs of correction or erasures on the stone.

[173] Repetition of the formula "from the time" in the middle of the entry.

[174] The verb "winning" is applied here to prevailing over a person; elsewhere, it is used for prevailing in a contest or in battle.

18. From the time Ale[x]a[nder, son of Alexander], dies, as well as another, (son) of Artabazus's daughter, Heracles, and Agathocles crossed over to Carched[on] (i.e. Carthage) . . . [4]6 [years] (= 310/9 BCE), when Hieromnemon was archon in Athens.

19. From the time the city of L[ysi]macheia was founded, and Ophelas . . . to [Ca]rch[edon] (i.e. Carthage) . . . and Ptolemy the son was born on Cos,[175] and Cl[eop]atra die[d] in Sardis . . . [45 years (= 309/8 BCE), when D]emetrius [was archon] in [A]then[s].

20. From the time Demetrius, son of Antigonus, besieged the [P]iraeus and seized it, . . .[176] [44 years (= 308/7 BCE)], when Caerimus [was archon] in Athens.

21. From the time Demetrius destroyed Munichia and seized Cyprus, and Phil[i]p . . . [4]3 [years] (= 307/6 BCE), when Anaxicratus was archon in Athens.

22. From the time Sosiphanes the poet wa[s born (?). . . . 42 years (= 306/5 BCE), when C]oroebus [was archon in Athe]n[s].

23. From the siege of Rhodes, and from the time [Pt]olemy t[o]ok ove[r] the kingdom, [41 year]s (= 305/4 BCE), [when Euxenippus was archon in Athens].

24. [From th]e ear[th]quake that [oc]cured in Ionia, and when Demetrius [sei]zed Chalc[is] by agreement and . . . of [De]metrius, 40 years (= 304/3 BCE), when Pherecles was archon in Athens.

25. From the time [a comet] ap[p]eare[d], and Lysimach[u]s [crossed over to Asia (?), 39 years (= 303/2 BCE), when] L[eost]r[atus was archon in Athens].

26. F[rom] the time a truce [occured] between Cassander and Demetrius . . . Cassan[d]er . . . [di]ed], 38 [years] (= 302/1 BCE), when Nicocles was archon in Athens.

---

[175] The birth of Ptolemy Philadelphus is the only instance noting the birth of a political personality (cf. the birth of Euripides at A50 and possibly of Sosiphanes II at B22).

[176] Jacoby's restored text reads: "when Demetrious of Phalerum was banished from Athens;" see note on the Greek text.

27. [From the time . . . of [Deme]trius's ascent to Chalcis, and the Athenians . . . Cas[sander] . . . Ptolem- . . . , 35 years (= 299/8 BCE), . . . [when Euctemon was archon in Athens].

Chapter 3
The Genre of the Parian Marble

1. The Chronicle as a Literary Genre

Features such as the catalogue-like format, the absence of authorial voice, the omission of controversies about facts or sources, are not exclusive to the Parian Marble. They characterize many other texts from ancient Greece and beyond. Most particularly, content and structure link the Parian Marble to the family of "chronography," one of the main types of ancient Greek historiographical writing.[1]

Chronography provided a framework for writing about the past when no absolute system for time reckoning existed. From the fifth century BCE on, chronological lists began to be written and were sometimes displayed on stone: lists of kings (such as the Spartan and the Athenian ones), of magistrates (Athenian archons, Spartan ephors), of priests (the list of priestesses of Hera in Argos, compiled by Hellanicus, and the stephanophoroi at Miletus), and of victors (at the Carnean festival in Sparta, compiled by Hellanicus; at the Pythian festival, compiled by Aristotle and Callisthenes, and at Olympia, by Hippias of Elis). Such lists went back in time, building on orally transmitted information and written records, and were occasionally supplemented by imagination. Although they had primarily administrative purposes, they often served as means of legitimation.[2] The setting of names in fixed chronological sequences made those lists particularly useful for time reckoning, as years could be identified by the corresponding eponym. With no fixed point of reference "each event had to be located in time in relation to other events, a relation expressed by intervals in years or generations."[3] When lists

---

[1] Fornara 1983. On ancient Greek chronography (to give but a small selection), see Momigliano 1966, Mosshammer 1979, Asheri 1991–1992, Grafton 1995, Möller and Luraghi 1995, Shaw 2003:19–46, Möller 2004, Christesen 2007:84–112, Feeney 2007:7–20, Clarke 2008:56–89, Burgess and Kulikowski, 2013:84–91. See Möller 2006 for Jacoby's fundamental contribution to the subject.

[2] Cf. Burkert 1995, Fowler 1998–1999.

[3] Möller 2004:171.

included names of people or events mentioned in other lists, correlations could be established.[4] Such synchronisms allowed linking between different systems, which in turn generated new information. Thus, intervals and synchronies were the essential tools of classical chronography. With them, as Astrid Möller puts it, "Ancient Greek scholars created a network of dates by drawing diachronic and synchronic lines, composing a temporal co-ordinate system similar to the spatial one used for geographical maps."[5]

The Parian Marble shares the basic mechanics of ancient Greek chronography. Indeed, it uses an eponymous list, namely the Athenian kings and archon list, which went far enough back in time and which must have been used by some of its sources too (e.g. by the Atthidographers, writers of Athenian local history). Furthermore, the author also chose to start counting years as intervals from a date close to or concomitant with the time of writing (I shall return to this point below). Finally, for most years noted—and not all years were—more than a single event was mentioned. Events often carried chronological value: they were not only dated, but could in themselves serve as a means of dating.

Unfortunately the extant text of the Parian Marble contains no self-referential term that could disclose how the author conceived of his work.[6] The traditional scholarly designation "Marmor Parium," i.e. Parian Marble, describes at the same time the place where it was set, the island of Paros (as the finding of section B made clear), as well as the material—marble from Paros—on which it was written.[7] The enduring use of these terms is indicative of the special status of this particular piece of Parian marble as historical document. The inscription has often been referred to as "Chronicon Parium," i.e. Parian Chronicle.[8] Rather than alluding to medium or origins, the term "chronicle" refers to a literary genre. However, in common use the referents of the term "chronicle" range from tabular registers of events to discursive narratives, as long as they are set in chronological order.[9] Since our inscription is a list, the technical term "annal"

---

[4] Asheri 1991–1992.

[5] Möller 2004:170, following the inspiring remarks of Mazzarino 1966:427 on the diastematic system of dating. See Momigliano 1966:16–17 for the metaphor of synchronisms as "bridges."

[6] A term like ἀναγραφή would not be as informative regarding genre as χρονικά or similar ones.

[7] In the first editions, the term "marmora" was applied to statues, reliefs, and inscriptions made in marble. Our inscription was published under the titles "Marmora Arundelliana" (Selden) and "Marmora Oxoniensia" (Prideaux, Maittaire). The term "marmor" was used more specifically for individual inscriptions.

[8] The chronographic character of the inscription was implied by the title "Epochae," given by Selden and used in the earliest editions.

[9] Cf. *Encyclopedia of the Medieval Chronicle*, s.v. "chronicles" (Dunphy 2010). The entry on the "Parian Marble" wrongly describes the stele as "small" (the original inscription was at least 2 m high, see chap. 1, sec. 1 above).

may be appropriate.[10] However, annals are expected to advance year by year, whereas the Parian Marble is selective regarding the years worthy of record.[11] A clarification of terms is thus necessary.

Burgess and Kulikowski made a most significant contribution to our understanding of the chronicle as genre. Dealing with Near Eastern, ancient Greek, Roman, late antique, and medieval materials, their study provides a common nomenclature independent of the specific field of study.[12] Burgess and Kulikowski note a number of salient features shared by most chronicles.[13] They are written in third-person prose and deal with large passages of time. Their format is annalistic, that is to say, the structure is given by the continuous counting of years. Chronicles lack fixed endings and were often conceived as collaborative efforts. Style is paratactic, events are not interconnected and there is no sense of progression or causality. Brevity is key to the genre, for it allows grasping long stretches of history at a single glance.[14]

These are salient features. Texts need not display all of them to be considered chronicles (e.g. the second-century BCE Apollodorus of Athens wrote his *Chronicle* in iambic trimeters).[15] In two respects the Parian Marble diverges

---

[10] See NP, s.v. "chronicles": "Chronicles are written histories structured on a yearly basis. They vary from mere lists of dates to miniature narratives for individual years: it is then, as annals—retrospective in the Roman period, ongoing and contemporaneous in the Carolingian—that they enter the realm of real historiography."

[11] In Hayden White's terms (1987:5), the Parian Marble would belong to the family of annals ("lists of events ordered in chronological sequence"), rather than chronicles, due to the lack of a narrative component (see chap. 4, sec. 3 below), although, unlike annals, our inscription is selective.

[12] Burgess and Kulikowski 2013:1–62. I am grateful to the authors for letting me read their work before it was published.

[13] Two definitions of Mesopotamian chronicles are illuminating:
"Three basic traits characterize chronicles. (1) They were written in prose, in the third person. This was the case even if this prose was reduced to a recurring formula and to a few more or less condensed chronological notes . . . (2) Priority was given to time. The essential thing was to note the date of every event selected. There was an increasing tendency to leave no year unaccounted. (3) Brevity was the norm. Restricting themselves to the events they summarized, and running the risk of appearing brief to the point of atomization, chronicles were a kind of handbook that reduced history to a series of facts" (Glassner and Foster 2004:38).
"A chronicle is a continuous register of events in chronological order. The events are simply enumerated in terse, often paratactic, sentences and the primary interest is in exact dating. A chronicle does not contain narrative; has no exposition about cause and effect; and offers no general background. It is a data base of facts about the past" (van der Spek 2008:277).

[14] As Burgess and Kulikowski note (2013:93–94), this feature is apparent in Cicero's comments on Atticus's *Liber Annalis* (Cicero *Brutus* 14–15). That book "briefly and very accurately embraced the whole memory of things" (omnem rerum memoriam breviter et . . . perdiligenter complexus est). It was useful because "it allowed to see everything at a single glance as the succession of time was unfolded" (ut explicatis ordinibus temporum uno in conspectu omnia viderem). See also Feeney 2007:25–28.

[15] See Rotstein 2010:10–11 for salient features in ancient Greek literary genres.

from the notional chronicle described above. First of all, it has a fixed ending that probably marks a specific event, rather than simply reaching the ephemeral present of composition (see chap. 1, sec. 4). That ending not only makes the Parian Marble a complete work, but also affects the very method by which time is reckoned. Second, the Parian Marble lacks the year-by-year framework when dealing with the distant past, although it is very close to giving an annual account in section B.[16]

For generic classification titles are crucial. They have a strong impact on the taxonomy of texts, as well as on the shaping of audience's expectations. Jacoby included the Parian Marble in a section of the FGrH entitled "Zeittafeln," i.e. timetables, rendering the Greek χρονικά and thus focusing on the chronographic character of the inscription.[17] More recently, Chaniotis included the Parian Marble in the category of "monumental historiography," that is, "historical works that were written on stone,"[18] This category accounts not only for the content of the Parian Marble, but its medium too. I decided to use the traditional name "Parian Marble" to remind us of the material quality of the text, inscribed on an artifact with a specific location and purposes.

To understand how typical a chronicle the Parian Marble was, we need to compare it with other instances of the genre.

The chronographic texts that are best attested and can, therefore, be used for comparison are the *Olympionikai*. The Olympic victor lists are, as Christesen puts it, "cumulative catalogs of victors at the Olympic Games."[19] First compiled by Hippias of Elis,[20] they were used for time reckoning from the fourth century BCE on, especially in literary and historical texts. Initially Olympiads were identified by the winner at the stadion race, considered by our sources the earliest event in the Olympic program. Later, Aristotle added numbers as additional means of identification (beginning with the first games at 776 BCE), and Eratosthenes subdivided each Olympiad into four years.[21]

---

[16] As Burgess and Kulikowski note, 2013:22n40.

[17] Among them, two epigraphical texts, the so-called Lindian Chronicle (99 BCE) and the Roman Chronicle (early first century CE). The Lindian inscription, however, is a catalogue of votive offerings and epiphanies (for a brief comparison with the Parian Marble, see Higbie 2003:271–273).

[18] Chaniotis 2005:220. The group includes the roughly contemporary IG II.2 677, Mnesiepes's inscription (see chap. 1, sec. 5 above), the later IMagnesia 17 and the Lindian Chronicle. In his earlier catalogue (Chaniotis 1988:87), the Parian Marble appears as a sole item under the heading "Universalgeschichte," along with the term χρόνων ἀναγραφή (adopted from Sosibius, FGrH 595 F 2).

[19] Christesen 2007:1. For a survey of the genre and the texts, see Christesen 2007:1–44, Möller 2004, Clarke 2008:59–67, with further references.

[20] Christesen 2005 illuminates Hippias's motivation for compiling the lists.

[21] Christesen (2007:26) distinguishes three categories of Olympic victor lists: standard catalogues, including victors in all events, chronographic catalogues or Olympiad chronography, including

The only surviving continuous work of ancient Greek chronography, besides the Parian Marble, happens to be an Olympic victor list that was included in the *Chronographia* composed by Eusebius in the early fourth century CE. The *Chronographia* was universal in scope and Christian in outlook (including Near Eastern lists of kings, as well as biblical history). Unlike most of the *Chronographia*, Eusebius' Olympic victor list came down to us through a Greek manuscript (Parisinus Graecus 2600).[22] Earlier chronographic authors survive only fragmentarily, such as Phlegon of Tralles. A few papyrological findings belong to this genre: the third-century CE Oxyrhynchus Chronicle (Chronicon Oxyrhynchi), which includes historical notices,[23] the fragmentary P.Oxy. XVII 2082,[24] and the recently discovered Leipzig Chronicle.[25]

Olympic victor lists display two salient features that are lacking from the Parian Marble: the annalistic structure and the cumulative quality. In this respect, the Parian Marble is utterly distinct. Having a fixed end, it has closure, which, as we have seen, is a principle of composition, because dates are computed backward from that particular time end. Furthermore, unlike victor lists, in which authors are free to choose what historical notices to add but not which years to count, in the Parian Marble there is an evident authorial choice of years, a choice that reflects a view on time and history (I will return to this point in Chapter 5).

The fixed ending and the selection of events set the Parian Marble apart from Olympic victor lists. These features, however, appear in two of the so-called Tabulae Iliacae: the Roman Chronicle (Chronicon Romanum)[26] and the Getty Table (Getty Tabula).[27]

---

stadion victors and other chronographic information (such as synchronies with, e.g. king lists), and Olympiad chronicles, which added notices of historical events.

[22] Mosshammer 1979:97, Christesen and Martirosova-Torlone 2006. On Eusebius' chronographic work, see chap. 6, sec. 1 below.

[23] P.Oxy. 12 = FGrH 255 (both include commentaries). English translations in Christesen 2007:337–340 and Burgess and Kulikowski 2013:313-315.

[24] FGrH 257a F 1, see Christesen 2007:335–336.

[25] P.Lips. 590, 1228, 1229, 1231, 1232 (text, commentary, and German translation of the Leipzig Chronicle in Colomo et al. 2010, Luppe 2010; assessment of genre and English translation in Burgess 2013).

[26] IG XIV 1297 = FGrH 252 = CIG IV 6855 d = Sarduska 18L (Museo Capitolino, Rome inv. 82). For the interpretation of text and images and for further references, see Sadurska 1964:78-83, Valenzuela Montenegro 2004:276–288 (with German translation).

[27] Also known as the Vasek-Polak Chronicle, SEG 33 802. It was first published by Burstein 1984. Valenzuela Montenegro 2004:289–295 studies text and images (with German translation). Burstein 1989 and Merkelbach 1989 study the inscription on the front (SEG 39 1072).

2. Miniature Parallels: The Roman Chronicle and the Getty Table

The Roman Chronicle (Plate 5) and the Getty Table (Plate 6) were inscribed on the back of miniature reliefs cut in limestone (palombino) in Rome or the Roman Campagna some time after 15/16 CE.[28] They are of very small dimensions: the Roman Chronicle is 8 cm high, 9 cm wide, 1.5 cm thick; the Getty Table is 7.5 cm high, 5 cm wide and 2 cm thick. The front of each table displays a horse in the center, surrounded by male figures, probably warriors (Plates 5 and 6).[29] Texts are given in columns on the back, in lines of irregular length, though never longer than 24–25 letters. Letters are very small: no more than 2 mm tall.[30] The narrow columns and the tiny letters form a papyrus–like layout. Columns may be missing from both chronicles, but opinions are divided as to their number. The lettering is irregular, and the Greek shows mistakes.[31]

The Roman Chronicle and the Getty Table are part of the so–called "Tabulae Iliacae," a group of 22 reliefs with Greek inscriptions of Roman provenance that, in spite of the traditional name, illustrate a range of themes from myth, epic poetry, and history.[32] Interest in the Tabulae Iliacae has grown in the last years, due to the combination of text and image.[33] The two chronicles, however, have not enjoyed similar attention, probably because they deal with historical rather than epic themes.[34] A closer look will help compare them with the Parian Marble.

The Roman Chronicle consists of two columns.[35] The left column (A) offers seven years of Roman events, from Sulla and the Mithridatic wars to the death of Soter Physkon (88/7 to 81/80 BCE). The right column (B) covers 200 years of

---

[28] Sadurska 1964:78, Burstein 1984:153, 157, Valenzuela Montenegro 2004:286–287, 307, Squire 2011:58–61. The *terminus post quem* for all Tabulae Iliacae is determined by the Chronicum Romanum's final year.

[29] Burstein (1984:157) argues that the two artifacts originated in the same workshop and were the work of Cutter d, in Sadurska's classification.

[30] The Getty Table: letters 1.5 mm height. Roman Chronicle: about 2 mm height (estimated from photographs).

[31] Jahn and Michaelis 1873:78, Burstein 1984:153.

[32] Main studies of the Tabulae Iliacae: Michaelis 1858, Jahn and Michaelis 1873, Sadurska 1964, Horsfall 1979 and 1983, Salimbene 2002, Valenzuela Montenegro 2004, Petrain 2006, Squire 2010 and 2011.

[33] Salimbene 2002, Valenzuela Montenegro 2004, Petrain 2006 and 2008, Squire 2010 and 2011:47–51 (very briefly on the chronicles).

[34] Petrain 2006 and Squire 2010 do not deal with the chronicles in detail.

[35] IG XIV 1297 = FGrH 252. See Sadurska 1964:78–79 for an account of the first publication and a description of the Roman Chronicle. Some of the difficulties in the study of this inscription derive from the various names in use: Tabula Capitolina, Chronicon Romanum, or even Greek Chronicle. The chronicle is studied by Sadurska 1964:78–83 and Valenzuela Montenegro 2004:279–288 (including a complete bibliography and German translation). Balcer 1972:101–103, Burstein 1984:162, Burgess and Kulikowski 2013:309-310 offer English translations.

Greek events, from Solon to the Gauls' conquest of Rome (from the sixth century to 385/4 BCE). While Roman chronology is very detailed and accurate, the inaccuracies in sixth century Greek chronology have long been noted.[36]

Roman Chronicle, column B:

```
1    ἀφ᾽ [οὗ] [- - -] το [- - -]
     ἀφ᾽ οὗ Σ[όλων Ἀθηναίων ἦρξεν καὶ]
     νόμου[ς αὐτοῖς ἔθηκεν, καὶ]
     Ἀνάχαρσις ὁ Σκ[ύθης εἰς Ἀθήνας (?)]
5    παρεγένετο, ἀφ᾽ [οὗ ἔτη - - -].
     ἀφ᾽ οὗ Κροῖσος Λυδῶν ἐβα[σίλευσεν, ἔτη - - -].
     ἀφ᾽ οὗ οἱ σοφοὶ ὠνομάσθησαν, [ἔτη - - -].
     ἀφ᾽ οὗ Πεισίστρατος ἐτυράννευσ[εν ἐν Ἀθή]-
     ναις, καὶ Αἴσωπος ὑπὸ Δελφῶν [κατεκρη]-
10   μνίσθη, ἔτη φοθ´.
     ἀφ᾽ οὗ Κροῖσος Κύρωι ὑποχείριος [ἐγένετο, ἔτη - - -].
     ἀφ᾽ οὗ Καμβύσης Αἴγυπτον κατ[εστρέψατο]
     καὶ Πυθαγόρας ἑάλω, ἔτη φμ´.
     ἀφ᾽ οὗ Ἁρμόδιος καὶ Ἀριστογείτων Ἵπ-
15   παρχον τὸν τύραννον ἀνεῖλον, [καὶ]
     Δαρεῖος ἐπὶ Σκύθας διέβη, ζεύξα[ς τὸν]
     Κιμμέριον Βώσπορον, ἔτη φκη´.
     ἀφ᾽ οὗ Ξέρξης κατὰ Ἄβυδον ζεύξας [τὸν]
     Ἑλλήσποντον διέβη, καὶ Θεμισ-
20   τοκλῆς ναυμαχίαι τοὺς βαρβά-
     ρους ἐνίκα, ἀφ᾽ οὗ ἔτη υϘ´.
     ἀφ᾽ οὗ Σωκράτης ὁ φιλόσοφος [καὶ Ἡρά]-
     κλειτος ὁ Ἐφέσιος καὶ Ἀναξα[γόρας]
     καὶ Παρμενίδης καὶ Ζήνων, ἔτη [- - -].
25   ἀφ᾽ οὗ ὁ Πελοποννησιακὸς πόλ[εμος]
     ἐνέστη, καὶ Θουκυδίδης ἦν, ἔτη [- - -].
     ἀφ᾽ οὗ Γαλάται Ῥωμαίους νική[σαντες]
     ἔσχον Ῥώμην, ἔτη υα´.
```

1   From [the time when] - - - the - - -
     From the time when S[olon was archon of the Athenians and
       made] law[s for them, and]
     Anacharsis the Sc[ythian] came

---

36   Sadurska 1964:81, Valenzuela Montenegro 2004:279–282.

5   [to Athens (?)], from [which time, - - - years].
       From the time when Croesus began to r[eign over the Lydians,
                                             [- - - years].
       From the time when the Wise Men became famous, [- - - years]
       From the time when Pisistratus became tyrant [in Athe]ns,
          and Aesop was hurled [down] a precipice
10   by the Delphians, 579 years.
       From the time when Croesus [became] subject to Cyrus, [- - - years].
       From the time when Cambyses con[quered] Egypt,
          and Pythagoras was captured, 540 years.
       From the time when Harmodius and Aristogeiton
15   killed Hipparchus the tyrant, [and]
          Darius crossed against the Scythians, having bridged the
          Cimmerian Bosporus, 528 years.
       From the time Xerxes, having bridged [the] Hellespont
          at Abydus, crossed, and Themis-
20   tocles defeated the barbarians
          in a sea battle, from which time, 490 years.
       From the time when Socrates the philosopher [and Hera-]
          clitus the Ephesian and Anaxa[goras]
          and Parmenides and Zenon (lived), [- - -] years.
25   From the time when the Peloponesian w[ar]
          began, and Thucydides lived, [- - -] years.
       From the time when the Gauls having defeated the Romans
          took Rome, 401 years.[37]

Let us now turn to the Getty Table.[38] Three columns remain, but only one is readable (IIB). The extant text offers only Greek events, from Phalaris to Darius's campaign against the Scythians.

---

[37] Translated by Burstein 1984:162 up to line 21, with minor changes.
[38] First published by Burstein 1984 (with English translation). See Valenzuela Montenegro 2004:291–294 for commentary, German translation, and further references.

Getty Table, IIB:[39]

5   Ἀφ' οὗ Φάλαρ[ι]ς [ἐτυράννευσεν],
     μέχ[ρι] τοῦδε, ἔτη [- - -]. [Ἀφ' οὗ οἱ σοφοὶ κ]–
     α[ὶ] Γίλων ν ΩΠΙ. Ἀφ' οὗ [Πεισίστρατος]
     ἐν Ἀθήναις ἐτυράνν[ευσεν, καὶ]
     Αἴσ{ι}ωπος ὑπὸ Δε⟨λ⟩φῶν κα̣[τεκρη]–
10   μνίσθη, μέχρι τοῦδε, ἔτη [- - -].
     Ἀφ' οὗ Κ̣ρ̣ῖσ̣ος, προδούσης τῆς [θυ]–[40]
     [γατρὸ]ς αὐτοῦ τὴν Σάρδεων ἀκ[ρό]–
     πολιν, δι' ἔρωτα Κύρῳ ὑποχείρι–
     ος γενόμενος, ἀπέβαλεν
15   τὴν ἀρχήν, ἐγένετο δὲ καὶ
     Σιμονίδης ὁ μηλοποιὸς καὶ
     Ἀναξίμανδρος ὁ φυσικὸς ἦν
     ἐτῶν ξ΄, μέχρι τοῦδε, ἔτη φξα΄.
     Ἀφ' οὗ Κῦρος ἐτελεύτησεν, διεδέ–
20   ξα̣τ̣ο δὲ τὴν ἀρχήν Καμβύσης,
     ἦν δὲ καὶ Ἀνάκρεων ὁ μηλοπο–
     ιὸς κα⟨ὶ⟩ Ἴβυκος ὁ Ῥηγεῖνος, ἔτη φμ΄.
     Ἀφ' οὗ Κῦρος ἐτελεύτησεν, Καμ–
     βύσης δὲ διαδεξάμενος, Αἴγυπ–
25   τον κατεστρέψατο, καὶ Πυθαγό–
     ρας ἑάλω σχολάζων καὶ τοῖς
     Μάγοις ἐπισχολάσας ἦλθεν εἰς
     Ἰταλίαν,[41] καὶ Καμβύσης ἐτελεύ–
     τησεν, Δαρεῖος δὲ ἐβασίλευ⟨σ⟩–
30   εν, καὶ Ξενοφάνης ὁ φυσι–
     κός· Ἀφ' οὗ ἔτη ν΄ ἅπαντα.

---

[39] The text follows the critical edition of SEG 33.802 (H. W. Pleket and R. S. Stroud). I marked lacunae after the word ἔτη in lines 6, 10, 34, and 36 (Haslam 1986:198n1). The stone is broken after lines 6 and 10, and is unreadable after lines 34 and 36. It seems that numerals are missing at the end of the four lines, as in lines 18, 22, and 31. The inscription includes a few misspellings: line 7 Γίλων = Χίλων; line 22 Ἴβυνος = Ἴβυκος. A few mistaken accents in Burnstein's editio princeps (ἄρχην in lines 15 and 20, φυσικὸς in line 31) were picked up by the SEG editors, further adding a double apostrophe in ἀφ' οὗ (lines 11 and 19) and ἦυ instead of ἦν (line 21) in the digital edition. However, the word μηλοποιός (lines 16 and 21) is thus written in the inscription. I am grateful to Barak Blum for these observations.

[40] I give lines 11–13 as restored by Haslam 1986 (for such probably legendary version of the events, see Parthenius 22).

[41] I follow Haslam 1986:198 in removing punctuation marks in the reference to Pythagoras; the translation differs from Burnstein's accordingly.

Ἀφ' οὗ Ἁρμόδιος καὶ Ἀριστογεί-
των Ἵππαρχον τὸν τύρανν-
ον ἀνεῖλαν, ἔτη [- - -].
35   Ἀφ' οὗ Δαρεῖος ἐπὶ Σκύθας ἐ-
στράτευσεν, ἔτη [- - -].

5   From the time Phalaris [became tyrant], [- - -] years until the
       present.
    [From the time the Wise Men a]nd Chilon [. . .].
    From the time [Pisistratus] became tyrant in Athens, [and] Aesop was
       hurled down a precipice by the Delphians,
10   [- - -] years until the present.
    From the time Croesus, his daughter having surrendered
       the acropolis of Sardis because of love, having (Croesus)
       been taken prisoner by Cyrus,
15   lost his realm; and there was also born Simonides, the lyric poet,
       and Anaximander, the natural philosopher, was sixty years old,
       561 years until the present.
20   From the time Cyrus died, Cambyses succeeded to the throne,
       and also Anacreon, the lyric poet, flourished and Ibycus of Rhegium,
       540 years.
25   From the time Cyrus died, and Cambyses, having succeeded,
       conquered Egypt; and Pythagoras was captured while lecturing
       and after studying the Magi went to Italy; and Cambyses died,
       and Darius began to reign; and
30   Xenophanes, the natural philosopher. From which time
       the total number of years, fifty.
    From the time Harmodius and Aristogiton killed Hipparchus,
       the tyrant, years [. . .].
35   From the time Darius campaigned against the Scythians, [- - -] years.[42]

The first editor of the Getty Table pointed out that it contains a fuller version of lines 6 to 16 of the Roman Chronicle.[43] Indeed, the same figures and events appear in exactly the same order: The sages (supplemented in the Getty Table just before Chilon), Pisistratus, Aesop, Croesus and Cyrus, Cambyses' conquest of Egypt, Pythagoras, Harmodius and Aristogeiton, Darius and the Scythians.

[42] Translated by Burstein 1984:158, except lines 11–13, and the reference to Pythagoras (which follows Haslam 1986:198n1). I changed the position of the word "years" and the numbers of years, and omitted restoration of number twenty in the translation of line 35.
[43] Burstein 1984:157.

The Getty Table expands some of the notices with participial constructions, as the following example illustrates:

> CR: from the time when Cambyses con[quered] Egypt, and Pythagoras was captured, 540 years (13–14).

> GT: From the time Cyrus died, and Cambyses, having succeeded, conquered Egypt; and Pythagoras was captured while lecturing and after studying the Magi went to Italy; and Cambyses died, and Darius began to reign (25–27).

Things are different in the following entries:

> CR: From the time when Harmodius and Aristogeiton killed Hipparchus the tyrant, [and] Darius crossed against the Scythians, *having bridged the Cimmerian Bosporus*, 528 years. (14–17)

> GT: From the time Harmodius and Aristogiton killed Hipparchus the tyrant, [- - -] years.

> From the time Darius campaigned against the Scythians, twenty years. (32–36)

Here, it is the Roman Chronicle that offers a somewhat more expanded version than the Getty Table, while conflating two notices into one.

In spite of the apparent similarity, the chronicles differ in two significant points. Although both mention Aesop and Pythagoras, the Getty Table adds Chilon, Simonides, Anaximander, Anacreon, Ibycus, and Xenophanes, whereas the Roman Chronicle adds Socrates, Heraclitus, Anaxagoras, Parmenides, and Zenon. Thus, each chronicle seems to harbor a different bias regarding cultural figures: the Roman Chronicle favors philosophers, the Getty Table, poets (see chap. 6, sec. 1 below). Another difference is the use of μέχρι τοῦδε in the Getty Table, lines 6, 10, and 18, instead of the pleonastic ἀφ' οὗ in lines 5 and 21 of the Roman Chronicle. Disregarding such differences, it has been maintained that the Roman Chronicle offers an abridged version of the Getty Table.[44] An equal and even more plausible view is that they both depend on a common source.

Until the discovery of the Getty Table, scholars postulated small exemplars (e.g. illustrated papyrus rolls) or big ones (e.g. monumental reliefs) as sources of the Tabulae Iliacae, including the Roman Chronicle.[45] Now, the possibility that the Roman Chronicle and the Getty Table depend on a third source may imply

---

[44] Burstein 1984:161, Pleket and Stroud 1983, commentary to column 2.
[45] Sadurska 1964:17, Horsfall 1979:43–48, Valenzuela Montenegro 2004:339–346, with further references.

that the work done at a textual level goes beyond the adaptation of smaller or larger visual models.[46] We cannot know whether abridgements of chronographic material were common practice, but as the two fragments suggest, chronicles circulated in the early first century CE, whether in handbooks or compiled from them, not necessarily connected to the illustrations. It seems that workshops catered to an audience with literary or antiquarian interests.

The Roman Chronicle has been known to scholars for over 150 years,[47] whereas the Getty Table was first published in 1984. Until then, the Roman Chronicle was the closest parallel to the Parian Marble (so it was for Jacoby).[48] Indeed, the texts share a number of significant features: the impersonal, factual style, the selective listing of events, more detailed when dealing with the recent past (i.e. the Roman column in the Roman Chronicle, section B of the Parian Marble), the backwards system of time reckoning, the beginning of entries with "from the time when" (ἀφ' οὗ), small letters that require close reading. Differences, however, are notable as well. Unlike the Parian Marble, which is a stele over two m high, the Roman Chronicle and the Getty Table were composed as miniatures.[49] They also include a visual component lacking in the Parian Marble, and their much shorter lines give them a bookish aspect. Though it is impossible to determine the original length of the Roman Chronicle and the Getty Table, it nonetheless seems that the Parian Marble embraces a more comprehensive time span. The Parian Marble is also more complex in method, as it uses both intervals from year 1 and an eponymous list, with which the other two dispense. Finally, the Roman Chronicle refers to both Greek and Roman history, whereas the Parian Marble seems to ignore Rome. The 250-year interval between the inscriptions and the Roman origins of the Roman Chronicle and the Getty Table may account for some of the differences. However, in one aspect the similarities among the three can illuminate the genre of chronicles to which the Parian Marble belongs. The three were set on stone to be seen "at one glance,"

---

[46] To be sure, the cutting of similar texts on different tables is a phenomenon already known for the Tabulae Iliacae. In a different workshop in the Roman Campagna (not the same workshop, as Burstein says), two similar texts were cut on the back of the Second Verona Table (IG XIV 285 II back, Sadurska 1964:55–58, 9D) and on the back of the Borgia Table (Sadurska 1964:58–61, 10K back, columns 1–4 or a–d). Incidentally, these tables tell of Cadmus's genealogy and the birth of Dionysos, dating the events with reference to a priestess of Argos, a method systematized by Hellanicus. Hence, the authors or their sources made use of earlier chronographic techniques.

[47] First reported by Secchi 1843, first published by Henzen 1854.

[48] Jacoby 1904b:96.

[49] Letters in the two Tabulae are at least one quarter the height of those in the Parian Marble, and the stones carrying the inscriptions are much smaller. Regarding numerals, the Parian Marble uses the acrophonic system, while the Roman Chronicle and the Getty Table use the alphabetic one.

uno in conspectu, in Cicero's words.[50] They made it possible for whole stretches of history to be taken in at once. Still, we may say that the Roman Chronicle and the Getty Table are examples of popular chronicles, probably compiled from handbooks, differing from sophisticated (i.e. Alexandrian) chronographic scholarship.

Where were the Tabulae Iliacae located? A number of hypotheses have been advanced.[51] They may have served didactic purposes, as *aide-mémoires* at schools. Alternatively, they could have had a votive function, set in ritual contexts. Or they could simply have been decorative, especially in libraries. Horsfall's suggestion that the Tabulae Iliacae were displayed at the houses of Roman *nouveaux riches* is widely accepted.[52] However, his anti-erudite view has been challenged recently by Salimbene and Squire, who recognize in some of the Tabulae Iliacae a sophistication that suits the context of culture, wealth, and leisure of the aristocratic Roman Villa.[53] The topics of literary education in most tables suggest, as Salimbene argues, locations such as libraries, meeting or lecture places.[54] Indeed, the reverse of one of the Borgia tables is consistent with a location in a library, as it displays a list of literary works, including authors, titles, and length, information typical of library inventories.[55] Salimbene made an interesting suggestion: that some of the Tabulae Iliacae may have been located on columns (thus, both sides of the tables could have been seen) situated in libraries, indicating the setting of volumes.[56] Going beyond content, Petrain examined the reliefs of the Tabulae Iliacae and found them consistent with decorative elements at Greek

---

[50] See n. 14 above.

[51] Sadurska 1964:18–19, Horsfall 1979:31–32, Valenzuela Montenegro 2004:402–407, Squire 2011:70–86, with further references.

[52] "... the libraries and dining rooms of the new rich, where ignorance is to be hidden and memories have to be jolted at every step" (Horsfall 1979:35). McLeod (1985:165) when discussing the so-called Borgia Table (10K) or "epic canon" concludes that it was "a pretense of literacy for the unlettered."

[53] Squire 2010:90 and 2011:70–86, following Guarducci 1974:502, Salimbene 2002, and the illuminating remarks of Valenzuela Montenegro 2004:408–412 on the audience and function of the Tabulae Iliacae.

[54] Salimbene 2002:30–33. Cf. Kontoleon 1964b:198–199, Squire 2011:73–74 (a different approach in Chaniotis 1988:94–99, 227–233).

[55] Without further analysis, Salimbene also suggests that the Roman Chronicle and the Getty Table show similarities with epigraphical bibliographical catalogues. The reverse of the Borgia is, however, much more similar. The large fragmentary inscription known as the Roman *Fasti* (IG XIV 1097, 1098, 1098a = IGUR 215–31 = Millis and Olson 2012:225-229), containing a list of comic poets probably derived from Aristotle's *Didaskaliai* through Callimachus's *Table and Register of Playwrights, Arranged Chronologically from the Beginning* was presumably cut on the walls of a major library (Pfeiffer 1968:132, Blum 1991:137–138, 170n103, with further references).

[56] The remains of a tenon, "presumably for mounting the monument in a slotted hand" can be observed on the Getty Table (Burstein 1984:153).

gymnasia and Roman libraries.[57] If the Roman Chronicle and the Getty Table were set in libraries, the references to philosophers and poets could somehow refer to the contents of the book-collections. Similarly, the parallel display of Greek and Roman history in the Roman Chronicle perhaps reflected the nature of a Greek and Latin collection. Speculation aside, it may be safer to assume more general locations characterized by literary culture.[58]

3. The Count-Down Chronicle

The Roman Chronicle and the Getty Table are the closest available parallels to the Parian Marble, from the point of view of form and chronographic method, as well as their epigraphic nature. Their affinities are such that it would be unreasonable to consider them unrelated, whereas their differences may be explained by the time and space between them. There is, however, no evidence to suggest origins in a common source. It would be safer not to draw genetic conclusions, but rather generic ones, and to suggest that they are instances of the same sub-genre, which I propose to call tentatively the count-down chronicle. While the Parian Marble appears more scholarly, none of the three achieved the sophistication of Alexandrian chronographic scholarship, as represented, for example, by Eratosthenes. The genre of the count-down chronicle may have been practiced by educated men and teachers. Regarding the location of the Parian Marble, the Roman Chronicle and the Getty Table, though belonging to a later period and to a Roman context, may suggest an interesting possibility. If indeed they were set at sites related to literary and cultural activities, this hypothesis would be consistent with the view that the Parian Marble was displayed at a site such as a mouseion, possibly the Archilocheion.

---

[57]   Petrain 2006:148–188.
[58]   Petrain 2006:158.

Chapter 4
The Parian Marble as a Literary Text

The Parian Marble offers the rare opportunity to explore the textual qualities of an ancient piece of Greek chronography. However, literary scholars seem to have so far been reluctant to study it as a verbal artifact, probably due to its catalogue style, simple syntax, and limited vocabulary. It is certainly possible to analyze the chronicle's style, themes, characters, and narrative technique, but in order to do so we have to align ourselves with non-Aristotelian poetics and relinquish any expectations of organic unity and poetic language. Thus, under the general umbrella of literary analysis this chapter will look into the textual qualities of the Parian Marble.

What are our units of analysis to be? Literary studies usually find such units in the divisions into books, sections, chapters, etc., especially if they belong to the originals. The Parian Marble offers little of this sort. There was an introduction, probably inscribed in characters bigger than the rest,[1] and possibly a conclusion, currently lost. One entry or another could be taken as marking a division in the text due to its historical[2] or chronographic[3] prominence, but at the risk of imposing our own perceptions, for the layout of the text does not display division into sections. The long lines follow each other continuously, without word separation as customary, and without leaving empty spaces. The only potential marks of internal division are the small blank spaces left between the introduction and the first entry (A1), and after the fall of Troy (A24).[4] The division of the text into entries, based on the recurrence of opening patterns and dating formulae, is the result of modern editorial work.[5] Entries provide

---

[1] Jacoby 1904a:26.
[2] Jacoby's table (cited in chap. 6, n. 22 below) marks a division before and after the battles of Plataea (A52) and Leuctra (A72 suppl., Jacoby FGrH 239 [commentary]:667).
[3] Such a chronological marker may be found in the beginning of the annual Athenian archonship, A32.
[4] See chap. 5, sect. 2 below.
[5] Editors either present the text of the Parian Marble graphically divided according to lines (Selden, Boeckh, Flach, Krispi and Wilhelm, Jacoby 1904a) or entries ("epochae," Prideaux, Hiller

useful and textually based small units of reference. For major units we are left with the partition suggested by the vicissitudes of transmission: the lost fragment (A1), the Ashmolean fragment (A2), and the Parian fragment (B). For the sake of convenience and based on changes of style and distribution of content, I refer in my analysis to broader sections of the text, such as the times before and after the fall of Troy, the sixth century BCE, or the period of Alexander the Great and his successors (which coincides with section B).

1. The Language and Style of the Parian Marble

Jacoby's seems to have been the first and so far the last discussion of the language of the Parian Marble.[6] He focused mainly on departures from Attic usage, which served him as evidence for his hypothesis of a Parian author, and briefly on morphology and syntax. In this section, I approach the structure of individual entries, and the syntactic and lexical features that help generate what we may term an objective style.

The deep structure of entries may be summed up as:

"Y years passed since X."

In most cases this is expressed by a temporal clause:

"From when X happened, Y years, when Z was archon (or king) at Athens."

E.g. "From the time Troy was conquered, 945 years."

ἀφ' οὗ Τροία ἥλω ἔτη ͲHHHHΔΔΔΔΓͰ, βασιλεύοντος Ἀθηνῶν ... (A24)

However, in nine occasions a noun with the preposition ἀπό (from) appears instead of the temporal clause:

"From X, Y years, when Z was archon (or king) at Athens"

E.g. "From Alexander's crossing to Asia"

ἀπὸ τῆς Ἀλεξάνδρου διαβάσεως εἰς τὴν Ἀσίαν (B3)

---

von Gärtringen, Jacoby FGrH). Occasionally the beginnings of lines coincide with the beginning of entries: A69, A74, B3, B22, B27.

[6] Jacoby 1904b:102–107. The assessment of divergences from Attic usage, which makes the language of the Parian Marble close to the koine, probably deserves revision in light of the many epigraphical and papyrological developments since 1904.

Both patterns are known from other chronographic texts, but temporal clauses seem characteristic of the count-down chronicle (so, e.g. in the Roman Chronicle, chap. 3, sect. 2 above), while nominal patterns seem typical of sources computing major intervals of time, as in a famous fragment of Eratosthenes's *Chronographiai* (FGrH 241 F 1a):

ἀπὸ μὲν Τροίας ἁλώσεως ἐπὶ Ἡρακλειδῶν κάθοδον ἔτη ὀγδοήκοντα.

The preposition + noun pattern appears only once in A, but 8 times in B (i.e. in thirty percent of B's entries).[7] This could indicate that different sources were used in B, or that the method of composition, and perhaps of making notes, changed along the composition of the chronicle.[8]

Individual entries usually close with the dating formula. In thirteen entries, however, additional information appears after the Archon's name (in Jacoby's words, postscripts):[9]

A36: Syracuse

A42: Hipponax

A48: Aeschylus's fighting in Marathon

A55: Epicharmus

A60: Socrates and Anaxagoras

A71: burning down of the temple at Delphi (suppl.)

A72: Alexander II

A79:]ΣΟΦΟΣ, possibly a philosopher

B7: foundation of Hellenis

B11: Ptolemy's going to Cyrene

B12: Agathocles appointed strategos at Syracuse

B14: Menander's victory

B15: Age of Sosiphanes at death

---

[7] A21, B3, B5, B8, B9, B12, B13, B23, B24 (suppl.).

[8] Repetition of "from X" in the same entry (sometimes with variation), is exclusive to B. We find repetition in the form "from X ... and from X ..." in B3, B9, B12 (with a third member in B12 introduced by "from when"), "from X ... and from when ..." in B23 (with suppl.), and two instances of "and when ..." (καὶ ὅτε) in B13 and B24. In B24, where a lacuna allows enough space for the dating formula, it is possible that repetition indicates a new entry.

[9] Jacoby FGrH 239 (commentary):668 gives a shorter list of postscripts, attributing them to the cutter.

Information after the dating formula appears from A36 on, becoming more frequent as the inscription advances: while only ten percent of entries in A display post-archon information (eight times in eighty entries), eighteen percent of B do so (five times in twenty-seven entries). Half of the instances have to do with cultural history, most specifically, with poets (A42, A48, A55, A60, B14, B15, perhaps A79),[10] although references are not agonistic, except for Menander. Three post-archon events have to do with Sicilian history (A36, A55, B12). Postscripts may be revealing regarding the process of composition. They may have resulted from consultation of additional sources of information, perhaps when revising the text before its engraving. Thus, additional information may have been available, especially for cultural and poetic history, Sicilian history, and particularly for the more recent past. This information may have been found in specific monographs or, as Jacoby suggested, in general works such as Ephorus's.[11]

Individual entries comprise one or more simple sentences, joined by coordinating conjunctions, in most cases καί. As for the coordinant δέ, it emerges in A36, appearing nine times in A[12] and eight times in B.[13] Half of all instances coordinate postscripts (A36, A55, A60, A71, B7, B11, B12, B14). The particle τε is rare (A14, A60).[14] Coordinants are so plentiful that they could easily be omitted in translation.[15] However, even though the general style is paratactic, the conjunctions occasionally convey additional meaning. In a few cases, καί seems consecutive or inferential and can be rendered by "hence."[16] This feature appears early in the text (A1, A3, A5, A6, A9), always connected to etymological aetiology. In one case, a coordinating conjunction may be epexegetic or explanatory, "namely" (τε in A14). In sum, there is variation in the distribution of conjunctions. While in the early part of A we find traces of consecutive coordination, in the second part of A that function disappears and δέ emerges, becoming proportionally more frequent in B. This feature of the text may partly derive from the sources, partly from the attempt to coordinate information from different sources.

---

[10] On Hellenistic historiography's tendency to conclude a year's account with reference to ancient intellectuals, see chap. 6, sect. 1 below.

[11] Jacoby 1904b:91.

[12] Introd., A36, A49, A55, A58, A60, A71, A74, A77.

[13] B1, B6, B7, B11, B12 (twice), B14, B27.

[14] Coordinating nouns, followed by καί: τε καί ... A60, τε ... καί ... καί ... A14 (supplements are not counted).

[15] As in Burgess and Kulikowski 2013:301–309. See Bartol 2013:409–413 for the use of the particle δέ as a mark of transition in [Plutarch] *On Music*, 1131e–1135d, with further references.

[16] For consecutive or inferential καί, see chap. 2, n. 131 (to the English translation of A1). Such an understanding of καί supports the supplement κωπ]ῶν in A9.

The structure of sentences is simple.[17] Besides occasional relative clauses,[18] syntactic subordination is achieved by participle constructions,[19] and attending circumstances are expressed by absolute genitives.[20] Events are given in aorist, with only few instances of imperfect and historical present.[21] Most verbal forms in the Parian Marble are active, eighty-seven percent.[22] The few passive forms (thirteen percent) are mainly concentrated in three semantic groups: "being named" or "being called" at the beginning of the inscription, "being set up," for contests and prizes in the sixth century BCE, and "being founded" in section B.[23]

Attribution is effected by the article followed by a qualifier,[24] by relative clauses,[25] and by attributive participles.[26] However, descriptive and figurative

---

17 Jacoby 1904b:106.

18 Relative clauses: A5, A19, A43, B12; formulaic indication of victory through relative clauses: A25, A46, A48, A51, A52, A72, B5, B9. One instance of relative instead of conjunction in postscript: A 48. In spite of its lacunose state, A19 clearly appears as the most complex sentence in the Parian Marble.

19 Concerted participles: Introduction (line 1), A1, A6, A9, A12, A19, A20 (twice; once suppl.), A30, A31, A36, A37 (suppl.), A48, A49, A54, A56, A57, A59 (in an erasure), A60, A63 (suppl.), A64, A66, A69, A76, B2 (twice), B10, B11 (twice), B15 (suppl.), B20.

20 Absolute genitives: A11, A36, A39 (twice), A44, A61, B2 (twice), and dating formulae along the inscription.

21 A5 (suppl., συνήγειρε either aor. or impf.), A10, A42 (suppl.), A49, A55, A58, A60 (suppl.), A61, A69, A72, A74 (suppl.), A77, B1, B14, B15, B16, B17, B18; ἐνίκων / ἐνίκα in subordinate clauses: A46, A48 (in an erasure), A51, A52, A72, B9.

22 186 active forms vs. 28 passive ones. All non-passive verbs and participles are considered active (only the most plausibly supplemented forms are counted).

23 "Being named" or "being called": A1 (twice), A3, A6 (twice), A9, A10, A13. Active form in A5.
"Being set," i.e. established: A37 (in an erasure), A38 (in an erasure), A39 (twice; once suppl.), A43 (suppl.); i.e. "buried": B11; for statues: A54. Active forms in A4 (temple, suppl.), A20 (agon), A22 (agon, suppl.), B13 (laws).
"Being founded": A73, B5, B7, B14 (twice), and B19. Active forms: A7, A11, A26, A27 (suppl.), A31 (suppl.).
Other passive forms include the notions of "being chosen" (A9), "being taken" (A24, B5), "being discovered" (A11), "being given" (A17), "being sent" (B10).

24 Article in attributive position: A1, A34, A37 (in an erasure), with ordinals (Introduction line 2, A10, A48, A64, A73), patronymics (A3, A6 suppl., A7, A12, A34, A53, A54, A56, A77, B18 suppl., B20; without article: A5, A31), kinship (A25 suppl., A48 suppl., A49 twice, first in an erasure, A77, B19), ethnics (A10 twice, A30, A34, A45 suppl., A46, A54, A56, A65, A68, A73, A74; without article: A47), locations (A26 suppl., A71 suppl., A75), mostly battles and sieges (A48, A51, A52, A72 suppl., B3, B5, B12, B23), professions (poets: A29, A42, A43, A48, A49, A50 three times, A55, A57, A59, A64, A70 partly suppl., B7, B14, B22; philosophers: B11 "the sophist"; king: A42; commander: A52). The attributive article is missing at A66, A69, B15.
The article with participle of γίγνομαι (B9, B24) may be a periphrastic rendition of the more usually pattern "from when ... took place" (A3, A4, A16, A17, A19, A48, A51, A52, A72).

25 See n. 18 above.

26 Participles used for stating age: ὤν with ordinal adjective A30, A31; ἐτῶν ὤν with numeral A48, A56, A60. Age is also stated through βιοὺς ἔτη with numeral (A57, A66, A69, B11, B15 suppl.) and βιώσας ἔτη with numeral (A59, A63 suppl.), A64, A76). In one case, ὤν is given a noun as predicate (A49, "being a poet himself").

language is missing from the Parian Marble, the range of adjectives being limited to ordinals[27] (occasionally adverbial), ethnics,[28] patronymics (see n. 24 above), and qualifiers that are part of conceptual units (e.g. the gymnic competition).[29] Pronouns are few,[30] and there is a small number of temporal adverbs.[31]

Cohesion is achieved in the Parian Marble by the formulaic character of the opening and closing of entries. Anaphoric references have their antecedents always in the same entry;[32] there are no forward looking references, and the only deictic is found in the phrase "up to now" (A5), which refers to the time of composition of the chronicle or its source.

The style of the Parian Marble is compressed, impersonal, and precise. Indeed, entries are composed of simple sentences, usually short, with more participles than subordinated clauses. There are no explanations but only succession, which sometimes invites *post hoc* interpretation. The author's voice disappears after the introduction; a simple enunciation of facts follows. Precision is achieved by dates and numbers, as well as by the lack of hedging (tentative language) and of figurative and descriptive language. Apart from the limited use of the passive voice (one of the main markers of scientific language in contemporary English), all other features form a style that may be termed objective, though it nevertheless expresses authorial subjectivity. Indeed, certain nuances (probably deriving from the sources used) emerge from minor variations of vocabulary, as the use of κυριεύειν for Alexander and Ptolemy, instead of the regular βασιλεύειν and τυραννεύειν,[33] and μεταλλαγή for Alexander's death (B8),[34] instead of the usual τελευτᾶν.[35] But as we shall see, it is the selection of characters and events, rather than the style in which they are presented, that expresses authorial subjectivity.

---

[27] τοῦ πρώτου Introd., Παναθηναίοις τοῖς πρώτοις γενομένοις A10, τρεισκαιδεκάτου A23, δευτέρου ⟨καὶ εἰκοστοῦ⟩ ἔτους A24, τρεισκαιδεκάτου A27, ἑνδέκατος A30, δέκατος A31, εἰκοστοῦ καὶ ἑνός A31, τοῦ προτέρου A36, τοῦ δευτέρου A38, καὶ ἆθλον ἐτέθη πρῶτον A39 (attributive or adverbial), πρῶτος A43, τοῦ προτέρου A43, τοῦ δευτέρου A48, τοῦ προτέρου A59, ὁ δεύτερος A73. Numerals, in addition to the numbers in the dating formula: τὰς δώδεκα πόλεις A20. Adverbial ordinals: τὸ πρότερον A1, A6, πρῶτος A10 (twice), πρ]ώτη A12, πρῶτον A16, A46, A50, A60, τότε πρῶτον B14.

[28] Phrygian (A10, twice), Idaean (A11), Argive (A30), Lesbian (A34), Pelasgian (A45), Chalcian (A46), Ceian (A54), Selinian (A65), Selymbrian (A68), Himerian (A73), Sicilian (A74).

[29] Ἄρειος Πάγος A3, A25, ὁ γυμνικὸς [ἀγών] A17, νόμισμα ἀργυροῦν A30, τοὺς νόμους τοὺ[ς κιθ]α[ρ]-ῳδ[ικ]οὺς καὶ αὐλητ[ικ A34, τὴν ἔμπροσθε μουσικὴν A34 (adverb), ⟨⟨ὁ ἀγὼν ὁ γυμνικὸς ἐτέθη χρ⟩⟩ηματίτης A37, [ὁ στε]⟨⟨φανίτης ἀγὼν A38, Μεγάλη πόλις A73, αὐτοκράτορα στρατηγόν B12.

[30] Pronouns: παν[τοί]ων Introd., ἄλλους A10, τῶι δ' αὐτῶι ἔτει τούτωι (B12), εἰς τὸ αὐτὸ A20, κατὰ τοῦτον A42, A55, τούτου A79, ἕτερος ... Ἡρακλῆς B18.

[31] Temporal adverbs κατ' ἐνιαυτὸν A32, ἔμπροσθε A34 (adverb), πάλιν A38, τότε A71, B14. Also: οὗ[περ] A5.

[32] τῶι δ' αὐτῶι ἔτει τούτωι B12, κατὰ τοῦτον A42, A55.

[33] Alexander: B4; Ptolemy: B17, B8 (κυριεύσεως).

[34] Jacoby already noted the pregnant meaning of the word (Jacoby 1904b:107).

[35] There is one instance of ἀποθνήσκω, B19.

2. The Contents of the Parian Marble

The limited repertoire of events recorded in the inscription allows for a quantitative semantic approach (see Appendix at the end of the book).[36] In my analysis, I distinguish as major themes religious, political, military, and cultural events. Natural events, which are few and proportionally more represented in B than in A, form a minor category: a flood (κατακλυσμός, A4), the eruption of Mount Etna (A52), a meteor (ὁ λίθος ἔπεσε, A57), fire (κατεκάη δὲ τότε κα[ὶ ὁ ἐν Δελφοῖς ναός], A71), an eclipse (ὁ ἥλιος ἐξέλιπεν, B16), an earthquake (with restoration: [ἀπὸ τῶ]ν σε̣ι̣[σ]μῶν, B24), and a comet (with restoration: [κομήτης ἀσ]τὴρ ἐφ[ά] ν[η], B25). In what follows, graphs are used to help comprehend the incidence of themes and their interaction.

Among religious events there are eighteen references to sacrifice, purification, epiphany, oracle consultation, as well as to the setting of festivals and contests: the Panathenaea, the ploughing festival at Eleusis, the Eleusinian mysteries, the gymnic agon at Eleusis, the contests at Isthmia, Nemea, and Delphi, and the Athenian contests of comedy, tragedy, and dithyramb. I count festival foundations also among cultural events but not among political ones, in spite of their political significance. Only one religious event, Croesus's *theoria* to Delphi (A41, with restoration), do I count as political.

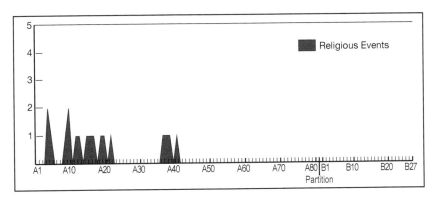

Table 1.

---

[36] Occasionally (A41), the nature of events is assessed through the most plausible restoration. The quantitative semantic analysis, as that of style, would benefit from digital encoding (e.g. using the Epidoc markup scheme, as in the "Digital Marmor Parium," edited by Monica Berti [Digital Humanities, University of Leipzig], announced as this book was going to press).

Religious events concentrate in two clusters: the times preceding the Trojan War, and the sixth century BCE (Table 1). Regarding the first cluster, the focus on religious events of aetiological nature is consistent with the practice of both local and universal historians when relating primeval times. The second cluster, which includes the establishment of contests at Delphi and Athens, probably benefited from the availability of documentary evidence—namely, victory lists kept at sanctuaries or reconstructed from local records (although the author most probably gathered the information from historiographical sources rather than from *didaskaliai* directly). Religious events from the fifth century BCE on, although implied in contexts of poetic victories, are not explicitly mentioned.

Political affairs (sixty-nine events), constitute the largest group of the inscription.[37] This category comprises references to ruling,[38] changes in form of government, and acts towards social cohesion.[39] Trials are considered as part of political life, even when situated in proto-historical times.[40] I include two political assassinations,[41] as well as the birth (B19) and death of political figures (*passim*). Foundations of cities belong here too.[42]

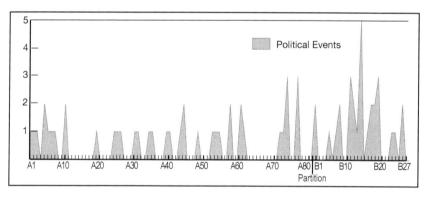

Table 2.

---

[37] I count the city foundations at A27 as a single event.

[38] As king, tyrant, *kyrios, passim.*

[39] Amphyction in Thermopylae, A5; Theseus's *synoikismos* and democracry in Athens, A20.

[40] Ares and Poseidon, A3; Orestes and Aegisthus's daughter, A25.

[41] Of Hipparchus, A45, of Bessus, B6. Other instances of political killing remain understated (e.g. Olympias and Cleopatra, B14 and B19).

[42] A foundation is possibly implied at A5; Cadmeia, A7; Apollonia, A11; Salamis, A26; Miletus and the Ionian cities, A27; Syracuse, A31; Megalopolis, A73; Alexandria, B5; Hellenis, B7; Lysimachia, B19.

The incidence of political events is very high, but their distribution uneven (Table 2). They are particularly frequent in section B. In section A, there are two plateaus. The first, between the Panathenaea and the fall of Troy (A10 to A24), with only three political events, at A11 and A20. The second, from Gelon and Hieron to the foundation of Megalopolis (A53 and A55 to A73), with only six political events (A58, A61, A62, A72). These plateaus of political events correspond to a high occurrence of religious and cultural events up to the fall of Troy, as well as of cultural events, mostly Athenian poetic competitions of the fifth and fourth centuries BCE.

Military affairs (forty-eight events, Table 3) include waging war and advancing with an army, battles, sieges, references to winning and to defeating, and specific conquests.[43]

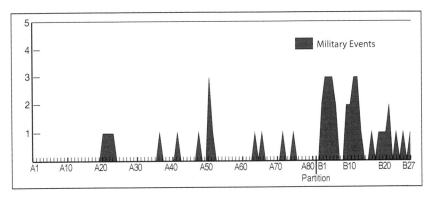

Table 3.

No military events are mentioned at the beginning of the inscription. They appear first in a cluster including the Amazons (A21), the Seven against Thebes (A22), and the Trojan War (A23, A24), very popular themes in the visual and literary arts. After that, they become sporadic, emerging in connection to Delphi, the Persian wars (including Marathon, Plataea, and Salamis), peaking with the Persian defeat (A51, A52) and Cyrus's anabasis (A64, A66). Section B includes a very high concentration of military events (thirty-three events, that is, sixty-nine percent of all military events, appear in B), with relatively high level of detail. In contrast, section A records only famous military conflicts from the mythical past and from the Persian wars, while few inter-city conflicts are mentioned (the battles at Leuctra [A72 suppl.] and Delphi [A75]).

---

[43] Phrased in terms of taking or destroying towns, taking dominion over an area, and prevailing over commanders.

Cultural affairs are the second most frequent type of event after political ones (fifty-six events). They include the organization of contests (considered religious events too), especially poetic competitions. Also included are references to *heuremata*, poets (their birth, "appearance" or *floruit*, victories, death, etc.) and other intellectuals, including philosophers.

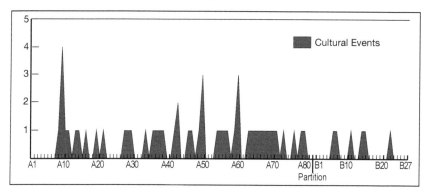

Table 4.

Cultural events are spread rather evenly in section A of the inscription (Table 4), with minor plateaus at the beginning (A1 to A8), between the fall of Troy and Hesiod (A24 to A28), at the beginning of B (B1 to B5), and towards its end. The section corresponding to the Classical period contains more cultural events, but fewer events of other types. Conversely, section B, with a very high frequency of military and political events, has much fewer cultural events (only six, that is, eleven percent of all cultural events, appear in B).

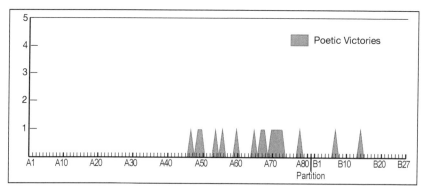

Table 5.

Among cultural events, the distribution of victories at poetic competitions deserves attention (Tables 5 and 6). They are concentrated in the period between 510/508 BCE and 370/369 BCE, and are restricted to victories in Athens. That is, no other *mousikoi agones* are mentioned in the Parian Marble. Perhaps most conspicuously absent are the Carneian contests at Sparta, whose list of victors was compiled by Hellanicus (see chap. 6, sect. 1 and 2.IV below).

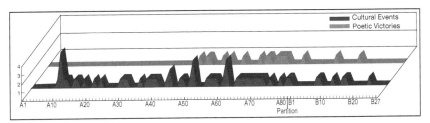

Table 6.

How are the major themes distributed in the Parian Marble? Table 7 helps to visualize their interaction, especially that between gaps and peaks.

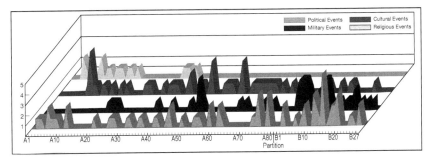

Table 7.

In the early periods of the chronicle, information is foundational, about emerging political entities, religious practices, and cultural institutions. The middle period is marked by cultural events and, to a lesser degree, by political ones. The more recurrent themes in the last part of the inscription (B) are political and military. However, in the entire text cultural events are almost as numerous as political ones, and gaps in the military and political series seem to be filled mostly by cultural events, and vice versa. The distribution of themes may derive partly from the sources used, yet authorial choice cannot be excluded, even though it was constrained by the availability of information. The emphasis on poetic events, as we shall see in Chapter 6, is idiosyncratic to the Parian Marble.

For the sake of the quantitative analysis of contents, I treated the four major themes as discrete. However, one notion seems to cross those semantic boundaries: the notion of conflict and competition, which appears in military, cultural, and political events. Winning is also a notion shared by various categories; twenty-two instances of winning occur in war, at musical contests, and in court.

3. Narrative and Characters

Unlike full-fledged literary historiography, the Parian Marble lacks narrative and authorial voice. The text has a beginning, a middle, and an end—a partly extant introduction, a body, and most likely a concluding section—yet the body itself, structured upon the succession of entries like a catalogue, has no plot. No story is told. Only the counting of years invests the text with a literary quality, that of closure, although the meaning of that closure is uncertain without the concluding section. And yet, although lacking a continuous narrative, individual entries include hints of story-telling. Indeed, some entries contain more detail than usual: Danaus and his daughters (A9), Demeter (A12), Minos and Athens (A19), Alexander and Thebes (B2), Alexander's victory at Arbela (B5). Furthermore, although events are, as a rule, located simply in the past, mostly through aorist verbs, a few nuances emerge. The adverbial τὸ πρότερον indicates previous states in the past. This is the case of two instances of "formerly named" (A1 and A6) located at the beginning of the inscription and probably deriving from sources, such as the writers of Atthis.[44] Occasionally, participle constructions or absolute genitives (see notes 19 and 20 above) refer to previous events, thus conveying very compressed tales. Sometimes, past processes are described through several actions by the same agent, one after another (B2, B5). At one point, the future relative to a past event emerges (ἀξιώσει, A19). In all these entries, information is included beyond the bare statement of events, with more details than needed for chronographic purposes. Such entries are actual kernels of narrative. Moreover, even though the Parian Marble never offers analysis or explanation, causality is implied by the succession of events. Perhaps those kernels of narrative result from a looser abridgement of sources, with story-telling occasionally taking over the chronographer.[45]

In the same way that there is no proper narrative in the Parian Marble, there are no main characters, even though a few names appear more than once, especially in section B (Alexander and Ptolemy are good examples). However, even if there are no real protagonists, we may explore the types of individual who are found worthy of record.

---

[44] Jacoby 1904b:89–91.
[45] Similar condensed narratives appear in the early sections of Jerome's *Chronicle*, e.g. the story of Proserpina (i.e. Persephone), with specific reference to Philochorus' second book of the *Atthis* (49l).

Among the 203 personal names mentioned in the inscription (or 117, if 86 kings and archons named for dating purposes are excluded),[46] only 9 entries include female characters: Danaus's daughters (Helike and Archedike, A9), the Mother of the gods (A10), Demeter and Neaera (A12), Amazons (A21), Erigone (A25), Sappho (A36), Alexander's mother Olympias (B14), Artabazus's daughter (B18), and Alexander's sister Cleopatra (B19). Females are more frequent in early times, a fact consistent with their strong presence in Greek mythology. They reappear after Alexander's death, in connection with his succession. Apart from the early period and the Macedonian dynasty, no female political actors are mentioned. Sappho is an exception, noted for her exile, rather than her poetry (unlike most poets in the inscription, she is not qualified as such).

Hence, males are the main protagonists of history, most of them rulers and military commanders. Their range crosses ethnic boundaries. It is their historical relevance from the Greek point of view and their position of power that makes them count, not their ethnic affiliation. A second group of protagonists includes cultural figures, mostly poets and musicians, and a few philosophers (we shall return to them in chap. 6, sect. 1).

Beside individuals a number of collective entities appear: Amphictyons (A5, A37), Greeks / Hellenes (A6, A17, A23, A51, suppl. A66), Athenians (A10, A19, A45, A48, A52, B9), Argives (A22), Lydians (A35), Icarians (A39), Persianas (A48, A51), Macedonias (A58, A61, B9), Lacedaimonians (A72), Thebans (A72, B2), Triballi (B2), Illyrians (B2), Syracusans (B12), Calchedonians (B13). References to ethnic groups are more frequent in the middle part of the inscription, whereas the military clashes of section B are presented rather as conflicts among individuals.[47] In this context are found two instances of individuals said to act by somebody else's will: Ptolemy sent Ophelas to Cyrene (B10) and Seleucus to Babylon (B16).

There is nothing idiosyncratic in the Parian Marble's approach to the protagonists of history. The focus on political and military affairs, typical of much ancient Greek historiography, calls for a certain type of character: leading and powerful male individuals and ethnic groups. There are no barbarians, no lexical marking of "the other," in the extant inscription. This interest in rulers is shared by ancient Near Eastern chronicles. In contrast, religious figures such as prophets are prominent in the Biblical, and later the Christian chronicles. Yet

---

[46] Numbers make no distinction between historical and mythological figures. Partially supplemented names are counted, but neither repetition of individual names nor patronymics. Female individuals account for 5 or 8.5 percent of all individuals attested in the inscription (from a total of 203 or 117; the Amazons are counted as one).

[47] Other groups besides *ethnoi* are the Amazons (A21), *choroi* (A39, A46), and the Pisistratids (A45).

the focus on poets, as we shall see in Chapter 6, although present in some works of Hellenistic historiography, is peculiar to the Parian Marble.

As we emphasized earlier in the analysis of style, the frequent use of the active voice strongly underlines human agency. Comparison of the voice usage in medieval chronicles is revealing. Hayden White, discussing non-narrative forms of historical representation in the Annals of Saint Gall concludes that they reflect "a world in which things happen to people, rather than one in which people do things."[48] The outlook on agency in the Parian Marble could not be more different.

4. Mapping Space in the Parian Marble

The Parian Marble charts human action in a chronological grid, and it does so by locating it in space. In this section, I explore geography in the Parian Marble and how the spatial focus changes as the inscription advances.

Up to the Trojan War (A23, A24), the chronicle dwells on central Greece, Northern Greece, and the Peloponnese,[49] referring only to two oversees locations, Egypt (A9) and Crete (A11 suppl.). After the Trojan War, the focus expands towards the East and West. First, by tracing the foundation of settlements in Cyprus (Salamis?, A26 suppl.), Ionia (A27), and Syracuse (A31). Second, by charting the rise and demise of rulers in Lydia,[50] Athens,[51] Persia,[52] Syracuse,[53] and Macedonia.[54] When section B opens, the chronicle is following closely Alexander's campaigns, North,[55] South,[56] East,[57] and further East.[58] After Alexander's death, the focus shifts back to the Mediterranean and the Aegean, to Syracuse,[59]

---

[48] White 1987:10. The question of whether White's assessment applies to most medieval chronicles is beyond the scope of this chapter.

[49] Athens (A1, A3, A4, A10 implied, A19, and A20); Attica (A1); Delphi (A2 implied, A4 implied), Thermopylae (A5), Phthiotis (A6), Thebes (A7, A22), Phrygia (A10), Eleusis (A13, A14 implied, A15, A17), Arcadia (A17), Argos (Nemea A22 suppl.).

[50] Alyattes (A35 suppl.) and Croesus (A41).

[51] Pisistratus and the Pisistratids, A40, A45.

[52] Cyrus, Darius, Xerxes: A42, A44, A49; Cyrus's anabasis: A64, A66; Artaxerxes's death: A77; Ochos: A77.

[53] The landowners, A36; Gelon, A53; Hieron, A55; Dionysius I and II, A62, A74.

[54] Alexander, Perdiccas A58; Archelaus A61; Philippus A77.

[55] Against the Triballi and Illyrians, B2.

[56] Against the Thebans, B2.

[57] The battles of Granicus and Issus, B3; the conquest of Phoenicia, Cyprus, and Egypt, B4; foundation of Alexandria, B5.

[58] The battle of Arbela, seizing of Babylon, B5; foundation of Hellenis, which may refer to Alexandria Eschate by the Iaxartes, B7 (cf. Krispi and Wilhelm 1897:192, Jacoby 1904a:125).

[59] B14, B18.

central and Northern Greece (Athens,[60] Boeotia,[61] Chalcis,[62] Macedonia)[63] the Hellespont,[64] Babylon,[65] Sardis,[66] and the Eastern Mediterranean,[67] with the prominence of Africa[68] and Carthage emerging towards the end of the extant text.[69] Thus, the geographical focus shifts as the text moves from central Greece to the Mediterranean basin, expands East with Alexander's campaigns, and returns to the Eastern Mediterranean, with Syracuse and Carthage in the West.

Athens is a major reference point in the Parian Marble. Not only is it mentioned in almost every entry as part of the dating formula, but it is also selected as the place where time begins to be reckoned. In addition, Athens is mentioned or implied in thirty-two further entries. The images of Athens that emerge from the Parian Marble conform to a common stereotype. Indeed, to a reader following its fate, Athens appears as the cradle of democracy, a major cultural center, a remarkable winner over the Persians for the sake of Greece, and little involved in interstate conflicts. Athens remains a cultural center (B7, B14) even when defeated (B9) and conquered (B10, B20). From a political point of view, however, the history of Athens *ab silentio* is one of demise, the focus moving to Macedonia and later to Ptolemaic Egypt. Among other Greek states, only Syracuse is followed consistently along the inscription.[70] Sparta's role is downplayed,[71] most conspicuously at Thermopylae (A51) and Plataea (A52). Lesbos appears at an early stage (A34, A36) in connection with cultural figures, Terpander and Sappho. Egypt is rarely mentioned in A but becomes central in B, particularly with Alexander (B4) and Ptolemy (B8).

The world depicted in the Parian Marble is one of movement. To be sure, it is not only travel that is implied in most military campaigns and city foundations, though in some cases it is mentioned explicitly. At the very beginning, movement towards Athens is charted, with Deucalion (A4) and Demeter (A12). Hellas is a destination for Danaus, coming from Egypt (A9), and later for Stesichorus

---

[60] B10, B13, B14, and the Piraeus (B20).
[61] The rebuilding of Thebes, B14.
[62] B24.
[63] B12, B14, including the foundation of Cassandreia at the site of Potidaea.
[64] B12, B13, and the foundation of Lysimachia, B19.
[65] B16.
[66] B19.
[67] Syria and Phoenicia, B12; Gaza, B16; and the Eastern Aegean: Amorgos, B9; Cos, B19; Rhodes, B23; and Cyprus, B17 suppl., B21.
[68] Egypt, B8, B11; Memphis, B11; Cyrene B10, B11.
[69] B18, B19 (partly restored).
[70] Jacoby, however, believed that no special source on the history of Sicily had been used (1904b:91).
[71] Jacoby sees the omission of the Dorian immigration, Lycurgus, and the very limited reference to Sparta (A72) as part of the inscription's anti-Spartan or anti-Dorian *Tendenz* (FGrH 239 [commentary]:667).

(A50). Two events dated to the seventh century BCE involve travelling across the Mediterranean, from Corinth to Syracuse (A31) and from Mytilene to Sicily (A36). The notion of crossing, implied in Croesus's *theoria* to Delphi (A41), dominates from the fifth century BCE onwards. Indeed, there is Xerxes's crossing the Hellespont (A51), Cyrus's anabasis (A64), and the return of the Greeks (A66), as well as the crossing of Alexander (B3) and Antigonus (B11) into Asia. The notion of crossing acquires a new direction with Agathocles's crossing from Sicily to Carthage (B18). Apart from Xerxes's crossing (A51), all travels are referred to in very general terms. This dynamic world, in which people and armies constantly move from place to place, is in sharp contrast with the rigid style of the Parian Marble.

Yet the geographical focus of the Parian Marble is something of a cliché, inviting comparison with that of contemporary historical handbooks. Let us look, for example, at the *Penguin Historical Atlas of Ancient Greece*, clearly influenced by ancient perspectives.[72] In the opening chapter, the first map in the section "Origins" is one of mainland Greece and the East coast of Asia Minor, from Macedonia and Thrace in the North and to Crete in the South.[73] Though Athens is not mentioned, the map actually centers on Attica. Furthermore, many headings in the table of contents have equivalent entries in the Parian Marble: "King Minos and Knossos," "The Trojan Wars," "Migration and Colonization," "Rise of the Tyrants," "Athens Ascendant," "Persia and the West," "Kingdom of Macedonia," "Campaigns of Alexander," "Alexander's Spoils," "Consolidation of the Kingdoms," "New Kingdoms, New Rivalries."[74] Thus, the shift in focus is similar, but the Parian Marble differs in downplaying "The Rise of Sparta," "Pericles and the Athenian Empire," and the "Peloponnesian War." Until Alexander, the reference to Egypt is minimal, and the West is limited to Syracuse, including Carthage only towards the end.

The geographical knowledge underlying the composition or the reading of the Parian Marble is not particularly rich. But precisely for that reason it may be seen as reflecting the knowledge of educated laymen, perhaps of teachers.[75]

---

[72] Morkot 1996.
[73] Morkot 1996:23.
[74] Morkot 1996:6–7.
[75] Thus, the Parian Marble provides an insight into the geographical knowledge possibly held by non-professionals in the Hellenistic period (cf. Dueck and Brodersen 2012:118–121).

5. Conclusions

The analysis of the Parian Marble in terms of style, themes, narrative technique, characters, and space shows that rather than remaining uniform, they vary as the inscription advances.

The opening, up to the Trojan War, sticks to the formulaic arrangement of entries, beginning with temporal clauses and ending with dating notices. Parataxis is the rule, achieved through καί, though occasionally consecutive and epexegetic meanings can be discerned, disclosing the aetiological orientation of the sources used. In this period, information concerns the emergence of political entities, religious practices, and cultural institutions. In terms of geography, the section focuses on central Greece, particularly on Attica and Athens. From the sixth century BCE on, the structure of entries loosens, postscripts emerge, and δέ appears, a conjunction almost unattested before A36. Both features perhaps testify to the difficulties of compiling information from diverse sources. From the point of view of content, cultural events dominate. In the Classical period, the festival culture of Athens is emphasized, whereas the political and military centrality of other areas emerges. Consequently, the geographical focus expands, covering the Mediterranean basin, from Syracuse to Persia. In section B entries have a much looser structure; nominalization frequently opens sections, and postscripts, usually coordinated by δέ, are more numerous. At the same time, information is more detailed, often more than needed for chronographic purposes. At times, entries resemble *hypomnemata.* The author's giving way to narrative may derive from his describing contemporary events, as well as from the wealth of available information. This period focuses particularly on the military and political realms, with events and people recorded from further east and west. It is reasonable to assume that much stylistic variation is due to the use of different sources.

The Parian Marble, as many have noted, may be disappointing as a historical source. People and events that we deem important are missing: Lycurgus, Solon, Cleisthenes, Pericles, the Peloponnesian wars, do not appear in the extant text.[76] What is more, chronology often differs from what we know from other sources.[77] In fact, the Parian Marble shows no deep historiographical aspirations. Events are dated, not explained. As a literary text, the inscription is equally disappointing. The objective style does not engage the poetically

---

[76] Other notable omissions: the Olympic games, the Argonauts, Heracles; see Jacoby FGrH 239 (commentary):666–667. In contrast, the later Roman Chronicle mentions Solon (B 2), Themistocles (B 19–20), the Peloponnesian war (B 25–26), and the Gauls' taking of Rome in 385/4 BCE (B 27–28).

[77] Cf. Jacoby FGrH 239 (commentary):669–670.

oriented mind, appreciative of the exceptional rather than the cliché. Whoever looks for originality of expression or thought finds nothing of the sort in the Parian Marble. The inscription partakes of the style of chronicles as a literary genre, sharing at the same time a world-view with ancient historiography, in terms of who and what counts. Nevertheless, to readers, ancient or modern, perusing it from beginning to end, the Parian Marble offers a compact version of Panhellenic history. In that sense, the inscription not only offers a chronology, as originally intended, but at the same time a historical overview. If read in this way, a notional hero emerges and a plot seems to form. The hero is Hellas, at times identified with Athens; the plot is the rise and fall of political powers.

The world of the Parian Marble is one of on-going confrontation. No didactic lesson is intended, yet a Herodotean moral is imparted, nonetheless: whatever rises is doomed to fall, whoever attains power eventually passes away. The comfort imparted by the rhythmical counting of years contrasts sharply with the instability of human endeavors. The objective style inspires authority, but knowledge of historical sources may yet raise a sense of dissonance.

Chapter 5
Time in the Parian Marble

Time is ubiquitous in the Parian Marble, as suits its genre and purpose; it structures the inscription at all levels. While individual entries open with "from when" and conclude with dating formulae (by Athenian kings or archons), the text as a whole is built upon the backward counting of years (see chap. 1, sect. 4 above). Scholarship has thus far focused on the denotational function of time references—that is, on the dates of events and their historical plausibility. Time, however, emerges as a theme of its own and, as such, has connotational functions too. Through an examination of time units, spans between events, and the ensuing time patterns, this chapter explores the social and cultural meaning of time in the Parian Marble.

1. Perceptions of Time

Creation of chronicles is based on the assumption that the continuum of time can be divided into discrete units that can thus be counted. What units are used for dividing and reckoning time in the Parian Marble, and what perceptions of time do they imply?

Years are the main unit for computing time in the Parian Marble, as in many ancient Mediterranean chronicles.[1] Events are dated by intervals with other events, which are expressed in numbers of years. Given the dating by Athenian kings and archons, the year must have been defined by the Athenian calendar, beginning when the annual archon assumed office, on the first of Hecatombaeum, with the new moon after the Summer solstice.[2] Such dependence on Athenian time has much to do with the sources used for the Parian

---

[1] Even regnal periods (see n. 7 below), the basic unit for reckoning time in ancient Mediterranean chronicles, count years (see Renger 2012 and Burgess and Kulikowski 2013:63-98 for useful summaries and further references). Olympic victor lists use the four-year cycle as basic time unit, noting each individual year within the cycle.

[2] On the Athenian calendar, see Samuel 1972, Hannah 2005:42–55, Clarke 2008:47–56, Stern 2012:25–70. Because the first Hecatombaeum fell during the Greek Summer (July), the BCE

Marble, more specifically, with the traditions of Athenian local historiography.[3] The Parian Marble is not unique in this respect; Apollodorus's use of Athenian archons for a chronicle of panhellenic scope is perhaps the most remarkable example.[4] Still, closing each individual entry with a reference to Athens contributes to making time Athenian, so to speak.[5] I shall return to this point at the end of this section.

Years imply calendars with months and days recurring in cycles. But in the Parian Marble, in contrast to calendars, years are distinctly identified. Such identification is achieved in the Parian Marble by two devices, year numbers and eponymous magistrates. The singularity of years as time units, along with the backward counting of time, suggests a metaphorical direction of time, and even an end to it. Time is linear, and it retreats towards year 1, a feature the Parian Marble shares only with the count-down chronicles discussed in Chapter 3. Without the final section of the inscription, we have no indication whether the end of a period has been reached, whether a new era is beginning, and perhaps more importantly, whether the decreasing numbers carry teleological implications.[6]

In addition to the counting of years, the inscription mentions or implies other modalities of time reckoning, the most prominent of which are regnal years.[7] Regnal periods are larger time units than individual years. Length of years is relatively constant, even with the addition of intercalary months,[8] whereas the span of regnal periods is necessarily contingent and unpredictable. In the Parian Marble up to A32, events are dated by reference to Athenian kings.[9] However, those references are not precise (e.g. "in the tenth year of Amphyction") but general ("when Amphyction was king of Athens"). As a result, events are recorded during the reigns of Amphyction (A5 to A8) and Erechtheus (A12 to A14), without noting the

---

equivalents are usually rendered with two numbers, thus the year 300/1 BCE refers to a year beginning in mid-300 BCE and ending in mid-301 BCE.

[3] Jacoby 1904b:88–91. Clarke's notion of "borrowed time," the use of local systems for panhellenic time reckoning, helps account for the usage of the Athenian chronological framework in an inscription set for a Parian audience (Clarke 2008:213–220; see chap. 1, sect. 4 above).

[4] In spite of Apollodorus's following of Eratosthenes, who used Olympiads.

[5] Rosenberger 2008:226–228.

[6] On linear vs. cyclic notions of time in ancient Greek historiography, see Momigliano 1966, Möller and Luraghi 1995:6–7.

[7] King lists are the most common form of time reckoning in Near Eastern chronography. See Renger 2012, sect. 3.1 for kings as a chronographic device in Near Eastern and Mesopotamian chronology and Clarke 2008:204–208 for regnal time in ancient Greek chronography. Eusebius' chronographic work was based on a broad range of ancient king lists (Burgess 2002:18–19 sums up those appearing in Jerome's translation of the *Canons*).

[8] That is, additions made for adjusting the year, built upon lunar months, with the solar year (see Hannah 2005:30–40).

[9] Jacoby (1902) published a reconstruction of the Athenian king list before concluding his work on the Parian Marble.

year within the reign. Such lack of specification is the rule, except for three events: the beginning of the Trojan War, dated to the thirteenth year of Menestheus (A23), the fall of Troy, dated to the twenty-third of Thargelion, in Menestheus's twenty-second year (A24), and the foundation of Syracuse, during the twenty-first year of Aeschylus (A31). Stating the number of generations or kings between Archias, the founder, and Temenus, one of Heracles's descendants, allows for the establishment of a connection with the return of the Heraclids (Macedonian claims may be alluded to, as well). These events, the Trojan War, the fall of Troy, and the return of the Heraclids are paramount temporal markers in ancient Greek historiography and chronography.[10] It seems that the author of the Parian Marble marked precise regnal years only for those major events that would allow for synchronisms with other chronological systems.[11]

Additional units of time larger than years are alluded to in A30 and A31, where Pheidon is said to be eleventh from Heracles and Archias, tenth from Temenus.[12] Indeed, generations lay behind royal succession. Well known as time reckoning devices in oral traditions,[13] generations were often used in ancient Greek historiography.[14] The references to Pheidon and Archias, probably stemming from local historiographical works, provide synchronisms with other significant chronological markers: Heracles and the Heraclids. The use of regnal years and generations for time reckoning implies a perception of time measured by human life.[15] References to the number of years lived by poets and philosophers display the same quality. Indeed, the formulaic "having lived" appears when noting the death of Simonides (A57), Aeschylus (A59), Sophocles (A64), Socrates (A66), Philoxenus (A69), Aristotle (B11), and Sosiphanes (B15). Age at death, whether derived from transmitted *vitae* or as a result of chronological computation (see chap. 6 below), conveys the notion of biographical time. To a biographical, perhaps even dynastic, perception of time belongs the reference to Ptolemy Philadelphos's birth (B19),[16] whereas the reference to the publication of Callippus's Astrology (B6) probably implies a supra-human unit of time: the cycle of 76 years that Callippus postulated for aligning the lunar calendar with

---

[10] Cf. Eratosthenes FGrH 241 F 1a (Clement *Stromateis* I 138, 1–3). See also Möller 2005, Clarke 2008:67–68, 144–147 , Burgess 2002:20–21 (Jerome's *Chronicle*).

[11] The regnal year in A27 is most probably a mistaken repetition from A23 (see note to Greek text). However, if the original entry included a regnal year number, the precision would serve the same purpose as the fall of Troy and the return of the Heraclids, since the Ionian foundation is an important chronological marker (Clarke 2008:211).

[12] See notes to Greek text.

[13] On measuring time in oral history, see Vansina 1965:100–102.

[14] Clarke 2008:195–203, with further references.

[15] Clarke 2008:204–208.

[16] The Parian Marble dates the birth of two historical figures, Euripides (A50) and Ptolemy II (B19).

the solar year.[17] The Callippean cycle is the result of observation and computation, thus a scientific construct, measured by the stars rather than by human life.

Only once do time units shorter than years appear in the inscription: a day and a month, the twenty-third (or seventh from the end) of Thargelion. The fall of Troy is the event dated with the highest resolution in the whole inscription, to the very day on which it occurred. That precision must be due to the major role played by the event as a chronological milestone, and is likewise found in other sources.[18] What source the Parian Marble follows is unclear, but dating the fall of Troy by the Athenian calendar was by no means unusual.[19] Similarly, references to poetic victories at competitive festivals imply the use of the Athenian sacred calendar.

Years and months as time units are ultimately based on natural phenomena. Seasons, the clearest sign of time passing other than day and night, are also alluded to in the inscription. Indeed, Athenian festivals, as well as the Eleusinian ploughing festival (probably mentioned in A12), were seasonal. Yet, months, seasons, and festivals, in their recurring cycles, are not instrumental for time reckoning in the Parian Marble. Nor are natural events, even though the inscription records a few: a flood (A4), Aetna's eruption (A52), a meteor (A57), a fire in Delphi's temple (A71, partly restored), an eclipse (B16), an earthquake (B24, partly restored), and a comet (B25, partly restored). Time is neither natural nor cosmic in the Parian Marble. It is not counted "from the beginning," that is, from the beginning of human life, from the first Athenians, from the origins of Athens itself, or from creation, as is the case in Christian chronicles.[20] The Parian Marble begins with Cecrops, taken as Athens's first king,[21] although the reference to Actaeus implies the existence of an earlier king (traditions regarding the first Athenian kings were diverse). If the information stems from Athenian local historiography, as does much of Apollodorus's account of the origins of Athens in *Library* 3.14, notions of cosmogonic beginnings are avoided, and autochthony emerges only from the qualification of Actaeus as "born from the earth" (A1).

In sum, the year is the basic time unit of the Parian Marble. Still, other longer or shorter units of time are mentioned or implied: regnal years, generations, the

---

[17] While the Parian Marble dates Callippus' *Astrology* to 330/329 BCE (B6), ancient astronomical sources allow for establishing the beginning of the first Callippean period in the summer solstice of 330 BCE (Fotheringham 1924:388, Goldstein and Bowen 1989, Jones 2000). The reference to Callippus's *Astrology* (B6) and to the beginning of the annual archonship in Athens (A32) are two instances of meta-chronographic references in the Parian Marble.

[18] Jacoby 1904a:146–149; cf. Burkert 1995, Clarke 2008:58.

[19] Cf. Hellanicus FGrH 323a F 21b, Lysimachus of Alexandria FGrH 382 F 13.

[20] Burgess and Kulikowski 2013:35–36, Clarke 2008:84–85 (Syncellus).

[21] Similarly, Apollodorus 3.141 and Jerome *Chronicle* 41b Helm (Philochorus may be his source, cf. 49g, l).

astrological Callippean cycle, the day, the month, seasons, the length of human life, all of which belong to different modalities of time reckoning. Time thus appears in the Parian Marble not only as a countable and divisible entity, but also as susceptible of multiple and often simultaneous forms of parcellation.[22] Furthermore, given that division and computation are for the most part dependent on the institutions of Greek cities (i.e. calendars and eponymous magistrates), time appears not only as a social cultural construct, but as a political one.[23] The dating formula's reference to Athenian archons suggests a connection with Athens, even for events that occurred elsewhere in the Mediterranean and the Near East. Colonized, so to speak, by Hellenic history, time is nonetheless marked as Athenian, even though the focus shifts from Athens to Macedonia and, later on, to Ptolemaic Egypt. Given the geographical and political span of events in the inscription, time may be termed universal, as the chronicle often is,[24] but such a use of the term is ethnocentric. When compared to other (admittedly late) chronicles, which combine a Hellenic framework with Egyptian and Macedonian kings (e.g. Porphyry of Tyre), or to other Near Eastern kingdoms (e.g. Castor of Rhodes) or to Biblical history (e.g. Eusebius)—even Roman history (e.g. Dionysius of Halicarnassus)—the Parian Marble does not seem universal, in the sense of multicultural; it does not offer global or world history.[25] Events outside the Greek-speaking world are dated for their impact on the Greek world.[26] Time is counted from within, often from an Athenian point of view. But if the hypothesis that the Parian Marble marks the beginning of a new era is accepted (see chap. 1, sect. 4 above), time would appear as a Ptolemaic appropriation. This is consistent with Ptolemy Philadelphos's interest in Egyptian chronography,[27]

---

[22] This is probably true of most of the ancient Greek chronographic tradition.

[23] A feature of most ancient Greek chronography (Clarke 2008:69–70) and time keeping through city calendars (Stern 2012:29–31). Conversely, the appropriation of time imagery for explaining political organization appears most clearly in Aristotle *Constitution of the Athenians* fr. 5 (Lexicon Patmense p. 152 Sakkel): four tribes at the number of seasons, twelve subdivisions as the number of months, thirty clans as the numbers of days of the month.

[24] E.g. Jacoby's FGrH 239 (commentary):666, Guarducci 1974:83. Clarke 2008:66n51 notes the lack of universal pretensions in the Parian Marble.

[25] Rome is missing from the extant inscription of the Parian Marble (cf. the reference to the Gauls' sack of Rome in 390/387 BCE in the Roman Chronicle, which has two parallel historical axes, Greek and Roman; chap. 3, sect. 2 above).

[26] This reinforces the impression that the intended chronicle was written not for professional chronographers, or even for historians, but for readers with a panhellenic frame of reference.

[27] The possibility of Ptolemaic patronage for Manetho's work on Egyptian chronography emerges from "Manetho" T 11a + F 25, T 12, which, according to Murray (1972:209n2), may reflect the attitude of the genuine works. I thank Jennifer Gates-Foster for suggesting possible connections between the chronographic project of Manetho with the Parian Marble and Ptolemaic ideology.

and his parading of personifications of time in the Grand Procession, in the figures of the Year and the Seasons.[28]

In sum, natural and cosmic time is superseded in the Parian Marble by historiographical and political time. Through the predictable cycles of time, the Parian Marble offers an account of the contingent occurrences of Hellenic history, in which time is construed simultaneously as Ptolemaic, Athenian, and panhellenic.

2. Proto-history in the Parian Marble

A striking feature of the chronicle, at least to the contemporary eye, is that it gives precise dates not only for historical events, but also for what we would consider mythical ones. As a result, figures such as Theseus, Heracles, and the Amazons have a status similar to that of Alexander or Ptolemy. In this, however, the Parian Marble is not exceptional. Historiographical projects of both local and universal scope usually began in legendary times,[29] as did Near Eastern chronicles.[30] Nonetheless, ancient Greek historians and chronographers held definite views about the beginning of *computable* time, the so-called *spatium historicum*.[31] For some, it was the fall of Troy, whenever dated.[32] For others, the return of the Heraclids or the foundation of the Olympic games.[33] The times before those chronological milestones could be termed legendary or mythical, but such terms imply a distinction between facts (history) and non-facts (myth or legend). However, for the ancients the difference seems to have been epistemological rather than ontological. A statement by Varro (fr. 3 = Censorinus *De die natali* 21) offers an alternative to binary thinking that focuses on the very ability of knowing the past, by distinguishing periods as obscure (*adelon*), mythical (*mythicon*), and historical (*historicon*).[34] It seems therefore preferable to adopt

---

[28] The procession opened with the Morning Star and closed with the Evening star (Athenaeus 197d). Between two groups of satyrs, a man called Eniautos ("Year") paraded, followed by a woman called Penteteris ('Four-year-cycle") and four Horai ("Seasons"). The procession was described by Callixenus of Rhodes (FGrH 627 F 2 = Athenaeus 198a–b); cf. Rice 1983:50–51, Clarke 2008:167.

[29] Clarke 2008:98–106.

[30] Burkert 1995:140, Burgess and Kulikowski 2013:63–98.

[31] Leyden 1949–1950.

[32] On the controversies surrounding the date of the fall of Troy, Burkert 1995 and Möller 2005:248–249 are insightful.

[33] For the traditions about the origins of the Olympic games, see Christesen 2007:18–21, Möller 2004.

[34] "Hic enim tria discrimina temporum esse tradit: primum ab hominum principio ad cataclysmum priorem, quod propter ignorantiam vocatur adelon, secundum a cataclysmo priore ad olympiadem primam, quod, quia multa in eo fabulosa referuntur, mythicon nominatur, tertium a prima olympiade ad nos, quod dicitur historicon, quia res in eo gestae veris historiis continentur." See

the term "proto-history" for times earlier than computable time (avoiding the implications of "pre-history").

In the manner of local and panhellenic historians, the Parian Marble dates time before proper computable time, covering proto-historical times too. A couple of markers may be understood as conveying a distinction between them. The first marker may be found in the level of resolution for dating the fall of Troy:

> A24. From the time Troy was conquered, 945 years (= 1209/8 BCE), when [Menesthe]us was king of Athens, in his ⟨twenty⟩ second year, in the month of Th[argeli]on, in the seventh day, (counting) from the end of the month.

The fall of Troy, the only event dated by the day, month, and regnal year, stands out as a marker of division between the times before and after.[35] The level of detail not only conveys the outstanding chronographic role of the event, but may also mark it as a watershed.[36] The layout of the inscription may further support the notion of a distinction between "history" and "proto-history." Indeed, in Selden's transcription there is a space equivalent to four or five letters between the fall of Troy in A24 and the following text, similar to the space between the introduction and A1. We know about these spaces only from Selden, notorious for his lack of accuracy (see introduction to chap. 2). However, since the transcriptions he published in 1628 show no other instances of blank spaces, Selden's report may well be trustworthy. As I have noted earlier (chap. 2, sect. 1 above), Selden did not use dots as representing exact numbers of letters, so the precise length of the space is unknown. If indeed the layout was part of the inscription's original intent, blank spaces may have been left as sense-divisions at significant points.[37] While space left between the introduction and the first entry (and presumably between the last entry and the concluding section too) would mark a structural division, the space left after the fall of Troy would mark a division in the stream of years—that is, a chronographic division.

Marincola 1997:117-127. For a distinction of historical stages in Herodotus (3.122.2, 1.5.3, 7.20), see Shimron 1973 (I am grateful to Rachel Zelnick-Abramovitz for the reference).

[35] The proximity of the four entries bearing specific dating suggests that they may all derive from the same source.

[36] A similar level of resolution with a similar role is found in Syncellus *Chronography* 1, where the resurrection is dated according to Hebrew, Greek, and Egyptian systems, to the day and month (Clarke 2008:84).

[37] On the use of uninscribed spaces as punctuation marks in inscriptions, see Dow 1936:62–66, Henry 1977:63–70 (third-century BCE decrees), Threatte 1980:83.

3. Patterns of Time

Time, as a mathematical entity, is homogeneous; not, however, in social memory, for which there are eventful and uneventful periods.[38] How are patterns of time construed in the Parian Marble?[39]

The extant text of the Parian Marble includes 107 entries (80 in A, 27 in B). For recording the first 900 years, until the beginning of the Athenian archonship, 32 entries suffice (28 years per entry on average). The rhythm grows faster from the seventh century BCE on. Indeed, 18 entries cover the 203-year period between the beginning of the Athenian archonship and Xerxes's invasion (from A32 to A51, 11 years per entry), 15 entries cover the period of approximately 74 years between Xerxes and Cyrus (from A51 to A64, 5 years per entry), 15 entries cover the last 49 years of section A (from A65 to A80, 3 years per entry), and 27 entries cover the 37 years of section B (1.4 years per entry). Thus, the closer the inscription approaches present time, the more information it contains. However, the dates of the early years are much more detailed than the times between the Trojan War and the Ionic immigration. Jacoby counts one entry for every 14.3 years from the beginning up to the Trojan War, but one entry for every 105 years for the following period.[40] The focus on the earliest periods and the nearest past coincides with the so-called "hour-glass" effect typical of oral traditions, where genealogies tend to emphasize the very early foundational times and the more recent past.[41] It is also similar to the pattern of commemoration in the modern nation state, which, as Zerubavel has shown, tends to focus on the very distant past and the last two hundred years.[42] Things are completely different in cultural history. In the preserved inscription, the period of the fifth and first half of the fourth centuries shows more information on poets and musicians. That distribution confirms what we already know: the Greek memory about cultural achievements tends to favor the "classical" period.[43] Memory, however, is not only about remembering but also about forgetting —omissions are revealing.[44]

---

[38] As Eviatar Zerubavel (2003:25–34) has shown in his inspiring book "Time Maps."
[39] Zerubavel 2003 uses the metaphor "topography of the past."
[40] Jacoby FGrH 239 (commentary):666.
[41] Henige 1974 (cf. Thomas 2001 for the application of the concept to Herodotus). Rosenberger 2008:226 distinguishes between two floating gaps in the Parian Marble. The first one would cover the last 80 years of the inscription, which would explain the high frequency of entries in early times. The second floating gap, the one Rosenberg considers the original one of Greek cultural memory, would have been "frozen" around 600 BCE.
[42] Zerubavel 2003:31.
[43] Jacoby FGrH 239 (commentary):667.
[44] As Jacoby noted, the period 477/6-370/69 contains more people and events pertaining to literary or cultural history than to general or political history (see Jacoby's table below, chap. 6, n. 22).

From the expulsion of the Pisistratids in A45 until the broken end of the inscription in A80, twenty-three references to poets appear, all but one (Epicharmus) connected to Athens, but only three Athenian political and military events are mentioned: the battles of Marathon and Plataea (A48 and A52) and the setting of statues in honor of Harmodius and Aristogeiton (A54). In contrast, that same period has four entries for Persian affairs (A49, A51, A66, A77), four entries for Sicilian affairs (A53, A55, A62, A74), and four for Macedonian affairs (A58, A61, A74, A77), as well as references to the battles of Thermopylae (A51), Plataea (A52), and Leuctra (A72 suppl.) and to two natural events (eruption of Aetna, A52, meteor in Aegospotami, A57). Hence, in thirty-five entries there are twenty-two references to poets active in Athens, but only three to other Athenian events, whereas seventeen events are mentioned from outside Athens (Persia, Sicily, and Macedonia). Thus, the view of Athenian cultural achievement in the classical period is accompanied by a void in the political realm. The period is markedly Athenian from the point of view of cultural history. As for general history, the focus is multiple and much broader.

In sum, the Parian Marble displays two different patterns of time. General history follows the pattern of social memory both in oral traditions and in the modern nation-state, focusing on beginnings as well as on the recent past. In contrast, literary history focuses on the so-called classical period.[45] The narrative pattern of general history may be described as "serial rise and fall," whereas literary history appears to have peaked only once: in classical Athens.

---

[45] The focus on the classical period corresponds to Zerubavel's "rise-and-fall" type of historical narrative (2003:18–20).

Chapter 6
Literary History in the Parian Marble

Biographies of ancient Greek poets and musicians frequently rely on informa-tion found in the Parian Marble.[1] The inscription is held as a reference point, even when the validity of dates is called into question.[2] Yet inquiry into how biographical details were attained rarely goes beyond matters of chronology and source criticism. In this chapter I shall explore the methods and attitudes that the Parian Marble shares with ancient Greek traditions of thinking about the literary past. I begin by discussing the nature of literary history in ancient Greece, and the extent to which it is of primary interest in the Parian Marble.

1. The Parian Marble as Literary History

Literary history as a discipline studies past processes and events related to the production, performance and reception of literature. It examines materials and contents (texts in both their oral and literate dimensions), agents (composers, writers, performers, sponsors, audiences, judges, readers, and interpreters), and institutions (occasions of performance, schools, libraries, etc.). In ancient Greece, literary history was not an intellectual discipline in its own right, but reflection on the literary past is attested from early times.[3]

Before the fourth century BCE, matters of literary history, including refer-ences to both poets and musicians, appear embedded in works of historians, such

---

[1] Known only from the Parian Marble are the poets Hypodicus of Chalcis (A46), Simonides the elder (A49), Stesichorus the second (A73), and the younger Sosiphanes (B22).

[2] Most notably, the Parian Marble serves as a reference point in reconstructing the chronology of dramatic Athenian contests (Capps 1900, Wilhelm and Kaibel 1906, Reisch 1907, Mette 1977, and, more recently, Millis and Olson 2012).

[3] Much of the evidence for ancient Greek literary history has been studied within the context of the history of ancient scholarship (Arrighetti 1987, Lomiento 2001, Pfeiffer 1968, Lanata 1963, Podlecki 1969, Blum 1991, Richardson 1994, Montanari 1993, Schenkeveld et al. 1995) and ancient biographies of poets (Graziosi 2002, Nagy 2009, Beecroft 2010, Kivilo 2010, Koning 2010, Lefkowitz 2012 [first edition: 1981]). For recent historiographical approaches to ancient Greek music, see Franklin 2010, Power 2010, and Barker 2014, published after completion of this book.

as Pherecydes, Hellanicus,[4] and Herodotus, as well as sophists, such as Theagenes of Rhegium and Hippias of Elis. Evidence is fragmentary and atomistic, often incidental, and always focused on famous individuals, rarely attaining abstraction and generalization through reflection on genres, periods, or styles. Main centers of interest were the genealogy of poets, their relative chronology, and first inventions.[5] In the last half of the fifth century BCE,[6] when issues of literary history were staged in Athenian comedies (Cratinus's *Archilochuses*, 450/449 BCE, and Aristophanes's *Frogs*, 405 BCE), questions of style (and perhaps of ideological stance too) seem to have prevailed over issues of chronology or development. Literary history fully emerged in the transition to the fourth century BCE, gaining independence from general historiography, especially in the works of Aristotle[7] and his school.[8] The lists of victors at the Pythian games compiled by Aristotle and Callisthenes[9] and the *Dionysiac Victories*, on Athenian Tragedy, Comedy, and Dithyramb,[10] both probably based on archival work, provided a chronographic grid, essential to historical research on poetry.[11] Of narrative nature were the monographs on poets, written by Glaucus of Rhegium, a precursor in the field,[12] as

---

[4]   Hellanicus's list of victors at the Carneian festival provided a framework for dating early poets and musicians (FGrH 4 F 85a = Athenaeus 635e; FGrH 4 F 86 = scholia V to Aristophanes *Birds* 1403). Some scholars believe it may have offered further information on the musical history of Greece (Ambaglio 1980:38–39, Möller 2001:245–246, *contra* Blum 1991:19). On Hellanicus's role in the historiography of music and his work on the Carneian Victors, see Franklin 2010:17–23. Franklin 2012 argues that Hellanicus focused on the Lesbian singers at the Carneia.

[5]   On Hippias's and Critias's concerns with matters of poetic history, see Lanata 1963:208–213, 218–223.

[6]   Ford 2002:139–146.

[7]   As I argue elsewhere (Rotstein 2007 and 2010:74–88), chapters 4 and 5 of the *Poetics* combine two different approaches to the history of poetry: one empirical or inductive, based on information partly available from public records, the other theoretical or deductive, based on perceived analogies between genres.

[8]   See Blum 1991:47–52 for the contribution of the so-called school of Aristotle to literary history.

[9]   Πυθιονικῶν ἀναγραφή (SIG³ 275 = FGrH 124 T 23; for a study of testimonies, see Hose 2002:108–109, 266–269), inscribed in 331 BCE. Cf. Diogenes Laertius's reference to a book entitled Πυθιονῖκαι μουσικῆς (5.1.26, we should disregard the common correction Πυθιονῖκαι ⟨α′ Περὶ⟩ μουσικῆς α′; the book was an incomplete catalogue or a summary, according to Homolle 1898:267). The inscription perhaps included legendary material (Gostoli 1986, Wilson 2004:270–271, Franklin 2013:221n43). On the role of these lists in ancient literary history, see Blum 1991:23.

[10] Νῖκαι Διονυσιακαί and Διδασκαλίαι may have used the same state archives as the so-called Fasti (IG II.2 2318), Didascaliae (IG II.2 2319–23a) and Victor list (IG II.2 2325), recently edited by Millis and Olson 2012 (for a study of testimonies, see Hose 2002:110–113, 270–280). On the Athenian didascalic records, see Sickinger 1999:41–47, with further references. The precise relationship between these catalogues and Aristotle's lists is a matter of dispute (cf. Blum 1991:24–43).

[11] Little is known about the Sikyon inscription (FGrH 550; cf. Chaniotis 1988:89–91), used by Heraclides of Pontus and known to us exclusively through [Plutarch] *On Music* 1131f–1132a.

[12] Towards the end of the fifth century BCE, Glaucus of Rhegium wrote a book "On Ancient Poets and Musicians" ([Plutarch] *On Music* 1132–1133; Glaucus's fragments are collected in FHG 2.23–24; see Lanata 1963:270–281, Huxley 1968, and more recently Franklin 2010:23–29). The peripatetic

well as by Aristotle, Phainias of Eresus, and Demetrius of Phalerum. Similar works on individual poets (or poets per genre, e.g. Lysanias of Cyrene's *On the Iambic Poets*) were written by Heraclides of Pontus, Chamaeleon of Heracleia, and the Epicurean Metrodorus of Lampsacus.[13] Judging from surviving fragments, those monographs added an interest in biographical detail, with a special inclination for anecdotes and aetiological explanation, to the common genealogical, chronological, and heurematic outlook. However, by the time these monographs were written a body of biographical interpretation had already conflated with local traditions, thanks to the well-known tendencies of extrapolating from poetic works biographical details, and explaining texts by details of their authors' biographies.[14]

Literary history is very prominent in the Parian Marble, as has long been noted.[15] However, its uniqueness in this respect among ancient chronographic material has not been fully appreciated. Literary history is entirely unprecedented in ancient Mesopotamian chronicles[16] and appears in the ancient Greek chronographers sparsely. The verse chronicle of Apollodorus (FGrH 244 F 1–61), written in the second century BCE, included some intellectual history, but the extant fragments focus particularly on philosophers[17] (Diogenes Laertius, the main intermediary, may be responsible for somewhat distorting the picture).[18]

---

scholars Phainias of Eresus (ca. 375–300 BCE, Wehrli 9:9–43) and Demetrius of Phalerum (ca. 360–280 BCE, FGrH 228, Fortenbaugh and Schütrumpf 2000) are credited with works *On Poets*. Little remains from Aristotle's book *On Poets* (fragments are collected by Rose 1967 frr. 70–75 and Breitenberger 2006:293–298, with commentary on pp. 332–346).

13   The two books of *On the Iambic Poets* by the third-century BCE Lysanias of Cyrene (Athenaeus 620c) are lost. The peripatetic Heraclides of Pontus (ca. 390–322 BCE, Wehrli 7, Schütrumpf 2008; see also Barker 2009 for musical history) and Chamaeleon of Heracleia (ca. 350–281 BCE, Wehrli 9:49–88, Martano, Matelli, and Mirhady 2012; and see Arrighetti 1987:141–159) wrote biographies on a number of poets. The fragments of the Epicurean Metrodorus of Lampsacus (ca. 331–278 BCE) are collected by Körte 1890.

14   One of the main difficulties in the study of ancient Greek literary history is the fact that aetiological explanations may have been responsible for much of the relevant information (see Arrighetti 1987:141–228, Martano, Matelli, and Mirhady 2012:426–430, for the so-called Method of Chamaeleon). The ancients did not distinguish the discipline of literary criticism from that of literary history. Ancient critics often employed seemingly historical arguments as explanatory tools. Such explanations may not indicate *how things really were*, but they certainly show how literary history was perceived (cf. Rotstein 2016). Graziosi 2002, Nagy 2009, Kivilo 2010, Koning 2010, and Lefkowitz 2012 (a precursor, originally published in 1981) are useful for assessing ancient biographies of poets with such distinctions in mind.

15   E.g. Dopp 1883:5. Katherine Clarke (2008:226–277) eloquently sums up the general impression: "The Parian Marble offers the most stunning demonstration of how the inscribed past, measured out primarily in terms of political power—first kings and then archons—could be heavily punctuated also by the history of invention and that of intellectual or literary prowess."

16   I have examined Grayson 1975 as well as Glassner and Foster 2004 (I am grateful to Matt Waters for the references).

17   Apollodorus's *Chronicle* mentions nineteen philosophers, ten poets, four historians, two doctors and two of the Seven Sages.

18   Clarke 2008:71–72. Wiseman (1979:158) considers Apollodorus's inclusion of philosophers and literary figures a "characteristically Hellenistic addition."

Thus, reference to ancient intellectuals (poets, philosophers, historians, and orators),[19] as Diodorus's occasional closing of a year's account by reference to cultural figures indicates,[20] seems to characterize the Hellenistic approach to chronography.[21] And yet, the Parian Marble is extraordinary in two respects. First, it displays a high number of cultural figures and events, in relation to political and military ones. Indeed, the inscription mentions fifty-six figures and events from the cultural field (twenty-nine percent), sixty-nine from the political field (thirty-six percent), forty-eight military events (twenty-five percent) and eighteen religious events (ten percent; distribution is discussed in detail in chap. 4, sect. 2).[22]

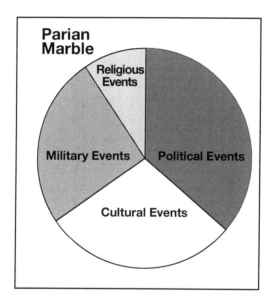

A second outstanding feature of the Parian Marble is that cultural figures and events belong almost exclusively to the fields of poetry, music, and drama.

---

[19] For the concept of "intellectual," see Zanker 1995:2.

[20] Diodorus 9.28.1: Aesop and the Seven Sages; 11.26.8: Pindar's *acme*; 13.103.4: Sophocles' death (age: 90); 13.103.5: Euripides' death (citing Apollodorus); 14.46.6: dithyrambic poets (see n. 166 below). For Diodorus' interest in intellectuals and literary figures, especially historians, and the possibility that they functioned as "chronological articulators" of his universal history, see Clarke 1999; cf. Clarke 2008:227n259.

[21] Clarke 2008:70.

[22] Jacoby's table provides an illuminating starting point (Jacoby FGrH 239 [commentary]:667):

Lines	Years BCE	Facts	
A 34–53	644/3 – 478/7	14 political	12 literary
A 54–73	477/6 – 370/69	11 political	18 literary
B 1–20	336/5 – 308/7	48 political	5 literary.

Indeed, the majority of cultural figures mentioned are poets and musicians, thirty-one in total:[23]

Hyagnis of Phrygia	(A10)
Orpheus	(supplemented in A14)
Mousaeus	(A15)
Hesiod	(A28)
Homer	(A29)
Terpander of Lesbos	(A34)
Sappho	(A36)
Susarion	(A39)
Hipponax	(A42)
Thespis	(A43)
Hypodicus of Chalcis	(A46)
Melanippides of Melos	(A47)
Aeschylus	(A48, A50, A59)
Simonides the elder	(A49)
Euripides	(A50, A60, A63)
Stesichorus	(A50)
Simonides of Ceos	(A54, A57)
Epicharmus	(A55)
Sophocles of Colonos	(A56, A64)
Telestes of Selinus	(A65)
Aristonous	(A67, partly restored)
Polyidus of Selymbria	(A68)
Philoxenus	(A69)
Anaxandrides	(A70)
Astydamas	(A71)
Stesichorus of Himera, the second	(A73)
Timotheus	(A76)
Philemon	(B7)

---

[23] I include Orpheus (A14) but neither Archilochus (Baumgarten, A33) nor Alexis (Capps, A78; see note to the Greek text of A78). I give poets' birthplaces only when the Parian Marble mentions them (as adjectives, e.g. Ύαγνις ὁ Φρύξ, A10). Three poets are given patronyms: Terpander (A34), Simonides of Ceos (A54), and Sophocles (A56). Qualified as "the poet" are Hesiod (A28), Homer (A29), Thespis (A43), Aeschylus, Simonides the elder ("being a poet himself"), Euripides (A50), Stesichorus (A50), Simonides (A57), Epicharmus (A55), Sophocles (A64), Sosiphanes I (only "poet," B15), Sosiphanes II (B22). Additional specifications have Hipponax, "the iambic poet" (ὁ ἰαμβοποιός, A42), Philoxenus, "dithyrambic poet" (διθυραμβοποιός, A69), Anaxandrides, Philemon, and Menander, each qualified as "the comedy poet" (ὁ κωμοιδοποιός (*sic*), A70, B7, B14). Poets from the West or connected to Sicily or Syracuse: Sappho, Stesichorus, Epicharmus, Telestes, Stesichorus the second, Philemon, and Sosiphanes I.

Menander	(B14)
Sosiphanes I	(B15)
Sosiphanes II	(B22)[24]

In contrast, only four intellectuals from other fields are named:[25]

Socrates	(A60, A66)
Anaxagoras	(A60)
Callippus	(B6)
Aristotle	(B11)

Other ancient chronological lists contrast sharply with the Parian Marble. The following examples, representative of chronological materials on stone and papyrus and of those known through indirect transmission, will clarify the tendency of early Greek chronography to record a broader spectrum of fields but many fewer intellectuals.

Let us begin with two epigraphical testimonies, the Roman Chronicle and the Getty Table, the only instances of the count-down chronicle, examined in our treatment of the genre of the Parian Marble (chap. 3).[26]

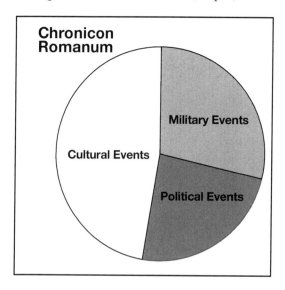

[24] Two tragic poets of similar name, *pace* Munro 1901b:361 (see note to the Greek text of B22). The Roman numbers are mine.
[25] A79 may have included a reference to a philosopher:]ΣΟΦΟΣ, perhaps Plato (Tod 1957:132n2), but Munro 1901b:360 had reservations (see note to Greek text). I do not count Demetrius of Phalerum, supplemented by Jacoby and others in B20.
[26] IG XIV 1297 = FGrH 252; after 15/16 CE. See chap. 3, sect. 2, for text, translation, bibliography, and further comparison with the Parian Marble.

Column B of the Roman Chronicle, covering 200 years of Greek history (from the early sixth century BCE until 385/4 BCE) in twelve entries and twenty-eight lines, mentions ten figures and events from the cultural field (forty-eight percent), five from the political field (twenty-four percent), six military events (twenty-eight percent).[27]

Cultural figures include:[28]

Anacharsis	(B, line 4)
the Wise Men	(B, line 7)
Aesop	(B, line 9)
Pythagoras	(B, line 13)
Socrates	(B, line 22)
Heraclitus	(B, line 23)
Anaxagoras	(B, line 23)
Parmenides	(B, line 24)
Zenon	(B, line 24)
Thucydides	(B, line 26)

Thus, the Roman Chronicle has a high proportion of cultural figures and events, but mostly from the field of Philosophy (seven out of ten),[29] whereas the Getty Table (II B)[30] includes an equal number of philosophers (three) and poets (three):[31]

the Wise Men	(II B, line 6 suppl.)
Chilon	(II B, line 7)
Aesop	(II B, line 9)
Simonides	(II B, line 16)
Anaximander	(II B, line 17)
Anacreon	(II B, line 21)
Ibycus	(II B, line 22)
Pythagoras	(II B, line 25)
Xenophanes	(II B, line 30)

---

[27] The extant text mentions no religious events. Among the political and military figures in the Roman Chronicle are Solon, Croesus (twice), Pisistratus, Cyrus, Cambyses, Harmodius and Aristogeiton, Hipparchus, Darius, Xerxes, and Themistocles.

[28] Solon is mentioned as archon and lawgiver, not as a poet (B, line 2).

[29] Cf. Tod 1957:32 (note, however, that Terpander is not the only representative of music in the Parian Marble, as Tod suggests).

[30] SEG 33 802. See chap. 3, sect. 2 for text, translation, and further comparison with the Parian Marble.

[31] Xenophanes is counted among philosophers. The extant text mentions no religious events. Among the political and military figures in the Getty Table are Phalaris, Pisistratus (line 7 suppl.), Croesus, Cyrus (three times), Cambyses (twice), Darius, Harmodius and Aristogeiton, and Hipparchus.

If these two miniature chronicles were located originally in libraries (see chap. 3), perhaps the content of the book collections influenced the emphasis of each tabula.

Let us now turn to a papyrus text known as the Oxyrhynchus Chronicle (Chronicon Oxyrhynchi),[32] an Olympic victor list with historical notices covering the period 355–315 in ten Olympiads. It was written in the first half of the third century CE. Six columns of text have been preserved, approximately thirty-six lines each. In more than 200 lines, we find only three figures from the cultural realm:

Plato	(1, Olympiad 108.1)
Speusippus	(1, Olympiad 108.1)
Isocrates	(2, Olympiad 110.3)

Things are similar in the Olympic victor list compiled by Eusebius of Caesarea in the first quarter of the fourth century CE, which is the most complete of its kind (from the first to the 249th Olympiad) and has reached us through the manuscript tradition.[33] Eusebius' list has few historical notices, among them only two references to cultural events: the first Carneian festival (26th Olympiad), an important event for ancient chronography since Hellanicus' *Carneian Victors*, and Nero's kitharodic victory (211th Olympiad).

It is only in Jerome's *Chronicle* (380/381 CE) that we find a continuous ancient chronographic text where intellectual history features prominently. This Latin work is a translation of Eusebius' *Canons* (*Chronici Canones*), completed by 325 CE.[34] The section of Jerome's *Chronicle* overlapping the thirteen centuries

---

[32] P.Oxy.12 = FGrH 255 (see chap. 3, n. 23). The recently discovered Leipzig Chronicle (P.Lips. 590, 1228, 1229, 1231, 1232, see chap. 3, n. 25) mentions Hesiod and Homer (II, line 17 and 20).

[33] Parisinus Graecus 2600. The extant text is a result of both trimming and expansion (Mosshammer 1979:138, Christesen 2007:248–249). A new edition of the Greek text in Christesen 2007:386–407, Christesen and Martirosova-Torlone 2006 (with English translation). The victor list was part of Eusebius' *Chronographia*. It survives also in a fifth-century Armenian translation (which Christesen and Martirosova-Torlone 2006 used in the constitution of the text).

[34] Eusebius' *Canons* are the second part of his *Chronicle*, the first being the *Chronographia*, of which only an Olympic victor list survived in a Greek manuscript (see note above). Jerome's Latin translation, as well as an Armenian translation, two Syriac epitomes and excerpts from Byzantine chronicles (the Paschal Chronicle, Syncellus and other) have been variously used for reconstructing the Greek original of Eusebius' *Canons* (on the witnesses to Eusebius' *Canons* and the apologetic and revolutionary nature of his work, see Mosshammer 1979:29-83, Burgess 1999:21-27, Christesen and Martirosova-Torlone 2006:34-48, Christesen 2007:232-250, with further references). Considering the difficulties involved in both source and textual criticism, it seems best to approach Jerome's *Chronicle* as a text of its own right. For an introduction to Jerome's *Chronicle* and the use of Helms's 1956 edition, see Burgess 2002. Burgess 1997 examines the dates of Eusebius' editions, Burgess and Kulikowski 2009 set Jerome's work in the context of the Latin chronicle tradition.

of Greek history presented by the Parian Marble mentions 100 intellectuals (they make about twenty-five percent of Jerome's historical notices).[35] Half of them are poets and musicians. Since an Armenian translation and a few Byzantine chronicles attest the vast majority of the references, they may well be considered as representing Eusebius' original. Eusebius, in turn, excerpted earlier chronographic sources, both Greek and Christian, among them Alexander Polyhistor, Castor of Rhodes, Diodorus, Porphyry and Iulius Sextus Africanus; some information may have been derived from Eratosthenes and Apollodorus.[36] It is indeed difficult to determine the stage of the tradition to which Jerome's selection of poets belongs, whether to Eusebius or any of his intermediaries or their sources. Still, albeit a late witness, Jerome's *Chronicle* supports the view that cultural history was conceived as an integral part of chronography in the late antiquity. The scope, however, is broader than that of the Parian Marble. Literary history includes pre-Homeric musicians (9, with Terpander and Aristoxenus for the historical period) and epic poets (8), and we find elegy, iambos and lyric poetry (19) better represented than the dramatic genres (12). Intellectual history is prominent as well, including

---

[35] Fifty poets and musicians (all references are to Helm's 1956 edition): Musicus (42i), Linus (48a, d; 56c), Zethus (48d), Amphion (48d; 53c), Phemonoe (51e), Philammon (55f), Orpheus (56b), Mousaeus (56b), Thamyris (57b), Homer (63d; 66a; 71b; 77c), Archilochus (67a, without parallel in the Greek sources; 94e), Hesiod (71b; 84c; 87f), Arctinus (86l; 87c), Eumelus (87c; 89d), Cinaethon (87g), Hipponax (93c, Greek sources give Archilochus), Simonides (94e; 102k; 103p; 108h), Aristoxenus (94e), Alcman (94i; 98e), Lesches (94i), Terpander (96e), Tyrtaeus (96i), Arion (97k), Stesichorus (98d; 102g), Sappho (99d), Alcaeus (99d), Eugammon (102b), Theognis (103l), Ibycus (103o), Phocylides (103p), Anacreon (104f), Aeschylus (107h; 109g), Pannyasis (108c), Pindar (108h; 109k), Choerilus (109a), Phrynichus (109a), Sophocles (109m, p; 116d), Euripides (109p; 113e; 116d), Bacchylides (110b; 112e; 114h), Diagoras Atheus (110b), Euenus (111f), Cratinus (111l), Plato (the comedy poet, 111l), Aristarchus (the tragedian, 112a), Crates (112e), Telesilla (112e), Eupolis (115d), Aristophanes (115d), Erinna (121g), Menander (125i; 128c).

Fifty intellectuals: Lycurgus (79c; 84f), Zeleucus (94f), Thales (96b; 100f; 103h), Draco (97g), Pittacus (98g), Solon (99g), Anaximander (101g), Aesop (102d), Anaximenes (102f), Chilon (102i), Xenophanes (103d, p: *Xenophanes physicus scriptor tragoediarum*, sic), Pythagoras (104i; 107f), Hellanicus (107e), Democritus (107e; 114d; 117f), Heraclitus (107e; 111e; 111i), Anaxagoras (107e; 111d), Diagoras (109b), Herodotus (110a; 113c), Zeuxis (110c), Socrates (110e; 114e; 118b), Empedocles (111h; 114d), Parmenides (111h; 114d), Zeno (111i; 114d), Pherecydes (111k), Abaris (112g), Melissus (113d), Protagoras (113e), Phidias (113g), Theaetetus (114b), Hippocrates (114d), Gorgias (114d), Hippias (114d), Prodicus (114d), Thucydides (115b), Plato (115g; 118l; 119g; 122c), Eudoxus of Cnidus (115i; 118i), Isocrates (117d; 119f), Xenophon (118a; 119g), Ctesias (118a), Diogenes (118e), Aristotle (120c), Demosthenes (121a, k), Speusippus (122c, h), Xenocrates (122h), Anaximenes (124b), Epicurus (124b), Theophrastus (125k), Demetrius of Phalerum (126a), Menedemus (126c), Theodorus Atheus (127a). In addition, Jerome mentions the Seven Sages (101be), natural philosophers (*physici philosophi*, 109ab), the Socratics (118d; 119g), and a change in the Athenian alphabet (117k).

[36] On the sources of Eusebius' *Canons*, see Mosshammer 1979:128-168, Burgess 1999:79-84, with further references.

philosophers (25), law-givers (3), sages (5), historians (6), sophists (4), orators (2), scientists (3). Even a painter and a sculptor are not missing.

As this brief survey indicates, the Parian Marble is rather idiosyncratic among ancient Greek chronographic materials. While Olympic victor lists, the best represented genre of ancient chronography, contain but few references to cultural figures, they feature prominently in the known examples of the countdown chronicle. Even if the use of cultural figures is typically Hellenistic, as Wiseman suggested, and as the much later *Chronicle* of Jerome may perhaps imply, the unusual prominence of poets and musicians in the Parian Marble suggests that literary history is essential to the text's original intent. An additional feature of the inscription further supports this claim.

As we have seen, by virtue of their synchronization with other people and events, poets and musicians often function as chronological milestones. However, in a number of entries (thirty percent, twelve out of thirty-seven entries) there is no correlation between poets and musicians and other people or events. Such is the case of Terpander (A34), the victories of Melanippides (A47), Telestes (A65), Aristonous? (A67), Polyidus (A68), and Anaxandrides (A70 suppl.); similarly, with the death of Aeschylus (A59), Euripides (A63), Philoxenus (A69), Timotheus (A76), Sosiphanes I (B15), and Sosiphanes II (B22). The references are unnecessary from a pure chronographic point of view, for they add no relevant intervals nor create synchronies. Were they absent, no significant gap would be noticed. Hence, the dating of poets in those cases is an end in itself. Most of the superfluous references are artists of the so-called New Music (Melanippides, Telestes, Polyidus, Philoxenus, Timotheus, and possibly Aristonous) and post-classical dramatists (Anaxandrides, Sosiphanes I and II), which reveals a special interest in contemporary performance poetry. If the Parian Marble was located in the Archilocheion (see chap. 1, sect 5 above), it may have promoted the performance of current poetry along with Archilochus's poems.

In sum, the high incidence of poets and musicians on the Parian Marble, many of them inconsequential from a purely chronographic point of view, strongly supports the notion that embedding literary history in panhellenic history was a main purpose of the inscription. Although information was culled from a number of sources, the emphasis on poets is probably a tendency of the author. The rest of this chapter will be devoted to examining the methods by which this purpose was achieved, in the context of the ancient Greek traditions of literary history.

2. Four Trends in Literary History

What kind of information about poets and musicians does the Parian Marble offer? At first sight, it seems biographical. We read about poets' births and deaths, travels and exiles and, most of all, victories. But perhaps this perception results from our own tendency to use the Parian Marble as a repository of biographical data. Yet, the value of such data depends on the sources of information used and on the methods by which it was obtained.[37] For the sake of the argument, I propose to distinguish four major tendencies, though things may be less clear cut than the following classification suggests.

I. Biographical/Chronographic Information

genealogy:	Orpheus (A14 suppl.), Mousaeus (A15)
acme:	Hesiod (A28), Homer (A29), Hipponax (A42), Epicharmus (A55)
birth:	Euripides (A50)
death:	Simonides (A57), Aeschylus (A59), Euripides (A63), Sophocles (A64), Philoxenus (A69), Timotheus (A76), Sosiphanes I (B15)
travel:	Sappho (A36), Stesichorus (A50)
military service:	Aeschylus (A48)

II. Bibliographical Information:

Orpheus (A14 suppl.), Mousaeus (A15), Callippus (B6)

III. Heurematic Information:

Hyagnis (A10), Terpander (A34), Susarion (A39)
First production/competition: Thespis (A43), Hypodicus (A46)

IV. Agonistic Information:

victory:	Melanippides (A47), Simonides the elder (A49), Simonides (A54), Sophocles (A56), Aristonous (A67), Polyidus (A68), Anaxandrides? (A70), Astydamas (A71), Stesichorus the second (A73), Philemon (B7); first victory: Hypodicus (A46), Aeschylus

---

[37] Mosshamer (1979:306) puts the problem most eloquently: "Tradition, record, and mathematical construction combine to produce chronological systems within which it is often difficult to distinguish the contemporary record from the scholarly inference."

(A50), Euripides (A60), Telestes (A65),
Menander (B14).

2.1. Biographical / Chronographic Information

Details regarding birth, death, travels, and military service may seem to have a documentary basis. However, much biographical information derives from traditional modalities of thought or stems from the application of techniques for chronological computation, one of which is the building of genealogies.

A pervading modality for making literary history, perhaps one of the earliest, is tracing the ancestry of poets and musicians. Indeed, genealogies of poets are a recurrent topic among the fragmentary historians.[38] Such genealogies may well reflect the concerns of later biographers, from whom information was actually received. Still, for some ancient historians such as Hellanicus, genealogy was part of their general approach to the past.[39] Genealogical thinking was predominantly used in the biographies of Homer and Hesiod, whom Hellanicus, Pherecydes, and Damastes asserted descended from Orpheus (and Mousaeus),[40] noting a span of ten generations between them. However, whether the 492 years between Orpheus and Homer in the Parian Marble involve some genealogical computation is unclear.[41] Thus, it remains uncertain whether the Parian Marble endorses Hesiod's and Homer's descent from Orpheus.

The dating of Orpheus (A14) and Mousaeus (A15) is rather unusual, when compared to other ancient testimonies. From the sixth century BCE on Orpheus

---

[38] See n. 40 below.

[39] Genealogy was one of the five genres of ancient Greek historiography, according to Jacoby 1909 (for criticism of his developmental approach, see Marincola 2012 with further references). On genealogical thinking and chronology, see Mosshammer 1979:101–105, Fowler 1998-1999, and Clarke 2008:201–203.

[40] "Hellanikos and Damastes and Pherekydes trace his [Homer's] ancestry to Orpheus. For they say that Maion the father of Homer and Hesiod's father Dios were sons of Apellis, son of Melanopos, son of Epiphrades, son of Chariphemos, son of Philoterpes, son of Idmonis, son of Eukles, son of Dorion, son of Orpheus" (FGrH 3 F 167 = FGrH 4 F 5b = FGrH 5 F 11b, translated by W. S. Morison, BNJ 3 F 167). Similarly, Hellanicus (FGrH 4 F 5a) claimed Hesiod's descent from Orpheus (ten generations stood between them), while Damastes (FGrH 5 F 11) claimed Homer's descent from Mousaeus with a ten-generations span. Tatianus accounts that Theagenes of Rhegium, Stesimbrotus of Thasos, and Antimachus of Colophon were among the earliest to write on Homer's poetry, genealogy, and chronology (FGrH 107 F 21 = FGrH 70 F 98). In contrast, Herodotus displays no interest in the genealogies of poets. Traditions regarding the genealogies of early poets are catalogued by Kivilo 2010, and analyzed by Lefkowitz 2012 (first published in 1981), Graziosi 2002 (Homer), Nagy 2009 (Hesiod), and Koning 2010 (Hesiod).

[41] Orpheus is dated to 1135 (= 1398/7 BCE) and Homer to 643 (= 907/6 BCE). The year for Mousaeus is lost, and for Hesiod is faulty. The series Orpheus, Mousaeus, Hesiod, Homer appears in Aristophanes' catalogue of beneficial poets in *Frogs* 1030–1036; see below.

was linked to the Argonauts.[42] Hence, he would have been active one generation before the Trojan War.[43] The Parian Marble, however, locates Orpheus and Mousaeus much earlier,[44] reflecting a view most probably promoted by Eleusis and received through Athenian historiographical sources (I shall return to this point in section 2.II of this chapter). Mentioning one after the other suggests a father and son genealogical link.[45] Thus, notwithstanding textual difficulties, genealogical thinking may lay behind the Parian Marble's reference to Orpheus and Mousaeus.

Why is this important? One could argue that genealogies have mere antiquarian interest. However, as studies in oral history suggest, genealogies were remembered, even partly invented, because they were useful.[46] As genealogies of kings or families supported claims to land ownership, to rights and power, genealogies of poets and musicians may have been disseminated at local sanctuaries, as well as by musical performers and rhapsodes, such as the Homeridai and the Lesbian kitharodes, who claimed descent from Homer and Terpander.[47] Furthermore, genealogies may provide a glimpse into the professional training of rhapsodes and musicians, who may have received it from their fathers or other male relatives.[48]

---

[42] Karanika 2010. Orpheus is linked to the Argonauts in the later chronographic tradition (Jerome *Chronicle* 56b).

[43] West 1983:20–24, 39–44. The dating was controversial, as apparent from the theory of two poets named Orpheus (Pherecydes FGrH 3 F 26), which Herodotus rejected (2.53). Herodotus (7.6.3) doubted the authenticity of poetry attributed to Orpheus and Mousaeus.

[44] Orpheus is a supplement first proposed by Prideaux 1676, a very plausible one considering the context. Le Paulmier suggests Πάμφως, a figure that later evidence connects to Athens and Demeter's cult, but Orpheus' link to Eleusis is much better documented. As for Mousaeus, his name is secure, but it remains doubtful whether Eumolpus was mentioned at the beginning of the entry and whether he was considered Mousaeus' son, as restoration suggests. In our sources Eumolpus is either son of Mousaeus (scholia to Sophocles *Oedipus at Colonus* 1053 = FGrH 10 F 13, Suda s.v. Μουσαῖος and Εὔμολπος; cf. West 1983:41), or Mousaeus' father (Philochorus FGrH 320 F 208 = scholia RV to Aristophanes *Frogs* 1033). Graf (1974:18) regards the latter as a secondary tradition. According to Henrichs (1985:6), the double genealogy indicates rival tendencies in fourth-century Eleusis.

[45] Orpheus is attested as Mousaeus' father from the first century CE (P.Berol 13044, cf. Diodorus 4.25.1; see West 1983:41n12, Currie 2011). For the complex genealogy of Mousaeus, see LIMC s.v.; testimonies in PEG II.3 Mousaeus fr. 19.

[46] Fowler 1998–1999.

[47] On the *Homeridai*, see Pindar *Nemean* 2.1, a reference explained by the scholion to the line, with Graziosi 2002:201–217. On Terpander's *apogonoi*, see Aristotle fr. 545 Rose = Gostoli T 60c, with Gostoli 1990:XLIX and Power 2010:331–332. If Tarditi's suggestion (1956:139) that the Mnesiepes inscription was set up by a rhapsodic thiasos is accepted, it then follows as a reasonable hypothesis that its members may have claimed descent from Archilochus.

[48] Heracleides' inference that Amphion was taught the art of kitharody by his father (Zeus) is illuminating (fr. 157 Wehrli = [Plutarch] *On Music* 1131f–1132a). The best-documented cases are the theatrical families of Athens, a phenomenon Sutton (1987) assesses as mainly educational.

Genealogies of poets, often modulated by local or professional patriotism, may also have a historiographical role. Through genealogies literary development can be seen diachronically, at a supra-individual level. The claim that Homer and Hesiod come from the same family and are descendants of Orpheus or Mousaeus perhaps attempts to account for the transmission of creative talent. Similarly with claims that Terpander descended from Homer or Hesiod (Suda s.v.)[49] and Stesichorus from Hesiod (Philochorus FGrH 329 F 213, a Locrian tradition).[50] Thus, genealogies afford quasi-genetic explanations of poetic history by applying a biological metaphor (with some historical basis on the professional training of poets and musicians) to cultural development. It may not be surprising that ancient and modern scholars alike resort to duplicating poets when faced with difficulties in their biographies, not only as homonymous but also as biologically related.[51] The notion that poetic creativity "runs in the family" underlies the mention of Simonides and his otherwise unknown grandfather (A49).[52] The inconsistency between Sosiphanes' death at B15 and his reappearance at B22, if not a cutter's mistake, suggests two poets of the same name, construed by some scholars as father and son.[53]

If genealogical thinking is a possible background of some references to poets and musicians in the Parian Marble, relative chronology is more pervasive. Indeed, any historical pursuit requires a systematic structure of time. Historical explanations, whatever form they take, require temporal scenarios. Literary history is no exception. Locating poets in a chronological grid has implications that go beyond the individual biographies of poets. Indeed, statements on influence, imitation, and parody make no sense unless set against a definite chronology. In ancient Greece, literary history had a peculiar connection to chronology. Backed up by poetic texts that were orally transmitted and widely known, as well as by living musical traditions, authors became milestones in the creation of general chronology.[54] The most outstanding examples of synchronism between poets and other people or events are found in Herodotus, whose

---

In contrast, *diadochai*, "succesions," may involve learning from a master (in the *Excerpts from Nicomachus* 1, Orpheus is said to have taught Thamyris and Linus, and Linos to have taught Hercules). I am grateful to John Franklin for the reference.

[49] Kivilo 2010:136–139.
[50] Kivilo 2010:11, 65–67.
[51] Main examples of duplicate poets are Orpheus (Herodorus FGrH 31 F 42), Homer (*Life of Hesiod* 3), Sappho (Suda, second notice), Alcman (Suda), Xenophanes (Diogenes Laertius 9.20), Euenus of Paros (Erathostenes *ap.* Harpocration s.v.), Melanippides (Suda); cf. LeVen 2008:38n126, Kivilo 2010:67n19.
[52] For the doubtful chronology, see note on the Greek text of A49.
[53] See note on the Greek text of B22.
[54] Clarke 2008:224–227, and *passim*.

references to almost all the poets appear synchronized: Archilochus and Gyges (1.12.2), Arion and Periander (1.23), Homer and Hesiod (2.53).[55]

Relative chronology is the backbone of literary history in the Parian Marble too. As we have seen, most entries mentioning poets synchronize them with other people or events (seventy percent). In the cases of Hipponax (A42) and Epicharmus (A55), the technique is made explicit through the expression κατὰ τοῦτον, synchronizing Hipponax with Cyrus's conquest of Sardis and Epicharmus with Hieron's seizing power in Syracuse. The fact that both references appear as postscripts suggests that they were added at a later stage of the chronicle's composition, a testimony to the high consideration poetic matters entertained.[56] Those synchronies, however, do not offer precise dating, but rather a general contemporaneity, probably referring to the period of creative peak, the *acme* (also known by the Latin *floruit*, "flourished"), set at the age of 40 by Apollodorus, possibly by Aristoxenus before him.[57]

In a system that dates poets by synchrony and intervals, controversies over antedating one or another, Hesiod or Homer, Archilochus or Terpander, had potential implications for the entire chronological scheme.[58] The relative positioning of poets also played a historiographical role. It often reveals a hierarchic view of cultural production, where "earlier" carries the added value of "better" or more authoritative.[59] Similar values may be attached to the genres that poets represented.[60] Such controversies, however, are absent from the Parian Marble, which records single views on dating, as suits its genre and purpose.[61]

The most famous controversy regarding the relative dating of poets involved Homer and Hesiod. The Parian Marble positions Hesiod one entry before Homer (between thirty-eight or thirty seven and thirty years earlier),

---

[55] Also: Sappho and Rhodopis (2.134), Anacreon and Polycrates (3.121), Olen, Arge, and Opis (4.35), Alcaeus and Pisistratus (5.95), Simonides and Eualcides, an athlete who died at the battle of Ephesus (5.102), Solon and the Cyprian revolt (5.113.2), Phrynichus and the fall of Miletus (6.21.2). Herodotus is not less concerned with matters of chronology, authenticity, and details of public performance (Legrand 1964:149–156) than with displaying his own cultural sophistication (Ford 2006), which may explain some of his seemingly incidental references.

[56] On postscripts in the Parian Marble, see chap. 4, sect. 1.

[57] Birth could then be calculated as forty years prior to the event that attests to poetic maturity, such as a first victory. On the theory of intellectual maturity, see Mosshammer 1979:119–127, with further references.

[58] Beecroft 2010:111.

[59] On the chronological and cultural implications of the dates proposed for Homer, see Graziosi 2002:90–124.

[60] Beecroft 2010:111–112.

[61] In contrast, the much later *Canons* of Eusebius, witnessed by Jerome's *Chronicle* (see chap. 6, sect. 1) gives voice to alternative views, often citing authorities, e.g. on the foundation of Carthage (58e, 69e, 71c, 81b) and the dating of Homer (63d, 66a, 69f, 71b, 77c).

possibly following Ephorus,[62] which is consistent with the *Contest of Homer and Hesiod* (45), where Homer is a younger contemporary of Hesiod.[63] Beyond the relative positioning of the poets (relative to each other, as well as to other events, such as the Trojan War, the Ionian migration, etc.), the Parian Marble does not offer specific biographical information. The verb used for Homer and supplied for Hesiod is ἐφάνη, "appeared."[64] It does not mean "came into being" or "was born," for which the inscription consistently uses ἐγένετο.[65] The "appearance" of Homer and Hesiod may point more generally to their creative peak or *acme*.[66]

The Parian Marble perhaps transmitted one side of the controversy regarding the relative chronology of Archilochus and Terpander. Supplementing Archilochus in A33, as Baumgarten suggests, would make him earlier than Terpander, in accord with Phainias of Eresos (FGrH 4 F 85b) and Glaucus of Rhegium (*ap.* [Plutarch] *On Music* 1132e).[67] Terpander, however, was considered later than Archilochus by Alexander Polyhistor (FGrH 273 = [Plutarch] *On Music* 1133a), and perhaps by Hellanicus too.[68] In either case, relative dating would result from synchrony with other events not mentioned in the inscription. Alternatively, it may stem from a view on the development or importance of the genres that Archilochus and Terpander represent, iambos and kitharody,[69] if not simply an instance of local patriotism. If Baumgarten's restoration of A33 is accepted, both Archilochus and Terpander would each occupy an entry of his own, which would indicate that they are dated for their own sake. That the Parian Marble mentioned Archilochus seems very plausible, due to the central role of Archilochus in ancient Greek chronography and the location of the inscription on his native Paros; A33 is the only suitable entry for supplementing his name. However, such considerations should not influence the constitution

---

[62] Jacoby 1904a:xiv, 152–158, Mosshammer 1979:195, but see Graziosi 2002:104–106.

[63] In the *Contest of Homer and Hesiod*, although the poets are said to be contemporary so as to compete together, Hesiod is at the end of his career, and Homer at its onset (cf. Graziosi 2002:104–107).

[64] A puzzling verb (it appears again in B25), probably derived from a source antedating the systematic chronographic use of *acme*.

[65] The verb ἐγένετο is used in the Parian Marble for "coming into being," either for an institution (Panionian league A27) or for people, i.e. "being born" (Euripides A50, Ptolemy II B19), and more generally for "happening," "taking place" (A3, A4, A16, A19, A48, A51, A52, A72).

[66] Dopp 1883:32. For the synchronisms and computations involved in the ancient datings of Homer and Hesiod, see Jacoby 1904a:152–158, Mosshammer 1979:193–197, Graziosi 2002, Nagy 2009, Kivilo 2010:45–52, Koning 2010, Koiv 2011.

[67] Mosshammer 1979:228 suggests Phainias or Glaucus to be the Parian Marble's sources on this point.

[68] Hellanicus recorded Terpander as the first victor at the Carneian Games and synchronized him with Midas (FGrH 4 F 85 b; cf. Mosshammer 1979:227). Gostoli 1990:2–7 collects and Kivilo 2010:158–163 studies the testimonies regarding the chronology of Terpander.

[69] Beecroft 2010:112, Kivilo 2010:160–161.

of the text.[70] Hence, the Parian Marble's position on the relative dating of Terpander *vis à vis* Archilochus remains uncertain.

Some of the information in the Parian Marble on the travels and deaths of poets seems to derive from biographical traditions. Sappho's travel or exile to Sicily (A36), not known from other sources,[71] is treated as factual by most biographers.[72] At any rate, information about a statue of her in Syracuse (Cicero *Verres* 1.4.1257), as well as the lack of local traditions regarding her death, suggest a death away from Lesbos.[73] As for the reference to Aeschylus' fighting at Marathon (A48), an event registered in his funerary epigram, it was probably transmitted in connection to the date of death, although the ultimate source could be Aeschylus' own poetry. Other dates of birth seem to result from chronological computation, of the author or his sources. Indeed, ancient chronographers often calculated birth backward, departing from the *acme*, or taking into account a generation interval from a figure considered older. The synchronism of Euripides' birth with Aeschylus' first victory (A50) raises suspicion that Euripides' year of birth is reached by a combination of backwards computation from Euripides' first victory (understood as *acme*) with the *acme* of Aeschylus.[74] In the same entry, Euripides' birth and Aeschylus' first victory are synchronized with Stesichorus' arrival in Greece. Although the date is too late,[75] information may derive from a tradition developed from an actual visit of Stesichorus to the Peloponnese, as argued by Bowra.[76]

The treatment of the thinking and techniques behind the dating of seemingly biographical events reveals many insights into the historiography of poetry and music, but offers little of factual weight. The travels of Sappho and

---

[70] The stone is broken at the point where Selden, whose dots not always represent a precise number of missing letters, reports ἀφ᾽ οὗ . . . . ο . . υ (see note to the Greek text of A33). Similarly cautious is Ornaghi 2009:276. If Archilochus's name appeared in A33, perhaps he was credited as well with one or more inventions in the realms of poetry or even music (on Archilochus's poetic and musical innovations, see Rotstein 2010:230–234, with further references).

[71] Kivilo 2000:182–183. The papyrus fragments [98 LP] mentioned by Mosshammer 1979:345n6 do not necessarily refer to Sappho's own exile.

[72] Mosshammer (1979:253) suggests as the source of this information Phainias of Eresus (Lesbos), who is also a possible source for another reference to Lesbos's literary history, i.e. the entry on Terpander. Information may ultimately stem from a Sicilian historiographical work (*contra* Jacoby 1904b:191).

[73] Kivilo 2000:182–183.

[74] Mosshammer 1979:307; Scullion 2002:82. On the use of chronographic construction instead of primary evidence, see Mosshammer 1979:113–127.

[75] Cf. Kivilo 2000:81.

[76] Bowra 1934:115, cf. 118–119, and West 1971:305. Stesichorus' travel could be taken metaphorically, as Bowie suggests (cf. Dopp 1883:47). His arrival to Greece would refer to the integration of his poetry into Athenian agonistic culture, in the choral competitions in which Hypodicus of Chalcis first won, according to A46 (Bowie, forthcoming). So far, no alternative has been proposed to Le Paulmier's ἀ[φίκετ]ο.

Stesichorus may reflect local traditions, but information on the early poets (Hyagnis, Orpheus, Mousaeus, Hesiod, and Homer) points towards scholarly views on their relative chronology (relative to other poets and other events). However, it seems that most references to the deaths of fifth- and fourth-century BCE poets (Simonides, A57; Aeschylus, A59; Euripides, A63; Sophocles, A64; Philoxenus, A69; Timotheus, A76; and possibly Sosiphanes I, B15) may have had some literary basis.[77] Indeed, year of death has a better chance of being remembered, recorded, and transmitted than year of birth. References to the years when poets died were probably used, along with dates of first victories, for the computation of some of the information regarding age at the time of death, as well as the year of birth (in the case of Euripides, A50).

2.II. Bibliographical Information

In my treatment of time in the Parian Marble (chap. 5), I suggested that the fall of Troy marks the beginning of the *tempus historicum* (A24, 1209/8 BCE). Before that, the inscription mentions three figures related to music and poetry, namely Hyagnis, the restored Orpheus, and Mousaeus (A10, A14 suppl., A15). How was their status understood by the author and his audience? Contemporary reference works regard them as mythical figures, but for many ancient audiences and scholars they were historical; they actually existed in the past.[78] As we have seen, some early historians placed Orpheus,[79] as well as Mousaeus,[80] in the genealogies of Homer and Hesiod, and they were often set at the very beginning of musical history.[81] We shall expand later in this chapter on the role of Hyagnis as inventor of the *aulos*. As for Orpheus, he was often held to be the inventor of the lyre and the hexameter, as well as the first kitharode.[82] Furthermore, hymns circulated under Orpheus' name, and oracles under Mousaeus'.[83] The distinction we drew in chapter 5 between ontology and epistemology will be of help here. Thus, rather than mythical figures that may have never existed, it may be

---

[77] Mosshammer 1979:308, Jacoby 1904a:xvi–xvii; Jacoby 1904b:93–94 suggests that much information on literary matters could have reached the author through Aristoxenus.

[78] For a call for caution when dealing with the historicity of "mythical poets," see Beecroft 2008:226.

[79] Pherecrates FGrH 3 F 167, Hellanicus FGrH 4 F 5.

[80] Gorgias B 25 DK, Damastes FGrH 5 F 11a.

[81] E.g. *Frogs* 1030–1036, [Plutarch] *On Music*. Other poets located at the early stages in the history of *mousike*, such as Demodocus and Phemius, result from reading the Homeric poems as referring to *realia* (Heraclides fr. 157 Wehrli = [Plutarch] *On Music* 1131f–1132c; see Gostoli 1986).

[82] Timotheus PMG 791, 221–233; Critias B 3 DK; Alexander Polyhistor FGrH 77 = [Plutarch] *On Music* 1132e–f.

[83] Sophocles fr. 1012 N², Aristophanes *Frogs* 1030–1033 (with scholia to Aristophanes *Frogs* 1033), Hippias FGrH 6 F 4, Plato *Apology* 41c, *Protagoras* 316d. Clement *Stromata* 1.132–135 distinguishes between Orpheus as author of poems and Mousaeus as author of oracles.

better to characterize Hyagnis, Orpheus, and Mousaeus as proto-historical poets and musicians, that is, figures about whom already in antiquity knowledge was known to be obscure.

It is therefore surprising that two of the proto-historical poets and musicians, Orpheus and Mousaeus (A14 suppl., A15), are not treated as first inventors, while Hyagnis is (that *heuremata* may have been mentioned in the lacunae in both entries cannot be ruled out). Instead, we have references to the publication of their work.[84] As for Orpheus, there is information about specific poems, their content, and even their titles, and similar information may have been given for Mousaeus' poetry in the lost parts of A15.

Three entries in the extant inscription allude to the dissemination of knowledge: the references to the poetry of Orpheus and Mousaeus, and to Callippus' *Astrology* (πο⟨ί⟩ησιν ἐξέθηκε, A14; ποιήσ[ει]ς ἐξέθηκ[εν, A15; ἀστρολογίαν ἐξέθηκεν, B6). Since ancient astronomical records indicate the summer solstice of 330 BCE as the beginning of the first Callippean year,[85] the *Astrology* may have consisted in Callippus' computations of the solar year. This was consequential for ancient professional chronography. What could be the rationale behind the reference to the publication of poetic texts by Orpheus and Eumolpus?

The status and date of Orpheus and Mousaeus were disputed in antiquity. Herodotus (2.53) participates in an ongoing polemic when he rejects the possibility of other poets (probably implying Orpheus and Mousaeus) preceding Homer and Hesiod.[86] While the figure of Mousaeus emerged with the Eleusinian cult, ancient sources from the sixth century BCE on connected Orpheus with the Argonauts—that is, one generation before the Trojan War. Such chronology does not appear in the Parian Marble, where Orpheus is dated 190 years before the fall of Troy. Instead, the Parian Marble places Orpheus, along with Mousaeus, at the beginnings of the Eleusinian cult, a connection attested in our sources from the fifth and fourth centuries BCE.[87] The unusual reference to the publication of Orpheus's works may be a residue of polemics regarding his date and, perhaps too, regarding the identity of the first Greek poet, which is resolved through

---

[84] The verb ἐκτίθημι means "expose," "exhibit," e.g. the text of the law, "expound," "put forward" an argument, while the middle voice is often used for citations. The simple use of active aorist with direct object, "made public poetry / poems / astrology" is rather unusual, and probably refers to the publication of texts either in oral or in written form. Cf. Jerome's *publicavit* with reference to Sophocles (*Chronicle* 109m), where the Paschal Chronicle (303.10) and Syncellus (305.12) have ἐπεδείξατο, referring to public performance.

[85] See chap. 5, n. 17.

[86] The polemics involved the authenticity of some of the poems and oracles attributed to Orpheus and Mousaeus (Herodotus 7.6.3, Aristotle fr. 7 Rose). In the case of Orpheus, the controversy was solved by Herodorus of Heraclea through the hypothesis of two poets of the same name (FGrH 31 F 42), see n. 51 above.

[87] West 1983:41. On the nature of that poem, see more recently Currie 2011.

an Attic and Eleusinian point of view. The Parian Marble's author was probably following a written source, perhaps the work of one of the Atthidographers, as Jacoby suggests (cf. Philochorus FGrH 328 F 77). Such a source may have supported the historicity and antiquity of Orpheus and Mousaeus precisely by appealing to oral or written evidence—namely, to their poetry.

2.III. Heurematic Information

The search for first inventors, *protoi heuretai*, is characteristic of ancient Greek thought on creativity and change.[88] Naming individuals as discoverers helps to visualize origins (*archai*) and causes (*aitiai*). *Heuremata* offer concrete answers to difficult questions: how did cultural products come into being? How did they develop? In the history of *mousike*, first inventors usually help to account for the origins of musical instruments and the emergence of genres of poetry and song.

On the historiographical role of *heuremata*, the second-century treatise *On Music* attributed to Plutarch is illuminating. We learn that discussion of first inventors was a desideratum in historical accounts of *mousike*.[89] An example clarifies the abstract tenet: Olympus skipped a note while playing the kithara in the diatonic genus and thus invented the enharmonic genre almost by mistake,[90] an extraordinary scene of a musician at work. *Heuremata*, then, are innovations or even contributions that introduce something new into preexisting forms. As a speaker of the dialogue puts it, music grows through inventions.[91] Another clear example appears in a passage from Proclus's *Chrestomathia*, where the definition of *nomos* involves a step-by-step account from Terpander to the New Music.[92] Thus, innovations and contributions were often construed as chains of

---

[88] Kleingünther 1933, Traede 1962, Bartol 2006. See Clarke 2008:226–227 for the history of discovery in Diodorus, D'Angour 2011 for *heuresis* in the Greeks' general attitude towards novelty, and esp. pp. 184–206 for novelty in the realm of music.

[89] ἄγε δὴ ὦ μουσικῆς θιασῶται, τίς πρῶτος ἐχρήσατο μουσικῇ, ἀναμνήσατε τοὺς ἑταίρους, καὶ τί εὗρε πρὸς αὔξησιν ταύτης ὁ χρόνος, καὶ τίνες γεγόνασιν εὐδόκιμοι τῶν τὴν μουσικὴν ἐπιστήμην μεταχειρισαμένων· ἀλλὰ μὴν καὶ εἰς πόσα καὶ εἰς τίνα χρήσιμον τὸ ἐπιτήδευμα ([Plutarch] *On Music* 1131e).

[90] [Plutarch] *On Music* 1134f–1135a.

[91] [Plutarch] *On Music* 1131f–1135e.

[92] Proclus *Chrestomathia* ap. Photius *Library* 320a: Δοκεῖ δὲ Τέρπανδρος μὲν πρῶτος τελειῶσαι τὸν νόμον, ἡρώῳ μέτρῳ χρησάμενος, ἔπειτα Ἀρίων ὁ Μηθυμναῖος οὐκ ὀλίγα συναυξῆσαι, αὐτὸς καὶ ποιητὴς καὶ κιθαρῳδὸς γενόμενος. Φρῦνις δὲ ὁ Μιτυληναῖος ἐκαινοτόμησεν αὐτόν· τό τε γὰρ ἑξάμετρον τῷ λελυμένῳ συνῆψε καὶ χορδαῖς τῶν ζ' πλείοσιν ἐχρήσατο. Τιμόθεος δὲ ὕστερον εἰς τὴν νῦν αὐτὸν ἤγαγε τάξιν.
A three-steps account of the kithara is offered by Timotheus of Miletos, beginning with Orpheus, through Terpander, and reaching Timotheus himself (PMG 791, 221–233, cf. recent work by LeVen 2008:82–85, Power 2010:336–345).

development.[93] Time and again, *heuremata* are far from simple *ex nihilo* creation, but rather help pinpoint stages in cultural processes.

Controversies about *protoi heuretai* were common not only within literary and musical history, as in *On Music*, but also among historians, as ancient sources on the origins of dithyramb indicate.[94] Even Pliny's later catalogue of inventions records contesting opinions (*Natural History* 7.191–215). In contrast, the simple matching of inventors and inventions, apparent in Clement's *Stromata* (1.74–80) is probably characteristic of the didactic use of *heuremata*.

The history of cultural inventions features prominently in the earliest part of the Parian Marble.[95] In some cases the inscription uses the language of invention (εὑρεῖν), in others *heuremata* are conveyed by the adverb "first," or supported by tradition.[96] *Heuremata* include:

Inventor	Invention	Entry	Place
	penteconter	A9 implied	Egypt
Erichthonius	chariot racing	A10 implied	Athens
Hyagnis	*auloi* and *nomoi*	A10	Phrygia
Idaean Dactyls	iron	A11[97]	Crete
Demeter	grain	A12 implied	Eleusis
Pheidon (Argos)	weights & measures	A30 implied	Aegina
Terpander	kitharodic and auletic *nomoi*	A34 implied	Lesbos
Susarion	chorus of *komoidoi*	A39	Athens, Icaria
Thespis	tragedy	A43 implied	in town (Athens)
Hypodicus	choruses of men	A46 implied	Athens

---

[93] On the history of the lyre, the first of the *Excerpts from Nicomachus* offers a combination of invention (Hermes), transmission (Hermes gave it to Orpheus, who taught Thamyris and Linos, who in turn taught Hercules), loss (after Orpheus' death), and rediscovery (by Terpander in Lesbos). The text may possibly go back to Hellanicus (Franklin 2003:306n12 and personal communication).

[94] Herodotus attributed the dithyramb to Arion of Methymna (Herodotus 1.23), while Lasus of Hermione was favored by Hellanicus in the *Carnean Victors*, as well as by Dicaearchus in *On Dionysiac Contests* as the first to have staged cyclic choruses (Hellanicus and Dicaearchus, FGrH 4 F 86 = scholia to Aristophanes *Birds* 1403). On the complex issue of the origins of the dithyramb and the early terminology, see the relevant testimonies collected by Ierano 1997, and the contributions by Kowalzig and Wilson 2013, with further references.

[95] Clarke 2008:329.

[96] *Heuremata* explicit through the verb "invented": A10 ("first invented" *auloi* and *nomoi*), A11 (twice), A39 (Susarion). *Heuremata* implicit through the adverb "first": A10 (first Panathenaic games), A12 (suppl.), A43 (Thespis), A46 (men's choruses). Three of the *heuremata* in the list are not marked as such in the text, but tradition allows their inclusion (A9, A30, A34). Simonides's invention of mnemonics (A54) appears as a qualification, rather than an event.

[97] The earliest invention attested in Greek literature, in a fragment of the anonymous *Phronis* (Kleingünther 1933:10, Bartol 2006:85).

Half of the *heuremata* in the Parian Marble regard two major themes in the history of *mousike*: the development of music, with Hyagnis and Terpander, and the emergence of Attic institutionalized choral and dramatic competition, with Susarion, Thespis, and Hypodicus. Let us first look into the two entries on musical history.

The Parian Marble attributes to Hyagnis (A10) the invention of *auloi* and certain auletic *nomoi*. The Phrygian nature of the invention is emphasized (the adjective Phrygian appearing three times), as well as the cultic link to the Mother of the gods, Dionysus, and Pan. Terpander (A34), in contrast, is described by details such as patronymic and city of origins ("Terpander son of Derdenes, the Lesbian"). His entry does not speak about beginnings but about change ("changed the music of old"). He belongs to a step-by-step account, comparable to those we mentioned before. Could the Parian Marble's source have construed both Hyagnis and Terpander, even though separated by more than 800 years, as stages in a single process? Apparently not. Hyagnis invented the *aulos* and auletic *nomoi*, whereas Terpander belongs to the history of the *kithara* and *kithara* playing. The Parian Marble, however, includes the word "auletic" in Terpander's entry (τοὺς νόμους τοὺ[ς κιθ]α[ρ]ω[ι]δ̣[ικ]οὺς καὶ αὐλητ[ικ), which was deleted by Wilamowitz, Hiller von Gärtringen, and Jacoby. Nonetheless, as Kivilo points out, two *nomoi* attributed to Terpander, the Apothetos and the Schoinion, were auletic.[98] The Parian Marble may well reflect a marginal tradition where Terpander made contributions to *aulos* music.[99] Furthermore, if A14 included a now lost reference to Orpheus' contribution to kithara music, Terpander could have represented a step in the development of both branches, kitharistic and auletic.

Unlike Terpander,[100] Hyagnis is rather marginal in the history of ancient Greek music.[101] For the invention of the *auloi* and auletic *nomoi*, other figures are usually named, such as the Phrygian Olympus and Marsyas, as well as Clonas,[102]

---

[98] Pollux 4.65 = Gostoli 38, cf. [Plutarch] *On Music* 1133d); see Kivilo 2010:137n6, 153, Ercoles 2014.

[99] A testimony by Sopater Rhetor (fourth century CE) speaks of Terpander as singing to the *aulos*: ὅτι τοῖς αὐλοῖς εἰς ὁμόνοιαν ἤγαγε τὴν Λακεδαιμονίων πόλιν κιθαρῳδὸς ὤν (5:21 Walz). The testimony, omitted by Gostoli, was noted by Slings 1991 and Campbell 1993. I am grateful to John Franklin for the references.

[100] Recent work on Terpander has contributed to understanding his emblematic role in the history of kitharody (Beecroft 2008:111–112, Power 2010:317–422). Although Terpander does not appear to be linked to any other poet or musician in the Parian Marble, the possible supplement of Archilochus in A33 would set Terpander as the younger poet. For the possibility that this, as well as some other references to literary and musical history in the Parian Marble, may go back to Hellanicus, see Franklin 2012.

[101] It is possible that the name Agnis (Ἄγνις) stands for Hyagnis (Ὕαγνις) in the third-century CE Monnus mosaic in Trier (CIL XIII 3710; cf. Kretschmer 1911:156–157, Daniel 1996:33).

[102] Clonas as first composer of aulodic *nomoi*, Heracleides *ap.* [Plutarch] *On Music* 1132a.

Ardalus of Troezen,[103] or Athena and Apollo.[104] These various *protoi heuretai* probably reflect regional traditions of musical history, as well as local patriotism.[105] The Phrygian branch of this tradition will eventually connect Hyagnis, Marsyas, and Olympus by genealogy or *diadoche*.[106] In its characteristic uncontroversial style, the Parian Marble's author follows a single tradition, known also from Aristoxenus,[107] Alexander Polyhistor,[108] and [Plutarch] *On Music*.[109] But most points of contact are found in an epigram of the late third-century BCE poet Dioscorides of Nicopolis:

> Αὐλοὶ τοῦ Φρυγὸς ἔργον Ὑάγνιδος, ἡνίκα Μήτηρ
> ἱερὰ τὰν Κυβέλοις πρῶτ' ἀνέδειξε θεῶν

Anthologia Palatina 9.340 1–2 = Dioscorides, xxxv
Gow and Page

> The *auloi* was the work of Phrygian Hyagnis, when the Mother
> of the gods revealed her sacred rites on Cybele.[110]

Noting that the epigram mentions Hyagnis's invention of the *auloi* in connection to the epiphany of the Mother of the gods on Cybele, Reizenstein concluded that Dioscorides and the Parian Marble must have used a similar source, the lost work *Peplos*,[111] attributed to Aristotle.[112] Let us briefly consider the nature of that book.

The *Peplos* was a miscellaneous work written in both prose and verse. It dealt with topics relating to the Trojan War: genealogies of commanders, the number of ships, including epigrams about them.[113] The scholiast to Aristides

---

103 [Plutarch] *On Music* 1133a.

104 [Plutarch] *On Music* 1135f.

105 Lasserre 1954:32.

106 Hyagnis was the father of Marsyas, according to [Plutarch] *On Music* 1132f, 1133e; Olympus was a disciple of Marsyas, Suda O. 219. The three are described as inventors of the *aulos* ([Plutarch] *On Music* 1135f) and the Phrygian harmony (Anon. Bellermanni 28).

107 Aristoxenus fr. 78 = Athenaeus 624b: Hyagnis invented the Phrygian harmony.

108 Alexander Polyhistor FGrH 273 F 77 (= [Plutarch] *On Music* 1132f): Hyagnis invented Phrygian music.

109 [Plutarch] *On Music* 1133f: Hyagnis as inventor of the *auletike*.

110 Adapted from Paton 1917 3:183. The last lines of the epigram allude to a polemic involving Marsyas, but the text is faulty.

111 Reitzenstein 1893:165–167; cf. Wendling 1891, Gow and Page 1968 II:236.

112 The fragments of the *Peplos* are collected in Rose 1967:394–407, frr. 637–644.

113 Porphyrius *ap.* Eustathius *Commentary on Homer's Iliad* β 557. The funerary epigrams may have been a later addition, perhaps no earlier than the second century BCE (Wilamowitz, Wendling 1891, Rose 1967, Cameron 1995). Focusing exclusively on the epigrams, as Gutzwiller (2010:223) has argued, does not give a whole picture of the entire work.

gives a list of ancient contests that derive from Aristotle's *Peplos*.[114] The list includes the order in which ten contests were founded and the occasion for their foundation. Wendling (1891) made a compelling case for the work's inclusion of a catalogue of inventions too. Thus, the *Peplos* seems to share with the Parian Marble an interest in genealogy, *heuremata*, and agonistic institutions. Authorship has been a matter of dispute. Only late writers, such as Porphyry, Eustathius, and Tzetzes, attributed the *Peplos* to Aristotle. Others attributed it to Theophrastus.[115] If the testimony of the scholiast to Aristides is given proper weight, the *Peplos* would be in tune with Aristotle's and his school's active role in recording agonistic information.[116] But considering the scanty evidence, it may be enough to conclude with Gutzwiller that the *Peplos* reflects peripatetic methods.[117]

Back to Hyagnis, the fact that both the Parian Marble and Dioscorides mention Hyagnis as *protos heuretes* of the *auloi* and do so in connection to the cult of Cybele suggests the use of a common source, perhaps a work of peripatetic orientation, such as the *Peplos* seems to have been.[118] A further point of contact will be apparent soon, as we discuss Thespis.

Let us now examine the entries on the emergence of Attic institutionalized choral and dramatic competitions. The Parian Marble mentions comedy first

---

[114] Scholia to Aristides *Panathenaic* Oration 189.4: ἐνδοξότατοι πάντων οἱ κατὰ τὴν Ἑλλάδα ἀγῶνες] ἡ τάξις τῶν ἀγώνων κατὰ Ἀριστοτέλην γράφεται· πρῶτα μὲν τὰ Ἐλευσίνια, διὰ τὸν καρπὸν τῆς Δήμητρος· δεύτερον δὲ τὰ Παναθήναια ἐπὶ Ἀστέρι τῷ γίγαντι ὑπὸ Ἀθηναίων ἀναιρεθέντα. τρίτος, ὃν ἐν Ἄργει Δαναὸς ἔθηκε, διὰ τὸν γάμον τὸν θυγατέρων αὐτοῦ· τέταρτος ὁ ἐν Ἀρκαδίᾳ τεθεὶς ὑπὸ Λυκάονος, ὃς ἐκλήθη Λύκαια· πέμπτος ὁ ἐν Ἰολκῷ, Ἰακάστου καθηγησαμένου ἐπὶ Πελίᾳ τῷ πατρί· ἕκτος ὁ ἐν Ἰσθμῷ, Σισύφου νομοθετήσαντος ἐπὶ Μελικέρτῃ· ἕβδομος ὁ Ὀλυμπιακός, Ἡρακλέους νομοθετήσαντος ἐπὶ Πέλοπι· ὄγδοος ὁ ἐν Νεμέᾳ, ὃν ἔθηκαν οἱ ἑπτὰ ἐπὶ Θήβας ἐπὶ Ἀργειόρῳ· ἔννατος ὁ ἐν Τροίᾳ, ὃν Ἀχιλλεὺς ἐπὶ Πατρόκλῳ ἐποίησε· δέκατος ὁ Πυθικός, ὃν οἱ Ἀμφικτύονες ἐπὶ τῷ Πύθωνος φόνῳ ἔθηκαν. ταύτην τὴν τάξιν εἰς πέπλους συνθεὶς ὁ Ἀριστοτέλης ἐξέθετο τῶν ἀρχαίων καὶ παλαιῶν ἀγώνων.

The Parian Marble mentions six of the ten contests that the scholiast attributes to the *Peplos*: Panathenaea (A10, perhaps A6 too, unless the reference is a cutter's mistake), Eleusis (A17), the Lycaea (A17), Isthmia (A20), Nemea (A22), and Pythia (A37).

[115] Wendling 1891:58–61. There is late evidence for a work entitled *Peplos* by Theophrastus.

[116] Nagy (2002:83–98) suggests that the title alludes to the climax of the major Athenian competitive festival, the peplos being a metaphor of rhapsodic composition.

[117] Gutzwiller 2010:227.

[118] Jacoby (1904a:51) rejected this hypothesis and proposed that a lost work on the history of music, written towards the end of the fifth century BCE, was the source for Dioscorides through Aristoxenus, whereas the author of the Parian Marble would have gotten the information through Ephorus, perhaps from a book *On Discoveries*. However, further similarities support the hypothesis of a common source. The entry mentioning Hyagnis in the Parian Marble refers also to the invention of the chariot and to the first Panathenaea, whereas the *Peplos* dealt with both *heuremata* and the history of ancient contests. Furthermore, another epigram by Dioscorides (*Anthologia Palatina* 7.410) mentions the same prizes that the Parian Marble does for comedy and tragedy (see below).

(A39), then a production by Thespis, i.e. tragedy (A43), and finally choruses of men (A46). As we shall see in the next section, these entries differ from agonistic references in their lack of formulaic language, which suggests a narrative source. They also differ from references to the foundation of festivals (Eleusis, Lycaea [?], Isthmia, Nemea, and Delphi) with the emphasis on individuals. Thespis, Susarion, and Hypodicus, however, are far from obvious choices for the origins of Athenian comedy and choral performances.

The entry on comedy (A39), though faulty at a crucial point ("a [cho]r[os] of *komo[idoi]* was [esta]blished in Ath[en]s," ἐν Ἀθ[ήν]αις κωμω[ιδῶν χο]ρ[ὸς ἐτ]έθη), seems to have been plausibly restored. The first competition is thus set in Athens between 582/1 and 561/0 BCE (archon's name and number of years are lost), that is, before comedy victor lists started to be kept and well before democracy (which the inscription sets fifty years later, A45). The Attic demos of Icarium appears as the first to have staged the competition [στε]σάν[των πρώ]των Ἰκαριέων. Susarion, though clearly conceived as an inventor, is an otherwise obscure figure, mentioned only by late sources.[119] The prize recorded is a basket of dried figs and a measure of wine. We shall soon return to this prize, but at this point it is important to note the qualification "at first," implying that prizes were later changed (not "the first prize," in contrast to other prizes in the same competition).[120]

Scholars have found it difficult to reconcile this portion of the Parian Marble with other literary and visual evidence on the origins of comedy, often dismissing the entry as too early and as making too unusual claims, or taking it as evidence for precursors of the Athenian competitive genre. For our purpose, it is important to note that this entry reflects a tradition on the origins of comedy as a competition first held by the demos Icarium, possibly in a Dionysiac context (as the prizes suggest), before the establishment of democracy and before tragedy.

The entry on tragedy (A43) locates Thespis' first production[121] between 540 and 520 BCE. It is not clear, however, whether the first production was conceived as invention or as a step in the consolidation of tragedy. The entry in its faulty

---

[119] Testimonies on Susarion are collected by Pickard-Cambridge 1962:280–284. Susarion was Icarian according to Clemens (*Stromata* 1.16.79). Some of the sources make Susarion a Megarian (fr. 1, transmitted by Tzetzes), perhaps endorsing the Doric, more specifically, Megarean claims mentioned by Aristotle (*Poetics* 1448a). See Piccirilli 1974 and Rusten 2006:43–44 for Susarion in the context of the Attic and Doric claims to have originated comedy. For Susarion as *heuretes* of iambic poetry, see Rotstein 2010:43–44.

[120] "The prize was at first" (adverbial), not "the first prize" (attributive).

[121] According to one possible restoration, which (following Connor 1990:26–32) I have omitted from the Greek text of the Parian Marble, Thespis's performance would have taken place "in town" (ἐν ἄ]στει), i.e. at the City Dionysia, in contrast to the rural celebration.

state displays no generic term (though Boeckh suggested δρᾶμ[α], but the reference to tragedy is clear. Unlike Susarion, Thespis is a more tangible figure in the literary record,[122] and although the inscription does not mention his hometown, tradition has him as Icarian. The prize established, a goat, has a long history in modern attempts to understand the origins of tragedy, linking the "goat song" to the performers or the prize offered,[123] or as a residue of the ritual context.[124] Whatever the *realia* behind the text, the Parian Marble here reflects a tradition that located this type of dramatic competition before the establishment of democracy.

The entries on Susarion and Thespis have much in common. They both refer to a stage prior to the documented competitions, usually believed to have emerged after democracy. Furthermore, the Parian Marble seems to follow a theory, which originated in Attica and is later attested, for example, by Athenaeus, that comedy preceded tragedy.[125] Furthermore, both genres would have had a common origin in the demos of Icarium.[126] Clues to the whereabouts of such a theory may be found in the tradition regarding the prizes of early comedy and tragedy. The prizes of figs and wine for comedy and a goat for tragedy are suitable to a Dionysiac context, though the connection may be aetiological.[127] Such prizes, which rarely appear in our sources, emerge in an epigram by Dioscorides on Thespis:

> Θέσπις ὅδε, τραγικὴν ὃς ἀνέπλασα πρῶτος ἀοιδὴν
> κωμήταις νεαρὰς καινοτομῶν χάριτας,
> Βάκχος ὅτε βριθὺν κατάγοι χορόν, ᾧ τράγος ἄθλων
> χὤττικὸς ἦν σύκων ἄρριχος ἆθλον ἔτι.
> εἰ δὲ μεταπλάσσουσι νέοι τάδε, μυρίος αἰὼν
> πολλὰ προσευρήσει χἄτερα· τἀμὰ δ᾽ ἐμά.

Anthologia Palatina 7.410 = Dioscorides, xx Gow and Page

I am Thespis, who first modeled tragic song, inventing a new diversion for the villagers, at the season when Bacchus led in the triennial chorus whose prize was still a goat and a basket of Attic figs. Now my juniors

---

[122] Pickard-Cambridge 1962:104–105, with sources on Thespis on 97–102.

[123] Pickard-Cambridge 1962:149–166.

[124] E.g. Burkert 1966:16–18, Sourvinou-Inwood 2003:141–200.

[125] Athenaeus 40a–b: ἀπὸ μέθης καὶ ἡ τῆς κωμῳδίας καὶ ἡ τῆς τραγῳδίας εὕρεσις ἐν Ἰκαρίῳ τῆς Ἀττικῆς εὑρέθη, καὶ κατ᾽ αὐτὸν τὸν τῆς τρύγης καιρόν.

[126] On the theory of the common origins of comedy and tragedy, see Pickard-Cambridge 1962:104–105.

[127] Jerome's *Chronicle* 100d and Syncellus 239a make explicit the etymological link between prize and genre's name.

remodel all this; countless ages will beget many new inventions, but my own is mine.[128]

In this epigram, Thespis asserts his invention of the tragic song, referring to a festival to Bacchus including a goat (tragedy) and a basket of figs (comedy) as prizes (later changed, cf. ἔτι, line 4). The same prizes are mentioned by Plutarch in a description of a Dionysiac procession (*Moralia* 527d).[129] Jacoby suggested Attic historiographical writings as a source for the dramatic *heuremata*.[130] Reitzeinstein, however, noting the similarities between the Parian Marble and Dioscorides' epigram on Thespis, suggested, as he also did with Hyagnis, that Dioscorides and our chronicle used the same source, namely, the *Peplos*.[131] It is possible that the *Peplos* or a similar miscellaneous work of Athenian origins and peripatetic inspiration acted as intermediary.

About Hypodicus of Chalcis (A46; Sutton 3, Ierano T 91) there is little to remark. He is a real *hapax* in the history of choral performance.[132] Although the choruses of men are usually understood as a reference to dithyramb, this need not be so.[133] The term may well refer to the category of competition also termed "cyclic choruses," only partly overlapping with the genre of dithyramb.[134] From the reference to choruses of men, some scholars made a misguided inference that choruses of boys were active beforehand. The qualification, however, may equally derive from viewing the past from a period in which there were competitions for choruses of both men and boys. Still, Hypodicus rightly deserves a place in accounts of the early dithyramb, as possibly reflecting Euboean choral traditions,[135] although his date may be too early.[136] Since the entry before Hypodicus mentions the end of Pisistratus's rule, it has been suggested that the Parian Marble refers to the first choral competition of this sort that was held under the democracy.[137]

---

[128] Paton 1917 2:221.

[129] Ἡ πάτριος τῶν Διονυσίων ἑορτὴ τὸ παλαιὸν ἐπέμπετο δημοτικῶς καὶ ἱλαρῶς· ἀμφορεὺς οἴνου καὶ κληματίς, εἶτα τράγον τις εἷλκεν, ἄλλος ἰσχάδων ἄρριχον ἠκολούθει κομίζων, ἐπὶ πᾶσι δ' ὁ φαλλός.
"The traditional festival of the Dionysia was paraded in a popular and lighthearted fashion, and there was an amphora of wine and a vine branch, then someone dragged a goat, another followed carrying a wicker basket of dried figs, and, to top it all off, the phallus" (translated by Rusten and Henderson 2011:95).

[130] Jacoby 1904a:XIIIn3, cf. Piccirilli 1974:1294.

[131] Reitzenstein 1893:166.

[132] Cf. Pickard-Cambridge 1962:25, 47, Ierano 1997:239–241, 209, 255.

[133] As noted by Osborne 1993:31, Ceccarelli 2013:159n26.

[134] See n. 94 above and n. 164 below.

[135] Wilson 2000:283–284.

[136] See Wilson 2000:17 for chronological difficulties.

[137] Privitera 1965:87.

The information we find in the Parian Marble regarding the earliest competitive performances of comedy, tragedy, and choruses of men is unorthodox, and
the dates are nowadays suspected as guesswork.[138] Some of the unusual details,
however, appear in Dioscorides, who also coincides with the Parian Marble
on much of the information given for Hyagnis. Dioscorides had a remarkable
interest in the history of poets and musicians.[139] Could the reference to the
first competition of choruses of men, won by Hypodicus, also derive from the
common source of Dioscorides and the Parian Marble?

The musical *heuremata* mentioned early in the Parian Marble regard developments outside Attica (Phrygia with Hyagnis, A10, Lesbos or perhaps Sparta
with Terpander, A34). In contrast, the *heuremata* relating to institutionalized
competition are located in Attica, deriving probably from a source tainted, as
many ancient discussion on the origins of poetry, by local patriotism.[140] From
that point on, with the sole exception of Epicharmus (A55), the inscription
remains focused on Athens.

2.IV. Agonistic Information

The epigraphical record was a major source for literary history in antiquity
no less than today.[141] Indeed, a great number of agonistic inscriptions (lists of
winners and prizes, dedications, etc.) outline a history without narrative.[142] But
extant official inscriptions, such as the Athenian Fasti and Didascaliae, are only
part of what must have been a broader record kept in archives of cities and sanctuaries.[143] From the fifth century BCE on, scholars combined archival materials,
inscriptional evidence, and oral traditions in works that established the dates of
poets, anchoring them in the general chronological setup. Hellanicus has been

---

[138] E.g. West 1989, Connor 1990, Scullion 2002; cf. Aristotle *Poetics* 1449a37–b1 for the lack of documentary evidence on the first stages of comedy.

[139] Dioscorides mentions Archilochus (*Anthologia Palatina* 3.351 = xvii Gow and Page), Philaenis (xxvi
Gow and Page, *AP* 7.450). Book 7 of the *AP* preserves seven epigrams on poets: Sappho (*AP* 7.407),
Anacreon (*AP* 7.31), Thespis (*AP* 7.410, 411), Aeschylus (*AP* 7.411), Sophocles (*AP* 7.37), Sositheus
(*AP* 7.707), and Machon (*AP* 7.708). Two of Dioscorides' epigrams on poets mention inventions,
AP 7.14 (Aeschylus) and 7.37 (Sophocles).

[140] Piccirilli 1974:1297.

[141] As soon as the Parian section of our inscription was published (1897), information was incorpo-
rated by Capps 1900, Wilhelm and Kaibel 1906, and Reisch 1907 in their works on the Athenian
dramatic records.

[142] The best-preserved agonistic inscriptions concern the dramatic competitions at the Athenian
Dionysia and Lenaea (Millis and Olson 2012). Wilson studied the institutional framework of dithyrambic and dramatic competitions in Athens and elsewhere (Wilson 2000; Wilson 2003, 2007a,
2007b, 2008). See Rotstein 2012 for the programs of non-dramatic contests in the fourth century
BCE.

[143] Sickinger 1999:41–47.

held as the founder of literary history[144] precisely because his *Carneian Victors*, a list of winners at the Carnean Games, provided a chronographic grid, essential to historical research on poetry.[145] Aristotle continued the tradition of research into competitive public performances (*Pythian Victories, Dionysiac Victories*, and *Didascaliae*),[146] as did his school (e.g. Dicaearchus' *On Musical Contests*) and perhaps Callimachus too (the lost *On Contests*, fr. 403 Pf.). Thus, the agonistic record in its literary or epigraphical form had a strong impact on ancient Greek literary history, making poetic victories the most widely attested literary event.[147]

This tendency is reflected in the Parian Marble, too. Indeed, fifteen out of thirty-one poets and musicians are mentioned in relation to victories at Athens. Most entries dealing with literary history from 510/508 BCE on (nineteen out of twenty-five entries, seventy-six percent) record poetic victories (see Table 5 in Chapter 4, section 2). Five of them are not synchronized with other events, which points to their intrinsic importance.

Agonistic information appears in the Parian Marble in rather formulaic terms, with the past verb "won" (ἐνίκησε/ν) and a qualification regarding contest or simply "in Athens." As we have seen above, references to Susarion, Thespis, and Hypodicus do not share this formula, which suggests that they derive from narrative sources and were, for that reason, discussed among *heuremata*.

Half of the agonistic entries in the Parian Marble include information about specific contests. In four instances, the category of competition is indicated in the dative case, namely tragedy (τραγωιδίαι, Aeschylus at A50, Sophocles A56, Euripides A60) and dithyramb (διθυράμβωι, Polyidus A68). In four cases, the category of competition may be inferred from the qualification ὁ κωμοιδοποιός (Philemon B7, Menander B14, Anaxandrides A70: ὁ κωμ[ ) and διθυραμβοποιός (Philoxenus A69).[148] However, the following victories are given without reference to the category in which they were achieved:

A47	Me[lan]ippid[es]	]εν Ἀθήνησιν
		(name securely supplemented)
A49	Simonides the elder	ἐνίκησεν Ἀθήνησι
A54	Simonides the younger	ἐνίκησεν Ἀθήνησι διδάσκων

---

[144] Kranz 1919:148, Lanata 1963:234–237.

[145] See n. 4 above.

[146] See nn. 9, 10 above.

[147] See, for example, Pausanias' history of the early Pythian agon (10.7.4–6), where the focus on winners suggests that it derives partly from available written records, even though, as Franklin suggests (personal communication), some of the material may have been fabricated. Ford (2002:272–293) assesses the impact of the agonistic tradition on ancient literary criticism.

[148] Capps (1900:60) suggested that A78 included a reference to Alexis: [. . . . . καὶ Ἄλεξις ὁ κωμοιδοποιὸς τότε πρῶτον] ἐνίκησεν.

A65	Telestes	ἐνίκησεν Ἀθήνησιν
A67	Ar[i]sto[nous]	] Ἀθήνησιν (name partly supplemented)
A71	Astydamas	Ἀθήνησιν ἐνίκησεν
A73	Stesichorus the second	ἐνίκησεν Ἀθήνησιν
A78	?	] ἐνίκησεν

Melanippides of Melos (61 Sutton, T 93a Ierano) is probably the New Music poet admired by Xenophon (*Memorabilia* 1.4.3).[149] His victory is most likely a dithyrambic one. The elder Simonides (7 Sutton, T 93b Ierano) of A49 is not attested elsewhere. He may be an older relative[150] of the famous Simonides of Ceos, easily identified in A54 by patronymic, birthplace, and the invention of mnemotechnics. The latter is also recorded as winning as *didaskalos*; thus, this was a choral competitive performance, most probably in the category of cyclic choruses. Telestes of Selinus (36 Sutton, T 78 Ierano) is known as a dithyrambic poet[151] and also as a musical innovator.[152] His victory could be dithyrambic, as well as kitharodic. Aristonous,[153] probably the famous kitharode who, according to Plutarch, won six times at Delphi (*Life of Lysander* 18.5),[154] may be the same Aristonous of Corinth whose hymns to Hestia and Apollo were inscribed on the Athenian treasury at Delphi and which are probably to be connected to the New

---

[149] Restoration of his name in A47 seems quite secure. The Suda speaks of two different poets named Melanippides (s.v. M 454 and 455). The elder was born (rather than flourished [γεγονώς], see below) in the sixty-fifth Olympiad (520–516 BCE), an author of dithyrambs, epic poems, epigrams, and elegies. The younger Melanippides, the dithyrambic poet known for his musical innovation, lived at the Macedonian court of Perdiccas (ca. 450–ca. 413 BCE). The Parian Marble's entry seems to offer an early dithyrambic victory by Melanippides the elder. However, as Rohde suggested, the fact that the two poets are given the same patronymic, Criton, and that the younger Melanippides is said to be a θυγατριδοῦς, a son of a daughter, yet with the same name as the grandfather, raises suspicion. Since no other source mentions two different poets named Melanippides of Melos, it seems best to follow Rohde and conclude that this is another instance of mistaken homonymous poets given by the Suda (Rohde 1878:213–214, Smyth 1906:453, LeVen 2008:38n26), see n. 51 above. *Contra* Jacoby 1904a:110–112, who takes this to be the elder Melanippides. Cf. Ierano 1997:209–210.

[150] Not necessarily his grandfather, see note to Greek text.

[151] Ctesias *ap.* Diodorus 14.46.6; Plutarch *Life of Alexander* 8.3; Athenaeus 637a cites from a dithyramb entitled *Hymenaeus*. In contrast, the Suda refers to him as κωμικός.

[152] Dionysius of Halicarnassus *On Literary Composition* 19.8 (= T 78 Ierano); cf. Barker 1984:97, Wallace 2003:87. Aristoxenus wrote a *Life of Telestes*. Ancient testimonies on Telestes are examined by Berlinzani 2008.

[153] So Munro 1901b:358; I cannot think of a better supplement than Aristonous for a poet whose name began with Ar[i]sto[or Ar[i]sta[and was victorious at or near 399/8 BCE (apart, perhaps, from a certain Aristarchus who won a dithyrambic victory at the Dionysia of 415 BCE [IG I.2 770a]).

[154] Käppel 1992:384ff, LeVen 2008:10n26 (*contra* Jacoby 1904a:116). Power 2010:453–454 analyzes Plutarch's anecdote.

Music.[155] The victory recorded in the Parian Marble is most probably a kitharodic one, perhaps achieved at the Panathenaea.[156] Two tragic poets named Astydamas are known in the fourth century, father and son (Suda A 4264, 4265); the reference in A71 is probably to the younger (TrGF 60).[157] Of Stesichorus the second nothing is known but the victory noted by the Parian Marble. In sum, the seven victories qualified as having taking place "in Athens" range from dithyrambic and kitharodic to tragic. Incidentally, three of these victories occupy an entry on their own: Melanippides (A47), Telestes (A65), and Aristonous (A67), all related to the so-called New Music.

In all probability, victories mentioned in the Parian Marble, even if not always qualified as "first," were at the time considered to be the first ones ever achieved by the poets, or the first at a given contest.[158] The inscription, however, makes no reference to specific festivals. For the dramatic and dithyrambic poets we may assume that it was the City Dionysia to which chronographers usually refer. If Aristonous's victory was indeed achieved at the Great Panathenaea, perhaps information may derive in this case from a Panathenaic victor list.

The Parian Marble is inconsistent in the range of agonistic information it offers, notwithstanding the formulaic language. Categories of competition are explicit sometimes, as with Aeschylus, Sophocles, Euripides ("in tragedy") and Polyidus ("in dithyramb"). Sometimes a qualification of the poet clarifies the type of competition, as with Philemon, Menander, and Anaxandrides (*komoidopoios*), as well as Philoxenus (*dithyrambopoios*). However, the victories of a few poets are generally qualified as achieved "in Athens" (Melanippides, Simonides the elder and the younger, Telestes, Aristonous, Astydamas, and Stesichorus the second). These three modalities in the agonistic references may ultimately derive from different sources. It is striking that no information on the festivals in which victories were achieved appears, nor any reference to choregoi or tribes for the dithyramb (apart from the qualification of Simonides as *didaskalos*). Such omissions of common didascalic information may indicate that none was available, perhaps because lists were used indirectly. Alternatively, information

---

[155] Furley and Bremer 2001 I:116–118, II:38–45, with further references; LeVen 2008:213–222 studies Aristonous' hymn to Hestia and the paean to Apollo.

[156] Power 2010:453n96.

[157] So Capps 1900:41–45, Mette 1977:30, based on the Parian Marble; *contra* Jacoby 1904a:117–119, Wilhelm and Kaibel 1906:186. The elder Astydamas's first production is dated to 398 BCE (Diodorus Siculus 14.43.5), and his first victory at the Dionysia between 376 and 362 BCE.

[158] Victories qualified as first: Hypodicus (A46), Aeschylus (A50), Euripides (A60), Telestes (A65), Menander (B14). Inconsistencies with information deriving mostly from other sources, especially Athenian victor lists, are usually resolved by the hypothesis that they refer to the Lenaea or to first productions (so, for example, the Parian Marble's placement of Philemon before Menander; Capps 1900:60, Wilhelm and Kaibel 1906:50, and more recently Iversen 2011:186–187, with further references).

about specific festivals may have been deemed unimportant outside Athens. Indeed, the specification that ten poets won their victories "in Athens"[159] makes better sense if the chronicle was composed for a non-Athenian audience.

The Parian Marble shows that agonistic documentation was probably the most visible manifestation of literary history within ancient Greek communities, both in the official memory maintained by public records and in the scholarly approach to the biographies of poets. From the end of the sixth century BCE, entries provide information almost exclusively on poetic victories, thus reflecting the cultural conditions of production of musical and poetic works and their consumption in classical Athens, as well as the construction of a history based upon them. In its emphasis on being first, implied both by poetic victories and *heuremata*, the Parian Marble reflects the general perception of literary history as a scene of competition.

3. Literary History in the Parian Marble

To conclude this chapter, a rather pragmatic question is in order. Can a literary historian trust, and to what extent, the dates transmitted by the Parian Marble? Most information regarding victories and deaths of poets seems to rest on solid traditions, written or oral. The dates are not necessarily right, but they do not appear to result from techniques of chronological computation, genealogical thinking, or synchronization. Not, perhaps, to be trusted are the dates before the fifth century BCE, including early *heuremata*, as well as the origins of choral and dramatic competitions. The real value of the Parian Marble, therefore, lies in the possible implications of its idiosyncratic choice of poets and events more than in their chronology.

The objective style of the inscription may seem to convey objective data, but literary history in the Parian Marble is intentional, not less than general history is (see chap. 4, sect. 5).[160] Beginning as a record of pan-Hellenic achievement, with Hyagnis, Orpheus, Mousaeus, Homer, Hesiod, Terpander, Sappho, and Hipponax, the chronicle limits its scope to Attica and Athens. If general history appears to stream centrifugally from Athens towards East and West, literary history seems to be drawn centripetally towards Athens. That author and audience may have construed such an Athenocentric view on the development of poetry as teleological would be an interesting, though speculative, suggestion.

---

[159] Melanippides (A47), Simonides the elder (A49), Simonides (A54), Telestes (A65), Aristonous (A67 suppl.), Polyidus (A68), Anaxandrides (A70), Astydamas (A71), Stesichorus the second (A73), Menander (B14).

[160] Gehrke 2001, cf. Foxhall, Gehrke, and Luraghi 2010 *passim*.

Limitation of scope is not only geographical. The extant inscription dispenses with orators and historians. Among philosophers, Socrates, Anaxagoras, and Aristotle are mentioned, but not Plato.[161] As for poetry, comparison with the so-called canonical authors is illuminating.[162] For epic poetry only the indisputable Homer and Hesiod are mentioned, not Antimachus, Panyassis, or Pisander. Iambic poetry is represented by Hipponax, but elegy is absent.[163] Lyric poetry features Sappho, Simonides, and Stesichorus, but the dithyramb seems to dominate,[164] and if Alcaeus[165] and Pindar are missing, the New Music is well represented, with Melanippides, Telestes, Polyidus, Philoxenus, Timotheus, and possibly Aristonous too.[166] Susarion and Epicharmus denote Comedy. Aristophanes is most conspicuously missing in the extant text, but New Comedy is represented or instantiated by at least three poets: Anaxandrides, Philemon, and Menander. Tragedy includes not only the triad of Aeschylus, Sophocles, and Euripides, but also the "modern" Astydamas, Sosiphanes I, and Sosiphanes II. In sum, the Parian Marble most clearly favors the competitive genres performed at Athenian festivals: tragedy, comedy, and dithyramb. Such an institutional approach to literary history, partly depending on the sources available, may explain why minor poetic genres were for the most part disregarded.[167]

The question whether the selection of poets and their distribution belongs to the author or his sources is difficult to gauge. The Parian Marble was composed within a tradition in which poets functioned as chronographic milestones, especially figures that could be synchronized with major historical events, such as Homer with the Trojan War. A great amount of information became available with the Athenian agonistic records of the fifth and fourth

[161] Cf. the range of intellectuals noted in Jerome's *Chronicle*, chap. 6, n. 35 above. Tod (1957:132n2) entertained the possibility that Plato was mentioned in A79 (see n. 25 above, and note to Greek text).

[162] Vardi 2003:151 sums up the lists of best authors found in Dionysius of Halicarnassus (fr. 6, II.204–214 U.-R.), Quintilian (*Institutio Oratoria* 10.1), Diomedes (*On Poems*, GL I.482–92), Caesius Bassus (*On Metres*, GL 6.312.7–9; cf. n35), Proclus (*ap.* Photius *Library* 239), Tzetzes (scholia to *Lycophron*, pp. 1–4, Scheer²), and the *Tractatus Coislinianus* 387.

[163] Unless one restores Archilochus in A33 and takes him as representative of both elegy and iambos.

[164] Hypodicus's choruses are not described as cyclic or as dithyrambic. In contrast, Polyidus and Philoxenus are explicitly connected to dithyramb. The victories by Melanippides and Simonides are most probably dithyrambic.

[165] Supplemented by Schoene in A36.

[166] According to Diodorus, the famous dithyrambic poets (οἱ ἐπισημότατοι διθυραμβοποιοί) Philoxenus, Timotheus, Telestes, and Polyidus flourished (ἤκμασαν) in the same year, the year concluding Ctesias of Cnidus' *Persian History* (*ap.* Diodorus 14.46.6 = FGrH 688 T 9).

[167] A similar reason may account for the near absence of lyric genres from the first chapters of Aristotle's *Poetics* (Rotstein 2004). The selection of poets in the post-sixth-century BCE entries of the Parian Marble may be an expression of the cognitive prism that I elsewhere denominate the "agonistic interface" (Rotstein 2012:120).

centuries precisely for the competitive genres of classical Athens. Research on the lives of poets by Glaucus of Rhegium and others surely provided materials for the biography of poets, including inventions and first victories. Similarities with Dioscorides suggest the *Peplos* or other similar works as possible intermediate sources in those realms. However, beyond the availability of information for literary history, many of the poets are chronographically unnecessary and were mentioned for their own sake, which may be an indication of authorial purpose. Similarly, the intriguing list of poets may be interpreted as the result of the author's choice. Indeed, it is striking that twelve poets are mentioned after the death of Euripides (A63) and Sophocles (A64). The number of poets is significantly smaller in the Parian fragment (B), which mentions only Philemon (B7), Menander (B14), Sosiphanes I (B15), and Sosiphanes II (B22). This may be due to the general change in focus to other parts of the Mediterranean (chap. 4, sect. 4), to the political demise of Athens, to the lack of appropriate sources for poetic victories in more recent periods, or to a combination of any of these factors. Still, a third of the poets and musicians mentioned in the Parian Marble are representatives of the late fourth-century poetry,[168] New Music, New Comedy, and perhaps New Tragedy, as well. In this sense, the Parian Marble's outlook differs utterly from the ancient lists of best authors developed in Hellenistic Alexandria.[169] These are much better reflected in the late antique *Chronicle* of Jerome (and its Greek original, the *Canons* of Eusebius) where we find fewer fifth-century dramatists than iambic, elegiac and lyric poets, and no fourth-century poets at all (see n. 35 above). The Parian Marble's alternative canon of poets, to use a somewhat provocative term, seems to have developed separately, combining chronographic traditions and techniques and available scholarly works with a taste for contemporary performance poetry. Such independence is consistent with the idiosyncratic count-down of years, the lack of chronographic sophistication, and perhaps also with the avoidance of papyrus format in the layout of the inscription.[170] Whether the Parian Marble's stance regarding literary history was unique remains a question for further investigation.

---

[168] Late fourth-century poets are studied by LeVen 2008 and, more recently, 2014, which I was unable to see before completing this book.

[169] See n. 162 above. On the concept of "selected authors," see Pfeiffer 1968:204–207; on notions of canon and canon-making, see Finkelberg and Stroumsa 2003, with further references.

[170] Jacoby noted the contrast between the unbookish layout of the Parian Marble, resulting from its very long lines, and the format of other inscriptions of the time (a late second-century BCE inscription on the foundation of Magnesia, IMagnesia 17) and the Epicurean inscription of Diogenes of Oinoanda (early second century CE), to which we may add the contemporary Mnesiepes inscription, with columns resembling a papyrus-leaf. Jacoby (1904b:90–91 with n1) suggested the author was unaware of the book practices current in Alexandria. The layout of the Parian Marble, however, was probably a default choice (see Rotstein 2014).

However, if the chronicle was conceived for display and consultation at a site for literary activities such as the Archilocheion (chap. 1, sect. 5 above), didactic concerns may have played a role in the selection of authors. Thus, along with the major events of panhellenic history and the classical poets, late fourth-century poetry appears to have been part of the knowledge expected from an educated man, perhaps even worthy of study, collection, and re-performance.

Final Words

The Parian Marble is a long inscription of unknown authorship, cut on a tall stele for display on the island of Paros. It may best be described as a selective chronographic list, annalistic in style and panhellenic in scope. It belongs to the families of ancient chronography and monumental historiography. The Parian Marble uses the basic techniques for time reckoning and the compressed, impersonal style typical of ancient chronicles, while sharing a world-view with ancient Greek historiography. The inscription dates events by Athenian kings and archons, yet a reference to a Parian archon at the very beginning anchors the chronicle in local history. Years are counted backwards down to year 1 (264/3 BCE), which must have been a meaningful date, perhaps marking the beginning of a new era established by Ptolemy II. We may consider the Parian Marble as the main representative of the "count-down" chronicle, a genre of which two miniature parallels survive, the Roman Chronicle and the Getty Table (early first century CE).

Unlike most ancient chronographic materials, the Parian Marble displays an exceptional emphasis on literary figures and events. Since many of them are unnecessary from a strictly chronographic point of view, presenting literary history embedded in panhellenic history appears to be one of the author's main concerns. The inscription may have been conceived for display and consultation at a site of literary activity, such as the Parian Archilocheion. Unlike the Mnesiepes and the Sosthenes inscriptions, which clearly foster local pride, the marked Athenian focus of the Parian Marble reflects the classicism typical of educational curricula, as well as the availability of sources for both general and literary history. Indeed, the Parian Marble focuses on the usual themes in the history of *mousike*, on the lives and chronology of poets, their inventions and victories. However, the record of poets is idiosyncratic. From the sixth century BCE, only the major competitive performance genres of Athens are represented, and the list of poets continues well after the death of Sophocles and Euripides. Thus, the Parian Marble displays a remarkably positive attitude towards late fourth-century developments in poetry and music. Such an attitude appears to have developed apart from the scholarly world of Alexandria, though in an atmosphere that likewise promoted literature under Ptolemaic rule.

Appendix
Thematic Classification of Events in the Parian Marble

Epoque	Political Event	Military Event	Cultural Events	Religious Event
A1	1	0	0	0
A2	1	0	0	0
A3	1	0	0	0
A4	0	0	0	2
A5	2	0	0	1
A6	1	0	0	0
A7	1	0	0	0
A8	1	0	0	0
A9	0	0	1	1
A10	0	0	4	2
A11	2	0	1	0
A12	0	0	1	1
A13	0	0	0	1
A14	0	0	1	0
A15	0	0	1	1
A16	0	0	0	1
A17	0	0	1	1
A18	0	0	0	0

Epoque	Political Event	Military Event	Cultural Events	Religious Event
A19	0	0	0	1
A20	1	0	1	1
A21	0	1	0	0
A22	0	1	1	1
A23	0	1	0	0
A24	0	1	0	0
A25	1	0	0	0
A26	1	0	0	0
A27	1	0	0	0
A28	0	0	1	0
A29	0	0	1	0
A30	0	0	1	0
A31	1	0	0	0
A32	1	0	0	0
A33	0	0	0	0
A34	0	0	1	0
A35	1	0	0	0
A36	1	0	1	0
A37	0	1	1	1
A38	0	0	1	1
A39	0	0	1	1
A40	1	0	0	0
A41	1	0	0	1
A42	0	1	1	0
A43	0	0	2	0

Epoque	Political Event	Military Event	Cultural Events	Religious Event
A44	1	0	0	0
A45	2	0	0	0
A46	0	0	1	0
A47	0	0	1	0
A48	0	1	0	0
A49	1	0	1	0
A50	0	0	3	0
A51	0	3	0	0
A52	0	1	0	0
A53	1	0	0	0
A54	1	0	1	0
A55	1	0	1	0
A56	0	0	1	0
A57	0	0	1	0
A58	2	0	0	0
A59	0	0	1	0
A60	0	0	3	0
A61	2	0	0	0
A62	1	0	0	0
A63	0	0	1	0
A64	0	1	1	0
A65	0	0	1	0
A66	0	1	1	0
A67	0	0	1	0
A68	0	0	1	0

Epoque	Political Event	Military Event	Cultural Events	Religious Event
A69	0	0	1	0
A70	0	0	1	0
A71	0	0	1	0
A72	1	1	0	0
A73	1	0	1	0
A74	3	0	0	0
A75	0	1	0	0
A76	0	0	1	0
A77	3	0	0	0
A78	0	0	1	0
A79	0	0	1	0
A80	0	0	0	0
Partition				
B1	2	0	0	0
B2	0	2	0	0
B3	0	3	0	0
B4	0	3	0	0
B5	1	3	0	0
B6	0	2	1	0
B7	1	0	1	0
B8	2	0	0	0
B9	0	2	0	0
B10	0	2	0	0
B11	3	3	1	0
B12	2	3	0	0

Epoque	Political Event	Military Event	Cultural Events	Religious Event
B13	1	1	0	0
B14	5	0	1	0
B15	0	0	1	0
B16	1	1	0	0
B17	2	0	0	0
B18	2	1	0	0
B19	3	1	0	0
B20	0	1	0	0
B21	0	2	0	0
B22	0	0	1	0
B23	1	1	0	0
B24	1	0	0	0
B25	0	1	0	0
B26	2	0	0	0
B27	0	1	0	0
Total	**69**	**48**	**56**	**18**

Plates

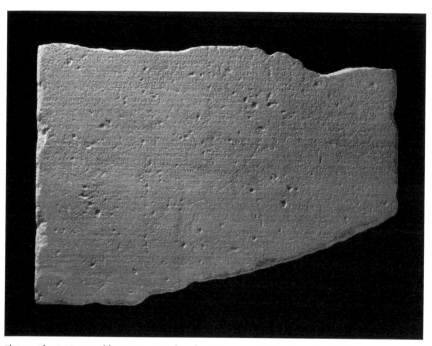

Plate 1. The Parian Marble, section A. Ashmolean Museum, University of Oxford, inv. ANChandler.2.23.

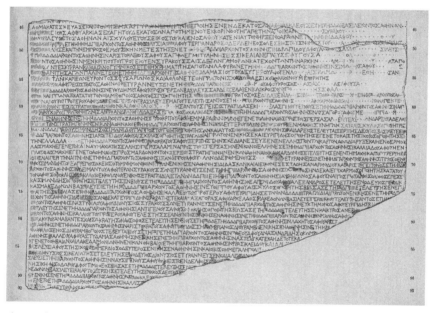

Plate 2. The Parian Marble, section A.

Plate 3. The Parian Marble, section B. Archaeological Museum of Paros, inv. no. A26.

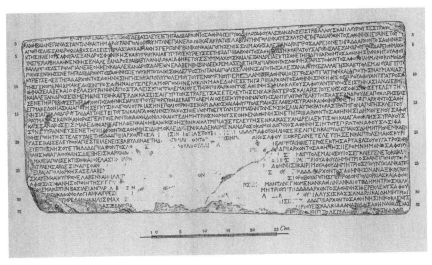

Plate 4. The Parian Marble, section B. Archaeological Museum, Paros.

Plate 5. Chronicon Romanum, recto (5a) and verso (5b). Capitoline Museum, Rome, inv. MC 342/S.

Plate 6. Getty Table, or "Tabula Iliaca" inscription, obverse (6a) and reverse (6b). The J. Paul Getty Museum, Villa Collection, Malibu, California, inv. 81.AA.113. Gift of Vasek Polak.

Plate 7. Mnesiepes Inscription, blocks E1 (7a) and E2 (7b). Archaeological Museum of Paros, inv. no. 175.

Plate 8. Mnesiepes Inscription, E1 III, lines 27–36. Original inscription in the Archaeological Museum of Paros.

Plate 9: Comparison of squeezes from the Parian Marble, Section B (top) and the
Mnesiepes Inscription (bottom).

Bibliography

Ambaglio, D. 1980. *L'opera storiografica di Ellanico di Lesbo*. Pisa.

Ameling, W. 2004. "Wohltäter im hellenistischen Gymnasion." In *Das hellenistische Gymnasion*, ed. D. Kah and P. Scholz, 129–161. Berlin.

Arrighetti, G. 1987. *Poeti, eruditi e biografi: momenti della riflessione dei Greci sulla letteratura*. Pisa.

Asheri, D. 1991–1992. "The Art of Synchronization in Greek Historiography: The Case of Timaeus of Tauromenium." *Scripta Classica Israelica* 11:52–89.

Athanassakis, A. N. 2001. "The *Marmor Parium*: A Reconsideration." In *Paria Lithos*, ed. D. U. Schilardi and D. Katsonopoulou, 187–191. Athens.

Austin, M. M. 2006. *The Hellenistic World from Alexander to the Roman Conquest: A Selection of Ancient Sources in Translation*. Cambridge.

Bagnall, R. S. 1976. *The Administration of the Ptolemaic Possessions outside Egypt*. Leiden.

Balcer, J. M. 1972. "The Date of Herodotus IV.1: Darius' Scythian Expedition." *Harvard Studies in Classical Philology* 76:99–132.

Barker, A. 1984. *Greek Musical Writings*. Vol. I: *The Musician and his Art*. Cambridge.

———. 2009. "Heraclides and Musical History." In *Heraclides of Pontus: Discussion*, ed. W. W. Fortenbaugh and E. E. Pender, 273–298. New Brunswick, NJ.

———. 2014. *Ancient Greek Writers on their Musical Past. Studies in Greek Musical Historiography*. Pisa.

Bartol, K. 2006. "The Lost World of Inventors: Athenaeus' Sentimental Heurematography." *Palamedes* 1:85–96.

———. 2013. "The Structure of Lysias' Speech in Pseudo-Plutarch's *On Music*." *Hermes* 141:401–416.

Beecroft, A. 2008. "Nine Fragments in Search of an Author: Poetic Lines Attributed to Terpander." *Classical Journal* 103:225–241.

———. 2010. *Authorship and Cultural Identity in Early Greece and China: Patterns of Literary Circulation*. Cambridge.

Berlinzani, F. 2008. "Teleste di Selinunte il ditirambografo." *Aristonothos* 2:109–140.

Berranger, D. 2000. *Paros II: prosopographie générale et étude historique du début de la période classique jusqu'à la fin de la période romaine*. Clermont-Ferrand.

Bertrand, J.-M. 1992. *Inscriptions historiques grecques*. Paris.

Blum, R. 1991. *Kallimachos. The Alexandrian Library and the Origins of Bibliography*. Translated by H. H. Wellisch. Madison, WI. Orig. pub. as *Kallimachos und die Literaturverzeichnung bei den Griechen*, 1977.

Bowie, E. L. Forthcoming. "Stesichorus at Athens." In *Stesichorus in Context*, ed. P. J. Finglass and A. D. Kelly. Cambridge.

Bowra, C. M. 1934. "Stesichorus in the Peloponnese." *Classical Quarterly* 28:115–119.

Bradeen, D. W. 1963. "The Fifth-Century Archon List." *Hesperia* 32:187–208.

Breitenberger, U. 2006. "Literaturwissenschaft, Sympotisches, Poesie." In *Aristoteles. Fragmente zu Philosophie, Rhetorik, Poetik, Dichtung*, ed. H. Flashar, U. Dubielzig, and U. Breitenberger, 289–331. Berlin.

Buckham, P. W. 1830. *The Theatre of the Greeks, or, The History, Literature and Criticism of the Grecian Drama, with an Original Treatise on the Principal Tragic and Comic Metres*. 3rd ed. Cambridge.

Burgess, R. W. 1997. "The Dates and Editions of Eusebius' *Chronici canones* and *Historia ecclesiastica*." *Journal of Theological Studies* NS 48: 471–504.

———. 1999. *Studies in Eusebian and Post-Eusebian Chronography*. Stuttgart.

———. 2002. "Jerome Explained: An Introduction to his Chronicle and a Guide to its Use." *Ancient History Bulletin* 16: 1–32.

———. 2013. "Another Look at the Newly-Discovered 'Leipzig World Chronicle.'" *Archiv für Papyrusforschung* 58:16–25.

Burgess, R. W., and M. Kulikowski. 2009. "The History and Origins of the Latin Chronicle Tradition." *The Medieval Chronicle* 6:153–177.

———. 2013. *Mosaics of Time. The Latin Chronicle Traditions from the Late Republic to the Early Middle Ages*, Vol. 1: *A History of the Chronicle from the Ancient Near East to the European Middle Ages*. Turnhout.

Burkert, W. 1966. "Greek Tragedy and Sacrificial Ritual." *Greek, Roman and Byzantine Studies* 7:87–121.

———. 1995. "Lydia Between East and West or How to Date the Trojan War: A Study in Herodotus." In *The Ages of Homer*, ed. J. B. Carter and S. P. Morris, 139–148. Austin.

Burstein, S. M. 1984. "A New 'Tabula Iliaca': The Vasek Polak Chronicle." *The J. Paul Getty Museum Journal* 12:153–162.

———. 1989. "'SEG 33.802' and the Alexander Romance." *Zeitschrift für Papyrologie und Epigraphik* 77:275–276.

Burzachechi, M. 1963. "Ricerche epigrafiche sulle antiche biblioteche del mondo greco." *Rendiconti della Classe di Scienze morali, storiche e filologiche dell'Accademia dei Lincei* 18:75–96.

——. 1984. "Ricerche epigrafiche sulle antiche biblioteche del mondo greco (continuazione)." *Rendiconti della Classe di Scienze morali, storiche e filologiche dell'Accademia dei Lincei* 29:307–338.

Cadoux, T. J. 1948. "The Athenian Archons from Kreon to Hypsichides." *Journal of Hellenic Studies* 68:70–123.

Cameron, A. 1995. *Callimachus and his Critics*. Princeton.

Campbell, D. A. 1993. Review of A. Gostoli 1990. *Gnomon* 65:70–71.

Capps, E. 1900. "Chronological Studies in the Greek Tragic and Comic Poets." *American Journal of Philology* 21:38–61.

Ceccarelli, P. 2013. "Circular Choruses and the Dithyramb in the Classical and Hellenistic Period: A Problem of Definition." In *Dithyramb in Context*, ed. B. Kowalzig and P. Wilson, 153–170. Oxford.

Chandler, R. 1763. *Marmora Oxoniensia*. Oxford.

Chaniotis, A. 1988. *Historie und Historiker in den griechischen Inschriften: epigraphische Beiträge zur griechischen Historiographie*. Stuttgart.

——. 2005. *War in the Hellenistic World: A Social and Cultural History*. Malden, MA.

——. 2007. Review of R. A. Hazzard 2000. *Classical World* 100:175–176.

——. 2009. "Travelling Memories in the Hellenistic World." In *Wandering Poets in Ancient Greek Culture: Travel, Locality, and Pan-Hellenism*, ed. R. L. Hunter and I. Rutherford, 249–269. Cambridge.

Christesen, P. 2005. "Imagining Olympia: Hippias of Elis and the First Olympic Victor List." In *A Tall Order: Writing the Social History of the Ancient World: Essays in Honor of William V. Harris*, ed. J.-J. Aubert and Z. Várhelyi, 319–356. Munich.

——. 2007. *Olympic Victor Lists and Ancient Greek History*. Cambridge.

Christesen, P., and Z. Martirosova-Torlone. 2006. "The Olympic Victor List of Eusebius: Background, Text, and Translation." *Traditio* 61:31–93.

Clarke, K. 1999. "Universal Perspectives in Historiography." In *The Limits of Historiography: Genre and Narrative in Ancient Historical Texts*, ed. C. S. Kraus, 249–279. Leiden.

——. 2008. *Making Time for the Past: Local History and the Polis*. Oxford.

Clay, D. 2004. *Archilochos Heros. The Cult of Poets in the Greek Polis*. Hellenic Studies 6. Washington, DC.

Cobet, J. 2002. "The Organization of Time in the *Histories*." In *Brill's Companion to Herodotus*, ed. E. J. Bakker, I. J. F. de Jong, and H. van Wees, 386–412. Leiden.

Colomo, D., L. Popko, M. Rücker, and R. Scholl. 2010. "Die älteste Weltchronik. Europa, die Sintflut und das Lamm." *Archiv für Papyrusforschung und verwandte Gebiete* 56:1–25.

Connor, W. R. 1990. "City Dionysia and Athenian Democracy." In *Aspects of Athenian Democracy*, ed. W. R. Connor, M. H. Hansen, K. A. Raaflaub, and B. S. Straus, 7–32. Copenhagen.

Constantakopoulou, C. 2012. "Identity and Resistance: The Islanders' League, the Aegean Islands and the Hellenistic kings." *Mediterranean Historical Review* 27:49–70.

Currie, B. 2011. "Perspectives on Neoanalysis from the Archaic Hymns to Demeter." In *Relative Chronology in Early Greek Epic Poetry*, ed. Ø. Andersen and D. T. T. Haug, 184–209. Cambridge.

D'Angour, A. 2011. *The Greeks and the New: Novelty in Ancient Greek Imagination and Experience*. Cambridge.

Daniel, R. W. 1996. "Epicharmus in Trier: A Note on the Monnus-Mosaic." *Zeitschrift für Papyrologie und Epigraphik* 114:30–36.

Dillery, J. 1999. "The First Egyptian Narrative History: Manetho and Greek Historiography." *Zeitschrift für Papyrologie und Epigraphik* 127:93–116.

Dinsmoor, W. B. 1939. *The Athenian Archon List in the Light of Recent Discoveries*. New York.

Dopp, E. 1883. *Quaestiones de Marmore Pario*. Bratislava.

———. 1905. Review of F. Jacoby 1904a. *Berliner philologische Wochenschrift* 25:531–536.

Dow, S. 1936. "New Kinds of Evidence for Dating Polyeuktos." *American Journal of Archaeology* 40:57–70.

Dueck, D., and K. Brodersen. 2012. *Geography in Classical Antiquity*. Cambridge.

Dunphy, R. G. 2010. *Encyclopedia of the Medieval Chronicle*. 2 vols. Leiden.

Ebert, E. 1987. "Der olympische Discus des Asklepiades und das Marmor Parium." *Tyche* 2:11–16.

Ercoles, M. 2014. "Notes on the Aulodic nomoi Apothetos and Schoinion." Greek And Roman Musical Studies 2:177–183.

Farnoux, A. 2002. "Homère à Délos." *Ktema* 27:97–104.

Feeney, D. 2007. *Caesar's Calendar: Ancient Time and the Beginnings of History*. Berkeley.

Finkelberg, M., and G. A. G. Stroumsa. 2003. *Homer, the Bible, and Beyond: Literary and Religious Canons in the Ancient World*. Leiden.

Flach, J. 1884. *Chronicon Parium*. Tübingen.

Ford, A. 2002. *The Origins of Criticism. Literary Culture and Poetic Theory in Classical Greece*. Princeton.

———. 2006. "Herodotus and the Poets." Princeton/Stanford Working Papers in Classics, http://www.princeton.edu/~pswpc/papers/authorAL/ford/ford.html. Accessed Dec. 9, 2006.

Fornara, C. W. 1983. *The Nature of History in Ancient Greece and Rome*. Berkeley.

Fotheringham, J. K. 1924. "The Metonic and Callippic Cycles." *Monthly Notices of the Royal Astronomical Society* 84:383–392.

Fowler, R. L. 1996. "Herodotos and his Contemporaries." *Journal of Hellenic Studies* 116:62–87.

———. 1998-1999. "Genealogical Thinking, Hesiod's Catalogue, and the Creation of the Hellenes." *Proceedings of the Cambridge Philological Society* 44:1–19.

Foxhall, L., H.-J. Gehrke, and N. Luraghi. 2010. *Intentional History: Spinning Time in Ancient Greece.* Stuttgart.

Franklin, J. C. 2003. "The Language of Musical Technique in Greek Epic Diction." *Gaia* 7:295–307.

———. 2010. "Remembering Music in Early Greece." In *The Historiography of Music in Global Perspective,* ed. S. Mirelman, 9–50. Piscataway, NJ.

———. 2012. "The Lesbian Singers: Towards a Reconstruction of Hellanicus' Karneian Victors." In *Poesia, musica e agoni nella Grecia antica: atti del IV Convegno internazionale di MOISA, 28-30 ottobre 2010,* ed. D. Castaldo, F. G. Giannachi, and A. Manieri, 719–764. Galatina.

———. 2013. "'Song-Benders of Circular Choruses': Dithyramb and the 'Demise of Music.'" In *Dithyramb in Context,* ed. B. Kowalzig and P. Wilson, 213–236. Oxford.

Fraser, P. M. 1972. *Ptolemaic Alexandria.* Oxford.

Furley, W. D., and J. M. Bremer. 2001. *Greek Hymns: Selected Cult Songs from the Archaic to the Hellenistic Period,* Vol. I: *The Texts in Translation.* Tübingen.

Gassendi, P. 1641. *Viri illustris Nicolai Claudii Fabricii de Peiresc.* Paris.

Gauthier, P. 2006. "Les Décrets de Colophon-sur-mer en l'honneur des Attalides Athènaios et Philétairos." *Revue des études grecques* 119:473–503.

Gehrke, H.-J. 2001. "Myth, History, and Collective Identity: Uses of the Past in Ancient Greece and Beyond." In *The Historian's Craft in the Age of Herodotus,* ed. N. Luraghi, 286–313. Oxford.

Gerber, D. E. 1999. *Greek Iambic Poetry. From the Seventh to the Fifth Centuries BC.* Cambridge, MA.

Glassner, J.-J., and B. R. Foster. 2004. *Mesopotamian Chronicles.* Atlanta. Orig. pub. as *Chroniques Mésopotamiennes,* 1993.

Goldstein, B. R., and A. C. Bowen. 1989. "On Early Hellenistic Astronomy: Timocharis and the First Callippic Calendar." *Centaurus* 32:272–293.

Gostoli, A. 1986. "La figura dell'aedo preomerico nella filologia peripatetica ed ellenistica: Demodoco tra mito e storia." In *Scrivere e recitare,* ed. G. Cerri, 103–126. Rome.

———. 1990. *Terpander: veterum testimonia et fragmenta.* Rome.

Gow, A. S. F., and D. L. Page. 1968. *The Greek Anthology. The Garland of Philip and Some Contemporary Epigrams.* 2 vols. Cambridge.

Graf, F. 1974. *Eleusis und die Orphische Dichtung Athens in vorhellenistischer Zeit.* Berlin.

Grafton, A. 1995. "Tradition and Technique in Historical Chronology." In *Ancient History and the Antiquarian: Essays in Memory of Arnaldo Momigliano,* ed. M. H. Crawford and C. R. Ligota, 15–31. London.

Graham, A. J. 1978. "The Foundation of Thasos." *Annual of the British School at Athens* 73:61–98.

Grayson, A. K. 1975. *Assyrian and Babylonian Chronicles.* Locust Valley, N.Y.

Graziosi, B. 2002. *Inventing Homer: The Early Reception of Epic.* Cambridge.

Guarducci, M. 1974. *Epigrafia greca III. Epigrafi di carattere privato.* Rome.

Gutzwiller, K. 2010. "Heroic Epitaphs of the Classical Age." In *Archaic and Classical Greek Epigram,* ed. M. Baumbach, A. Petrovic, and I. Petrovic, 219–249. New York.

Hannah, R. 2005. *Greek and Roman Calendars: Constructions of Time in the Classical World.* London.

Harding, P. 1985. *From the End of the Peloponnesian War to the Battle of Ipsus.* Cambridge.

Haslam, M. W. 1986. "The Fall of Sardis in the Roman Chronicle." *Zeitschrift für Papyrologie und Epigraphik* 62:198.

Hawkins, T. 2009. "This is the Death of the Earth: Crisis Narratives in Archilochus and Mnesiepes." *Transactions of the American Philological Association* 139:1–20.

———. 2011. "The Judgement of Paros." Paper presented at San Francisco State University, April 2011.

Hazzard, R. A. 2000. *Imagination of a Monarchy: Studies in Ptolemaic Propaganda.* Toronto.

Helm, R., ed. 1956. *Die Chronik des Hieronymus. Hieronymi Chronicon.* Berlin. (1st edition: 1913–1926).

Henige, D. P. 1974. *The Chronology of Oral Tradition: Quest for a Chimera.* Oxford.

Henrichs, A. 1985. "Zur Genealogie des Musaios." *Zeitschrift für Papyrologie und Epigraphik* 58:1–8.

Henry, A. S. 1977. *The Prescripts of Athenian Decrees.* Leiden.

Henzen, W. 1854. "Eine neuentdeckte griechische Zeittafel." *Rheinisches Museum* 9:161-178.

Hewlett, J. 1789. *A Vindication of the Authenticity of the Parian Chronicle.* London.

Higbie, C. 2003. *The Lindian Chronicle and the Greek Creation of Their Past.* Oxford.

Hiller von Gärtringen, F. 1903. "444. Chronicum Parium," in *Inscriptiones Graecae.* Vol. XII.5, *Inscriptiones Cycladum praeter Tenum,* 100–111. Berlin.

———. 1934. "Noch einmal das Archilochosdenkmal von Paros." *Nachrichten aus der Altertumswissenschaft Göttingen, philologisch-historische Klasse* 1:41–56.

Homolle, T. 1898. "Inscription de Delphes." *Bulletin de correspondance hellénique* 22:260–270.

Horsfall, N. 1979. "Stesichorus at Bovillae?" *Journal of Hellenic Studies* 99:26–48.

———. 1983. "Tabulae Iliacae in the Collection Froehner, Paris." *Journal of Hellenic Studies* 103:144–147.

Hose, M. 2002. *Aristoteles. Die historischen Fragmente.* Berlin.

Hunter, R. L., and I. Rutherford. 2009. *Wandering Poets in Ancient Greek Culture: Travel, Locality, and Pan-Hellenism.* Cambridge.

Huss, W. 2001. *Ägypten in hellenistischer Zeit 332–30 v. Chr.* Munich.

Huxley, G. 1968. "Glaukos of Rhegion." *Greek, Roman and Byzantine Studies* 9:47–54.

Ierano, G. 1997. *Il ditirambo di Dioniso: Le testimonianze antiche.* Pisa.

Iversen, P. A. 2011. "Menander's Thaïs: 'Hac Primum Iuvenum Lascivos Lusit Amores.'" *Classical Quarterly* 61:186–191.

Jacoby, F. 1902. "Die Attische Königsliste." *Klio* 2:406–439.

———. 1903. "Sosiphanes." *Rheinisches Museum* 58:459–461.

———. 1904a. *Das Marmor Parium.* Berlin.

———. 1904b. "Über das Marmor Parium." *Rheinisches Museum* 59:63–107.

———. 1909. "Über die Entwicklung der griechischen Historiographie und den Plan einer neuen Sammlung der griechischen Historikerfragmente." *Klio* 9:80–123.

———. 1955. FGrH IIIb Kommentar, 415–416 (Notes). Leiden.

Jahn, O., and A. Michaelis. 1873. *Griechische Bilderchroniken.* Bonn.

Jones, A. 2000. "Calendrica I: New Callippic Dates." *Zeitschrift für Papyrologie und Epigraphik* 129:141–158.

Käppel, L. 1992. *Paian: Studien zur Geschichte einer Gattung.* Berlin.

Karanika, A. 2010. "Inside Orpheus' Songs: Orpheus as an Argonaut in Apollonius Rhodius' Argonautica." *Greek, Roman and Byzantine Studies* 50:391–410.

Kimmel, F. 2008. *Morts, tombeaux et cultes des poètes grecs. Étude de la survie des grands poètes des époques archaïque et classique en Grèce ancienne.* Ph.D. diss., Université Jean Moulin, Lyon 3.

Kivilo, M. 2000. "Certamen." *Studia Humaniora Tartuensia* 1:1–5.

———. 2010. *Early Greek Poets' Lives: The Shaping of the Tradition.* Leiden.

Kleingünther, A. 1933. *ΠΡΩΤΟΣ ΕΥΡΕΤΗΣ. Untersuchungen zur Geschichte einer Fragestellung.* Leipzig.

Körte, A., ed. 1890. *Metrodori Epicurei fragmenta.* Leipzig.

Koiv, M. 2011. "A Note on the Dating of Hesiod." *Classical Quarterly* 61:355–377.

Koning, H. H. 2010. *Hesiod, the Other Poet: Ancient Reception of a Cultural Icon.* Leiden.

Kontoleon, N. M. 1952 [1955]. "ΝΕΑΙ ΕΠΙΓΡΑΦΑΙ ΠΕΡΙ ΤΟΥ ΑΡΧΙΛΟΧΟΥ ΕΚ ΠΑΡΟΥ." *Archaiologike ephemeris* 32–95.

———. 1956. "Zu den neuen Archilochosinschriften." *Philologus* 100:29–39.

———. 1964a. "Archilochos und Paros." In *Archiloque*, 37–86. Fondation Hardt, Entretiens sur l'antiquité Classique 10. Geneva.

———. 1964b. "Zu den literarischen anagraphai." In *Akte des 4. internationalen Kongresses für griechische und lateinische Epigraphik*, 192–201. Vienna.

Kowalzig, B., and P. Wilson. 2013. *Dithyramb in Context*. Oxford.

Kranz, W. 1919. "Die Urform der attischen Tragödie und Komödie." *Neue Jahrbücher für die klassische Altertumsgeschichte und deutsche Literatur und für Pädagogik* 22:145–169.

Kretschmer, P. 1911. "Griechisches." *Glotta* 2:156–164.

Krispi, M. K., and A. Wilhelm. 1897. "Ein neues Bruchstück der Parischen Marmorchronik." *Athener Mitteilungen* 22:183–217.

Lämmer, M. 1967. "Der Diskos des Asklepiades aus Olympia und das Marmor Parium." *Zeitschrift für Papyrologie und Epigraphik* 1:107–109.

Lanata, G. 1963. *Poetica pre-Platonica. Testimonianza e frammenti*. Florence.

Lanzillotta, E. 1987. *Paro dall' età arcaica all' età ellenistica*. Rome.

Lasserre, F. 1954. *Plutarque, De la Musique*. Lausanne.

Lefkowitz, M. R. 2012. *The Lives of the Greek Poets*. 2nd ed. London.

Legrand, P. E. 1964. *Hérodote, Histoires*. Paris.

LeVen, P. A. 2008. *The Many-Headed Muse: Tradition and Innovation in Fourth-Century B.C. Greek Lyric Poetry*. Ph.D. diss., Princeton University.

———. 2014. *The Many-Headed Muse: Tradition and Innovation in Late Classical Greek Poetry*. Cambridge.

Leyden, W. von. 1949–1950. "Spatium Historicum: The Historical Past as Viewed by Hecataeus, Herodotus, and Thucydides." *Durham University Journal* 11:89–104.

Liddel, P. 2014. "From Chronography to Liberal Imperialism: Greek Inscriptions, the History of Greece, and Historiography from Selden to Grote." *Journal of the History of Collections Advanced Access* (first published online April 26, 2014).

Lomiento, L. 2001. "Da Sparta ad Alessandria. La trasmissione dei testi nella Grecia antica." In *La civiltà dei Greci. Forme, luoghi, contesti*, ed. M. Vetta, 297–355. Rome.

Lorber, C. C. 2007. "The Ptolemaic Era Coinage Revisited." *The Numismatic Chronicle* 167:105–117.

Luppe, W. 2010. "Korrekturen und Ergänzungen zur Leipziger Weltchronik." *Archiv für Papyrusforschung und verwandte Gebiete* 56:200–206.

Macridy, T. 1905. "Altertümer von Notion." *Jahreshefte des Österreichischen Archäologischen Institutes* 8:155–173.

Maittaire, M. 1732. *Marmorum Arundellianorum Seldenianorum aliorumque Academiae oxoniensi donatorum cum variis commentariis & indice.* 2nd ed. London.

Marincola, J. 1997. *Authority and Tradition in Ancient Historiography.* Cambridge.

———. 2012. "Introduction: A Past without Historians." In *Greek Notions of the Past in the Archaic and Classical Eras: History without Historians,* ed. J. Marincola, L. Llewellyn-Jones, and C. A. Maciver, 1–13. Edinburgh.

Marquaille, C. 2008. "The Foreign Policy of Ptolemy II." In *Ptolemy II Philadelphus and his World,* ed P. McKechnie and P. Guillaume, 39–64. Leiden.

Martano, A., E. Matelli, and D. C. Mirhady. 2012. *Praxiphanes of Mytilene and Chamaeleon of Heraclea: Text, Translation, and Discussion.* New Brunswick, NJ.

Mazzarino, S. 1966. "L'intuizione del tempo." In *Il Pensiero storico classico,* 2.2.:412–461. Rome.

McLeod, W. 1985. "The 'Epic Canon' of the Borgia Table: Hellenistic Lore or Roman Fraud?" *Transactions of the American Philological Association* 115:153–165.

Merkelbach, R. 1989. "Der Brief des Dareios im Getty-Museum und Alexanders Wortwechsel mit Parmenion." *Zeitschrift für Papyrologie und Epigraphik* 77:277–280.

Merrit, B. D. 1977. "Athenian Archons 347/6–48/7 B.C." *Historia* 26:161–191.

Mette, H. J. 1977. *Urkunden dramatischer Aufführungen in Griechenland.* Berlin.

Michaelis, A. 1858. *Inscriptiones Tabulae Iliacae.* Rome.

———. 1882. *Ancient Marbles in Great Britain.* Cambridge.

Miller, P. N. 2005a. "Nicolas-Claude Fabri de Peiresc and the Mediterranean World: Mechanics." In *Les grands intermédiaires culturels de la République des Lettres. Études de réseaux de correspondances du XVIe au XVIIIe siècles,* ed. C. Berkvens-Stevelinck, H. Bots, and J. Häseler, 103–126. Paris.

———. 2005b. "Peiresc, the Levant and the Mediterranean." In *The Republic of Letters in the Levant,* ed. A. Hamilton, 103–122. Leiden.

Millis, B. W., and S. D. Olson. 2012. *Inscriptional Records for the Dramatic Festivals in Athens: IG II2 2318-2325 and Related Texts.* Leiden.

Möller, A. 2001. "The Beginning of Chronography: Hellanicus' *Hiereiai.*" In *The Historian's Craft in the Age of Herodotus,* ed. N. Luraghi, 241–262. Oxford.

———. 2004. "Greek Chronographic Traditions about the First Olympic Games." In *Time and Temporality in the Ancient World,* ed. R. M. Rosen, 169–184. Philadelphia.

———. 2005. "Epoch-making Eratosthenes." *Greek, Roman and Byzantine Studies* 45:245–260.

———. 2006. "Felix Jacoby and the Ancient Greek Chronology." In *Aspetti dell'opera di Felix Jacoby,* ed. C. Ampolo, 259–275. Pisa.

Möller, A., and N. Luraghi. 1995. "Time in the Writing of History: Perceptions and Structures." *Storia della Storiografia* 28:3–15.

Momigliano, A. 1966. "Time in Ancient Historiography." *History and Theory* 6:1–23.

Montanari, F. 1993. "L'erudizione, la filologia, la grammatica." In *Lo spazio letterario della Grecia antica. Vol. I tomo 2. La produzione e la circolazione del testo. L'Ellenismo*, ed. G. Cambiano, L. Canfora, and D. Lanza, 235–281. Rome.

Mørkholm, O. 1975–1976. "The Ptolemaic 'Coins of an Uncertain Era.'" *Nordisk numismatisk årsskrift* 23–58.

Morkot, R. 1996. *The Penguin Historical Atlas of Ancient Greece*. London.

Mosshammer, A. A. 1979. *The Chronicle of Eusebius and Greek Chronographic Tradition*. Lewisburg, PA.

Munro, J. A. R. 1901a. "Notes on the Text of the Parian Marble. I." *Classical Review* 15:149–154.

———. 1901b. "Notes on the Text of the Parian Marble. II." *Classical Review* 15:355–361.

———. 1905. Review of Jacoby 1904a. *Classical Review* 19:267–269.

Murray, O. 1972. "Herodotus and Hellenistic Culture." *Classical Quarterly* 22:200–213.

Nagy, G. 1979. *The Best of the Achaeans*. Baltimore.

———. 2002. *Plato's Rhapsody and Homer's Music: the Poetics of the Panathenaic Festival in Classical Athens*. Hellenic Studies 1. Washington, DC.

———. 2009. "Hesiod and the Ancient Biographical Traditions." In *Brill's Companion to Hesiod*, ed. F. Montanari, A. Rengakos, and C. Tsagalis, 271–311. Leiden.

Nicolai, R. 1987. "Le biblioteche dei ginnasi." *Nuovi annali della scuola speciale per archivisti e bibliotecari* 1:17–48.

Niese, B. 1888. "Die Chronographie des Eratosthenes." *Hermes* 23:92–102.

Ohnesorg, A. 1982. "Der dorische Prostylos des Archilocheion auf Paros." *Archäologischer Anzeiger* 271–290.

———. 2008. "The Architectural Form of the Archilocheion of Paros." In *Archilochos and His Age. Proceedings of the Second International Conference on the Archaeology of Paros and the Cyclades*, ed. D. Katsonopoulou, I. Petropoulos, and S. Katsarou, 303–324. Athens.

Ornaghi, M. 2009. *La lira, la vacca e le donne insolenti: contesti di ricezione e promozione della figura e della poesia di Archiloco dall'arcaismo all'ellenismo*. Alessandria.

Osborne, M. J. 1989. "The Chronology of Athens in the Mid-Third Century B.C." *Zeitschrift für Papyrologie und Epigraphik* 78:209–242.

Osborne, R. G. 1993. "Competitive Festivals and the Polis: A Context for Dramatic Festivals at Athens." *Tragedy, Comedy and the Polis.* ed. A. H. Sommerstein, S. Halliwell, J. Henderson, and B. Zimmermann, 21-38. Bari.

Parke, H. W. 1958. "The Newly Discovered Delphic Responses from Paros." *Classical Quarterly* 8:90–94.

Paton, W. R. 1917. *The Greek Anthology.* 5 vols. London.

Peek, W. 1955. "Neues von Archilochos." *Philologus* 99:4–50.

———. 1976. "Epigramm aus Chios." *Zeitschrift für Papyrologie und Epigraphik* 23:87–90.

Petrain, D. 2006. *Epic Manipulations: The Tabulae Iliacae in their Roman Context.* Cambridge, MA.

———. 2008. "Two Inscriptions from the 'Tabulae Iliacae' the Epic Canon of the Borgia Tablet (IG 14.1292.2) and the Roman Chronicle (*SEG* 33.802B)." *Zeitschrift für Papyrologie und Epigraphik* 166:83–84.

Pfeiffer, R. 1968. *History of Classical Scholarship. From the Beginnings to the End of the Hellenistic Age.* Oxford.

Pfohl, G. 1966. *Griechische Inschriften als Zeugnisse des privaten und öffentlichen Lebens: Griechisch-Deutsch.* Munich.

Piccirilli, L. 1974. "Susarione e la rivendicazione megarese dell'origine della commedia greca (Arist., poet., 3, p.1448a 29–48b 2)." *Annali della Scuola Normale Superiore di Pisa* 4:1289–1299.

Pickard-Cambridge, A. W. 1962. *Dithyramb, Tragedy, and Comedy.* 2nd ed. Oxford.

Pleket, H. W., and R. S. Stroud. 1983. "802: Rome and the Roman Campagna. Tabulae Iliacae, Early 1st cent. A.D." *SEG* 33.

Podlecki, A. J. 1969. "The Peripatetics as Literary Critics." *Phoenix* 23:114–137.

Pohlmann, E. 1994. *Einführung in die überlieferungsgeschichte und in die Textkritik der antiken Literatur.* Darmstadt.

Power, T. C. 2010. *The Culture of Kitharôidia.* Hellenic Studies 15. Washington, D.C.

Prêtre, C., and M. Brunet. 2002. *Nouveau choix d'inscriptions de Délos : Lois, comptes et inventaires.* Athens.

Prideaux, H. 1676. *Marmora Oxoniensia ex Arundellianis Seldenianis aliisque conflata.* Oxford.

Privitera, G. A. 1965. *Laso di Ermione nella cultura ateniese e nella tradizione storiografica.* Rome.

———. 1966. "Archiloco e le divinità dell' Archilocheion." *Rivista di filologia e di istruzione classica* 94:5–25.

Reisch, E. 1907. "Urkunden dramatischer Aufführungen in Athen." *Zeitschrift für die österreichischen Gymnasien* 58:289–315.

Reitzenstein, R. 1893. *Epigramm und Skolion. Ein Beitrag zur Geschichte der Alexandrinischen Dichtung.* Giessen.

Renger, J. 2012. "Introduction: Sources for the Reconstruction of Ancient Near Eastern Chronological Systems." In *Brill's New Pauly*, Suppl. 1, Vol. 1: *Chronologies of the Ancient World—Names, Dates and Dynasties*, ed. W. Eder and J. Renger. Leiden. Accessed online.

Rice, E. E. 1983. *The Grand Procession of Ptolemy Philadelphus*. Oxford.

Richardson, N. J. 1994. "Aristotle and Hellenistic Scholarship." In *La Philologie grecque à l'époque hellénistique et romaine*, ed. F. Montanari, 7–28. Vendoeuvres-Geneva.

Robert, J., and L. Robert. 1955. "178. Paros." *Revue des études grecques* 68:248–250.

Roberts, W. 1791. *Marmorum oxoniensium inscriptiones graecae ad Chandleri exemplar editae*. Oxford.

Robertson, J. 1788. *The Parian Chronicle, or The Chronicle of the Arundelian Marbles; with a Dissertation Concerning its Authenticity*. London.

Rohde, E. 1878. "Γέγονε in den Biographica des Suidas." *Rheinisches Museum* 33:161–220.

Rose, V. 1967. *Aristotelis qui ferebantur librorum fragmenta*. Stuttgart. Orig. ed.: Leipzig, 1886.

Rosenberger, V. 2008. "Panhellenic, Athenian, and Local Identities in the Marmor Parium?" In *Religion and Society: Rituals, Resources and Identity in the Ancient Graeco-Roman World*, ed. A. H. Rasmussen and S. W. Rasmussen, 225–233. Rome.

Rotstein, A. 2004. "Aristotle, *Poetics* 1447a13–16 and Musical Contests." *Zeitschrift für Papyrologie und Epigraphik* 149:39–42.

———. 2007. "A história da poesia no capítulo 4 da Poética de Aristóteles (*Poética* 1448b20–1449b9)." In *II Simpósio de Estudos Clássicos da USP*, ed. M. e. a. dos Santos, 21–37. São Paulo.

———. 2010. *The Idea of Iambos*. Oxford.

———. 2012. "*Mousikoi Agones* and the Conceptualization of Genres in Ancient Greece." *Classical Antiquity* 31:92–127.

———. 2014. "The Parian Marble and the Mnesiepes Inscription." *Zeitschrift für Papyrologie und Epigraphik* 190:3–9.

———. 2016. "The Ancient Literary History of Iambos." In *Greek Iambus and Elegy: New Approaches*, ed. L. Swift and C. Carey. Oxford.

Rusten, J. 2006. "Who 'Invented' Comedy? The Ancient Candidates for the Origins of Comedy and the Visual Evidence." *American Journal of Philology* 127:37–66.

Rusten, J. S., and J. Henderson. 2011. *The Birth of Comedy: Texts, Documents, and Art from Athenian Comic Competitions, 486–280*. Baltimore.

Sadurska, A. 1964. *Les tables iliaques*. Warsaw.

Salimbene, C. 2002. "La Tabula Capitolina." *Bollettino dei musei comunali di Roma* 16:5–33.

Samuel, A. E. 1972. *Greek and Roman Chronology: Calendars and Years in Classical Antiquity*. Munich.

Schenkeveld, D. M., J. G. J. Abbenes, S. R. Slings, and I. Sluiter. 1995. *Greek Literary Theory after Aristotle: A Collection of Papers in Honour of D. M. Schenkeveld*. Amsterdam.

Scholz, P. 2004. "Elementarunterricht und intellektuelle Bildung im hellenistischen Gymnasion." In *Das hellenistische Gymnasion*, ed. D. Kah and P. Scholz, 103–128. Berlin.

Schütrumpf, E., ed. 2008. *Heraclides of Pontus: Texts and Translation*. New Brunswick.

Scullion, S. 2002. "Tragic Dates." *Classical Quarterly* 52:81–101.

Secchi, G. 1843. "Sulla cronachetta di palombino testè scoperta a Roma." *Bulletin de l'Institut de correspondance archéologique*. Rome.

Selden, J. 1628. *Marmora Arundelliana, sive, Saxa Graecè incisa*. London.

Shaw, P.-J. 2003. *Discrepancies in Olympiad Dating and Chronological Problems of Archaic Peloponnesian History*. Stuttgart.

Shimron, B. 1973. "πρῶτος τῶν ἡμῖς ἴδμεν." *Eranos* 71:45–51.

Sickinger, J. P. 1999. *Public Records and Archives in Classical Athens*. Chapel Hill.

Slings, S. R. 1991. "Review of *Greek Lyric with an English Translation*, Vol. II: *Anacreon, Anacreontea, Choral Lyric from Olympus to Alcman* by D. A. Campbell." *Mnemosyne* 44:172–176.

Smith, M. F. 1996. *The Philosophical Inscription of Diogenes of Oinoanda*. Vienna.

———. 2003. *Supplement to Diogenes of Oinoanda. The Epicurean Inscription*. Naples.

Smyth, H. W. 1906. *Greek Melic Poets*. London.

Sourvinou-Inwood, C. 2003. *Tragedy and the Athenian Religion*. Lanham, MD.

Squire, M. 2010. "Texts on the Tables: The *Tabulae Iliacae* in Their Hellenistic Literary Context." *Journal of Hellenic Studies* 130:67–96.

———. 2011. *The* Iliad *in a Nutshell: Visualizing Epic on the* Tabulae Iliacae. Oxford.

Stern, S. 2012. *Calendars in Antiquity: Empires, States, and Societies*. Oxford.

Sutton, D. F. 1987. "The Theatrical Families of Athens." *American Journal of Philology* 108:9–26.

Tarditi, I. T. 1956. "La nuova epigrafe archilochea e la tradizione biografica del poeta." *La Parola del Passato* 11:122–139.

Thomas, R. 2001. "Herodotus' Histories and the Floating Gap." In *The Historian's Craft in the Age of Herodotus*, ed. N. Luraghi, 198–210. Oxford.

Threatte, L. 1980. *The Grammar of Attic Inscriptions*. Berlin.

Tod, M. N. 1946. *A Selection of Greek Historical Inscriptions*. 2 vols. 2nd ed. Oxford.

———. 1951. "Epigraphical Notes from the Ashmolean Museum." *Journal of Hellenic Studies* 71:172–177.

———. 1957. "Sidelights on Greek Philosophers." *Journal of Hellenic Studies* 77:132–141.

Toomer, G. J. 2009. *John Selden: A Life in Scholarship*. New York.

Traede, K. 1962. "Das Lob des Erfinders. Bemerkungen zur Analyse der Heuremata-Kataloge." *Rheinisches Museum* 105:158–186.

Treu, M. 1959. *Archilochos*. Munich.

Valenzuela Montenegro, N. 2004. *Die Tabulae Iliacae: Mythos und Geschichte im Spiegel einer Gruppe frühkaiserzeitlicher Miniaturreliefs*. Ph.D. diss., Munich University.

van der Spek, R. J. 2008. "Berossus as a Babylonian Chronicler and Greek Historian." In *Studies in Ancient Near Eastern World View and Society*, ed. R. J. van der Spek, 277–318. Bethesda, MD.

van Wees, H. 2002. "Herodotus and the Past." In *Brill's Companion to Herodotus*, ed. E. J. Bakker, I. J. F. d. Jong, and H. v. Wees, 321–349. Leiden.

Vanderpool. 1955. "New Inscriptions concerning Archilochos." *American Journal of Philology* 76:186–188.

Vansina, J. 1965. *Oral tradition: A Study in Historical Methodology*. London.

Vardi, A. D. 2003. "Canons of Literary Texts at Rome." In *Homer, The Bible and Beyond: Literary and Religious Canons in the Ancient World*, ed. M. Finkelberg and G. Stroumsa, 131–152. Leiden.

Verbrugghe, G., and J. M. Wickersham. 1996. *Berossos and Manetho, Introduced and Translated: Native Traditions in Ancient Mesopotamia and Egypt*. Ann Arbor.

Vickers, M. 2006. *The Arundel and Pomfret Marbles*. Oxford.

Waddell, W. G. 1956. *Manetho*. Cambridge, MA.

Wallace, R. W. 2003. "An Early Fifth-Century Athenian Revolution in Aulos Music." *Harvard Studies in Classical Philology* 101:73–92.

Walz, C., ed. 1893. *Scholia ad Hermogenes status seu artem rhetoricam*, Rhetores Graeci, vol. 5 (Stuttgart, 1883).

Wendling, E. 1891. *De Peplo Aristotelico quaestiones selectae*. Argentorati.

West, M. L. 1971. "Stesichorus." *Classical Quarterly* 21:302–314.

———. 1983. *The Orphic Poems*. Oxford.

———. 1989. "The Early Chronology of Attic Tragedy." *Classical Quarterly* 39:251–254.

White, H. V. 1987. "The Value of Narrativity in the Representation of Reality." In *The Content of the Form: Narrative Discourse and Historical Representation*, 1–25. Baltimore.

Wilhelm, A. 1909. *Beiträge zur griechischen Inschriftenkunde mit einem Anhange über die öffentliche Aufzeichung von Urkunden*. Vienna.

Wilhelm, A., and G. Kaibel. 1906. *Urkunden dramatischer Aufführungen in Athen*. Vienna.

Wilson, P. 2000. *The Athenian Institution of the Khoregia: The Chorus, the City and the Stage*. Cambridge.

————. 2003. "The Politics of Dance: Dithyrambic Contest and Social Order in Ancient Greece." In *Sport and Festival in the Ancient Greek World*, ed. D. J. Phillips and D. Pritchard, 163–196. Swansea.

————. 2004. "Athenian Strings." In *Music and the Muses*, ed. P. Wilson and P. Murray, 269–306. Oxford.

————. 2007a. "Sicilian Choruses." In *The Greek Theatre and Festivals: Documentary Studies*, ed. P. Wilson, 351–377. Oxford.

————. 2007b. "Performance in the *Pythion*: The Athenian Thargelia." In *The Greek Theatre and Festivals: Documentary Studies*, ed. P. Wilson, 150–182. Oxford.

————. 2008. "Costing the Dionysia." In *Performance, Iconography, Reception. Studies in Honour of Oliver Taplin*, ed. M. Revermann, 88–127. Oxford.

Wiseman, T. P. 1979. *Clio's Cosmetics: Three Studies in Greco-Roman Literature*. Totowa, N.J.

Yegül, F. K. 1992. *Baths and Bathing in Classical Antiquity*. New York.

Zanker, P. 1995. *The Mask of Socrates: the Image of the Intellectual in Antiquity*. Berkeley.

Zelnik-Abramovitz, R. 2014. "Look and Listen: History Performed and Inscribed." In *Between Orality and Literacy: Communication and Adaptation in Antiquity*, ed. R. Scodel, 175–196. Leiden.

Zerubavel, E. 2003. *Time Maps: Collective Memory and the Social Shape of the Past*. Chicago.

Index